Sic et Non

Encountering *Dominus Iesus*

Stephen J. Pope
Charles Hefling
Editors

ORBIS BOOKS
Maryknoll, New York 10545

Founded in 1970, Orbis Books endeavors to publish works that enlighten the mind, nourish the spirit, and challenge the conscience. The publishing arm of the Maryknoll Fathers and Brothers, Orbis seeks to explore the global dimensions of the Christian faith and mission, to invite dialogue with diverse cultures and religious traditions, and to serve the cause of reconciliation and peace. The books published reflect the opinions of their authors and are not meant to represent the official position of the Maryknoll Society. To obtain more information about Maryknoll and Orbis Books, please visit our website at www.maryknoll.org.

Library of Congress Cataloging in Publication Data

Sic et non : encountering Dominus Iesus / Stephen J. Pope, Charles Hefling, editors.
    p. cm.
  Includes text of Dominus Iesus.
  Includes bibliographical references and index.
  ISBN 1-57075-424-1 (pbk.)
    1. Jesus Christ—Person and offices. 2. Catholic Church—Doctrines. I. Pope, Stephen J.,
1955- II. Hefling, Charles C. III. Catholic Church. Congregatio pro Doctrina Fidei.
Dominus Iesus.

BT203 .S53 2002
230'.2—dc21

2002019874

To
the memory of
ANTHONY J. SALDARINI
who did much
to promote inter-religious understanding

CONTENTS

PART THREE
SIC ET NON: THEOLOGICAL DISCUSSION OF DOMINUS IESUS

PREFACE

This book offers a serious examination of a serious document—the Vatican declaration *Dominus Iesus*, issued by the Congregation for the Doctrine of the Faith on September 5, 2000. A range of theological and religious considerations must be entertained if the claims and contents of the declaration are to be properly addressed, and that is what the essays here aim to do. Taken together, they constitute an example of theological reflection on topics of concern to the wider public, the academy, and the church.

The relevance of these topics to the public at large is indicated by the attention that *Dominus Iesus* received in the media and the responses it elicited from the major religious authorities throughout the world. Our topics are also of concern to the academy, both the academic world of Catholic and Christian colleges and universities, which often sponsor talks, courses, symposia, and publications on these matters, and even in more secular academic quarters, which are beginning to realize that avoiding matters of religion has left them improperly positioned to reflect on major features of human experience, values, and culture.

Finally, the essays of this book obviously address matters of concern to the church. They offer for consideration arguments and theses that pertain to a number of ongoing and vital theological conversations about Christ, the church, the nature of salvation, the relation between the church and the Kingdom of God, etc. Criticisms of Vatican documents are sometimes confused with disloyalty or religious intolerance or aggression; sometimes they are properly so identified. Yet historians have shown that at times critical research and writing have also played an important role in the development of Christian doctrine by stimulating fresh approaches to problems and new hypotheses for consideration by the mind of the church. It is not going too far to say that treating a document of this kind with care and attention is one way of showing respect for the teaching office of the church. We do not argue about ideas that we consider trivial or discuss them with people whom we do not acknowledge to be intellectually serious.

The declaration *"Dominus Iesus:* On the Unicity and Salvific Universality of Jesus Christ and the Church" teaches that Jesus Christ is Lord, that the Body of Christ is one, and that the Roman Catholic Church, and only the Roman Catholic Church, possesses the full means of salvation desired by Christ. It explicitly denies most other Christian traditions the status of "churches" and it holds that, while other religions can receive divine grace, *"objectively speaking* they are in a gravely deficient situation in comparison with those who, in the Church, have the fullness of the means of salvation" (§22; emphasis in original). Cardinal Ratzinger, prefect of that Congregation, explained that the declaration was written because Pope John Paul II had "wanted to offer the world a great and solemn recognition of Jesus Christ as Lord at the culminating moment of the Holy Year."

Despite the utterly uncontroversial nature of the claim that "Jesus Christ is Lord" (uncontroversial among Christians, at least), *Dominus Iesus* was immediately received with criticisms, complaints, and, in some cases, outrage. Clearly not only one but many nerves had been struck. Jewish leaders postponed indefinitely their participation in a planned Jubilee Jewish-Christian dialogue scheduled for October in Rome. Criticisms were issued by the archbishop of Canterbury, the general secretary of the Lutheran World Federation, the general secretary of the Alliance of Reformed Churches, and the World Council of Churches. Criticism came from progressive Catholic theologians, but, more surprisingly, reservations were also registered publicly by prominent members of the Roman Catholic hierarchy, among them Cardinal Carlo Maria Martini, archbishop of Milan, and Cardinal Edward Cassidy, president of the Pontifical Council for Promoting Christian Unity. (Many more prelates, of course, rallied to its defense.)

One of the issues raised by the declaration concerns its understanding of who, or what, actually constitutes the church. Cardinal Ratzinger had previously written a letter to bishops asking them to refrain from referring to Protestant communions as constituting "sister churches." "The one, holy, catholic and apostolic universal church," he wrote, "is not sister but 'mother' of all the particular churches." *Dominus Iesus* continued this train of thought, but in the wider context of Christological doctrine.

Criticisms came especially from within sectors of Catholic theology most involved with ecumenical theology, Jewish-Christian relations, and inter-religious dialogue. *Dominus Iesus* was not intended to undercut these efforts; on the contrary, as the Pope explained in a response to critics of the document, it was written to offer a proper framework for meaningful dialogue: "The document clarifies the essential Christian elements, which do not obstruct dialogue but illustrate its foundations, because a dialogue without foundations would be destined to degenerate into empty verbosity." Whether it succeeds is open to discussion.

Some of those interested in developing mutual understanding between Catholics and adherents of other religious traditions have applauded the Pope for taking this initiative, but others are unsatisfied. Perhaps one reason for this negative response lies in the expectations that have been built up over recent years. Catholics are no longer taught, nor would they any longer accept, the discredited claim that there is no salvation outside the church (a phrase that itself, we should remember, has been subject to multiple interpretations). The Second Vatican Council made great strides in *Unitatis redintegratio,* the Decree on Ecumenism, and *Nostra aetate,* the Declaration on the Church in Relation to Non-Christian Religions. The Council communicated a critical acknowledgment of the integrity of other religious traditions. The Council Fathers recognized that God grants saving grace to adherents of other religions "in ways known to Himself." They also acknowledged that beyond the borders of the Roman

Catholic Church "many elements can be found of sanctification and truth." Indeed, *Lumen gentium,* the Dogmatic Constitution on the Church, teaches that "Those who, through no fault of their own, do not know the gospel of Christ or his Church, but who nevertheless seek God with a sincere heart, and, moved by grace, try in their actions to do his will as they know it through the dictates of their conscience—these too may attain eternal salvation" (§16). Expectations were also raised by the work of Pope John Paul II himself, from the encyclical *Ut unum sint,* which acknowledged that "certain features of the Christian mystery have at times been more effectively emphasized" outside the Roman Catholic Church than inside it, to the visitation of the synagogue in Rome and the inter-religious World Day of Prayer for Peace at Assisi in 1986.

The Vatican issued *Dominus Iesus* in order to correct the problems it believes flow from relativism that regards all religious positions as equally valuable and legitimate. The increased Vatican focus on this issue was indicated in the excommunication of the Sri Lankan priest-theologian Tissa Balasuriya (subsequently reinstated) and the investigation into the writings of Jaques Dupuis, S.J., the Belgian theologian who worked for thirty-six years in India and authored a book entitled *Toward a Theology of Pluralism.* In fact, *Dominus Iesus* is said to have been written in response to the work of Asian bishops who have been struggling with issues of pluralism and fidelity in largely non-Christian contexts. How does one communicate, at one and the same time, both wholehearted respect for the other, including the other's religious tradition, spirituality, and beliefs, and unswerving fidelity to the core Christian belief that Jesus Christ is the Savior of all human beings (and not only of Christians)? In many ways *Dominus Iesus* simply repeats various aspects of this core Christian message that Christ is Lord and universal Savior and therefore says nothing new. Why, then, so much controversy?

Answers that have been proposed are that the message of *Dominus Iesus* was substantively correct but expressed without nuance, or missing key qualifications, or poorly timed, or misinterpreted by a hostile and secular press, or misunderstood by overly suspicious progressive theologians. All these suggestions may or may not be true, but they do not gainsay the fact that there are also significant theological reasons for the controversy that ensued. It may be, then, that the controversy concerns issues of great theological import. Given the complexity of these topics, it would be better to describe this as a series of connected controversies rather than a single controversy. In fact, simply establishing the terms of the discussion, the relevant questions that ought to be asked of the declaration, the array of arguments that bear on their resolution, and the kinds of evidence relevant to reflection on them offers an extensive and substantial agenda.

The authors of these essays illustrate the range of issues raised by *Dominus Iesus* as well as suggest something of the plurality of religious perspectives that have attempted to come to terms with it. This collection is hardly comprehensive, however. The most that could be hoped for from a volume of this sort would be a selection of chapters that would provide a "sampler" of theological examinations of some of the central teachings of the declaration. We have tried to present helpful analyses of key theological themes as treated in the declaration. Catholic theologians thus examine its ecclesiology (Sullivan), its relation to major themes in the theology of Karl Rahner (Egan), its use of scripture (Perkins), its relation to matters of Trinitarian theology (Lawrence), its Christological doctrine (Imbelli), and its relevance to inter-religious dialogue (Clooney), specifically Jewish-Christian dialogue. The second half of the book widens the perspective considerably. It offers Anglican (Hefling), Protestant (Heim), Jewish (Langer), and Muslim (Huda) responses to the declaration.

None of the contributors to this volume, of course, presents an "official" or religiously authoritative response to *Dominus Iesus* on behalf of their religious communities. And none attempt to offer anything remotely resembling a rigorously systematic and fully comprehensive interpretation of how their traditions might respond to the claims of *Dominus Iesus*. Yet they do give an indication of how a range of scholars from a variety of religious perspectives—not only Roman Catholic, but also Anglican and Protestant, and not only Christian, but also Jewish and Muslim—have come to think about *Dominus Iesus*.

Most of the chapters of this book are based on papers presented at one of two panels at Boston College in the fall semester of 2000. The presentations were of such high quality, and the conversations they inspired so fruitful, that their authors agreed to develop their papers at greater length and to allow them to be published so that they could be made widely available for study. We hope, then, that this book will play a modest but significant role in developing the kind of understanding that is essential for the discipline of theology, the life of the church, and the ongoing conversation among the religions of the world.

ABBREVIATIONS

AAS   *Acta Apostolicae Sedis*

AG   *Ad gentes*

CCSL   Corpus Christianorum Series Latina

CDF   Congregation for the Doctrine of the Faith

DP   Instruction "Dialogue and Proclamation"

DH   *Dignitatis humanae*

DI   *Dominus Iesus*

DS   Denziger-Schönmetzer, *Enchiridion Symbolorum, definitionum et declarationum de rebus fidei et morum* (1976)

DV   *Dei verbum*

EN   *Evangelii nuntiandi*

FR   *Fides et ratio*

GS   *Gaudium et spes*

LG   *Lumen gentium*

NA   *Nostra aetate*

PG   J. P. Migne, ed., Patrologia Graeca (Paris: 1857–1866)

PL   J. P. Migne, ed., Patrologia Latina (Paris: 1841–1855)

Q   Qur'ân

RM   *Redemptoris missio*

SC   *Sources Chrétiennes*

UR   *Unitatis redintegratio*

UUS   *Ut unum sint*

PART ONE

THE TEXT OF *DOMINUS IESUS*

DECLARATION

"DOMINUS IESUS"

On the Unicity and Salvific Universality
of Jesus Christ and the Church

INTRODUCTION

1. The *Lord Jesus*, before ascending into heaven, commanded his disciples to proclaim the Gospel to the whole world and to baptize all nations: "Go into the whole world and proclaim the Gospel to every creature. He who believes and is baptized will be saved; he who does not believe will be condemned" (Mk 16:15-16); "All power in heaven and on earth has been given to me. Go therefore and teach all nations, baptizing them in the name of the Father, and of the Son, and of the Holy Spirit, teaching them to observe all that I have commanded you. And behold, I am with you always, until the end of the world" (Mt 28:18-20; cf. Lk 24:46-48; Jn 17:18, 20, 21; Acts 1:8).

The Church's universal mission is born from the command of Jesus Christ and is fulfilled in the course of the centuries in the proclamation of the mystery of God, Father, Son, and Holy Spirit, and the mystery of the incarnation of the Son, as saving event for all humanity. The fundamental contents of the profession of the Christian faith are expressed thus: "I believe in one God, the Father, Almighty, maker of heaven and earth, of all that is, seen and unseen. I believe in one Lord, Jesus Christ, the only Son of God, eternally begotten of the Father, God from God, Light from Light, true God from true God, begotten, not made, of one being with the Father. Through him all things were made. For us men and for our salvation, he came down from heaven: by the power of the Holy Spirit he became incarnate of the Virgin Mary, and became man. For our sake he was crucified under Pontius Pilate; he suffered death and was buried. On the third day he rose again in accordance with the Scriptures; he ascended into heaven and is seated at the right hand of the Father. He will come again in glory to judge the living and the dead, and his kingdom will have no end. I believe in the Holy Spirit, the Lord, the giver of life, who proceeds from the Father. With the Father and the Son he is worshipped and glorified. He has spoken through the prophets. I believe in one holy catholic and apostolic Church. I acknowledge one baptism for the forgiveness of sins. I look for the resurrection of the dead, and the life of the world to come."[1]

---

1. First Council of Constantinople, *Symbolum Constantinopolitanum*: Henricus Denzinger (ed.) and Adolfus Schönmetzer (original ed.), *Enchridion symbolorum definitionum et declarationum de rebus fidei et morum* (Freiburg in Breisgau: Herder, 36th ed., 1976), number 150 (hereafter abbreviated "DS" followed by the article number of the reference).

2. In the course of the centuries, the Church has proclaimed and witnessed with fidelity to the Gospel of Jesus. At the close of the second millennium, however, this mission is still far from complete.[2] For that reason, Saint Paul's words are now more relevant than ever: "Preaching the Gospel is not a reason for me to boast; it is a necessity laid on me: woe to me if I do not preach the Gospel!" (1 Cor 9:16). This explains the Magisterium's particular attention to giving reasons for and supporting the evangelizing mission of the Church, above all in connection with the religious traditions of the world.[3]

In considering the values which these religions witness to and offer humanity, with an open and positive approach, the Second Vatican Council's Declaration on the relation of the Church to non-Christian religions states: "The Catholic Church rejects nothing of what is true and holy in these religions. She has a high regard for the manner of life and conduct, the precepts and teachings, which, although differing in many ways from her own teaching, nonetheless often reflect a ray of that truth which enlightens all men."[4] Continuing in this line of thought, the Church's proclamation of Jesus Christ, "the way, the truth, and the life" (Jn 14:6), today also makes use of the practice of inter-religious dialogue. Such dialogue certainly does not replace, but rather accompanies the *missio ad gentes*, directed toward that "mystery of unity," from which "it follows that all men and women who are saved share, though differently, in the same mystery of salvation in Jesus Christ through his Spirit."[5] Inter-religious dialogue, which is part of the Church's evangelizing mission,[6] requires an attitude of understanding and a relationship of mutual knowledge and reciprocal enrichment, in obedience to the truth and with respect for freedom.[7]

3. In the practice of dialogue between the Christian faith and other religious traditions, as well as in seeking to understand its theoretical basis more deeply, new questions arise that need to be addressed through pursuing new paths of research, advancing proposals, and suggesting ways of acting that call for attentive discernment. In this task, the present Declaration seeks to recall to Bishops, theologians, and all the Catholic faithful, certain indispensable elements of Christian doctrine, which may help theological reflection in developing solu-

---

2. Cf. John Paul II, Encyclical Letter *Redemptoris missio*, 1: *Acta Apostolicae Sedis* 83 (1991), 249-340. (*Redemptoris missio* is hereafter abbreviated "RM" with the article number in the standard edition following; *Acta Apostolicae Sedis* is hereafter abbreviated "AAS" followed by a page number.)

3. Cf. Second Vatican Council, Decree *Ad gentes* (hereafter abbreviated "AG") and Declaration *Nostra aetate* (hereafter abbreviated "NA"); cf. also Paul VI Apostolic Exhortation *Evangelii nuntiandi* (hereafter abbreviated "EN"): AAS 68 (1976), 5-76; John Paul II, RM.

4. NA 2.

5. Pontifical Council for Inter-Religious Dialogue and the Congregation for the Evangelization of Peoples, Instruction *Dialogue and Proclamation* (hereafter abbreviated "DP"), 29: AAS 84 (1992), 424; cf. Second Vatican Council, Pastoral Constitution *Gaudium et spes* (hereafter abbreviated "GS"), 22.

6. Cf. RM 55.

7. DP 9.

tions consistent with the contents of the faith and responsive to the pressing needs of contemporary culture.

The expository language of the Declaration corresponds to its purpose, which is not to treat in a systematic manner the question of the unicity and salvific universality of the mystery of Jesus Christ and the Church, nor to propose solutions to questions that are matters of free theological debate, but rather to set forth again the doctrine of the Catholic faith in these areas, pointing out some fundamental questions that remain open to further development, and refuting specific positions that are erroneous or ambiguous. For this reason, the Declaration takes up what has been taught in previous Magisterial documents, in order to reiterate certain truths that are part of the Church's faith.

4. The Church's constant missionary proclamation is endangered today by relativistic theories which seek to justify religious pluralism, not only *de facto* but also *de iure* (or "in principle"). As a consequence, it is held that certain truths have been superseded; for example, the definitive and complete character of the revelation of Jesus Christ, the nature of Christian faith as compared with that of belief in other religions, the inspired nature of the books of Sacred Scripture, the personal unity between the Eternal Word and Jesus of Nazareth, the unity of the economy of the Incarnate Word and the Holy Spirit, the unicity and salvific universality of the mystery of Jesus Christ, the universal salvific mediation of the Church, the inseparability—while recognizing the distinction—of the kingdom of God, the kingdom of Christ, and the Church, and the subsistence of the one Church of Christ in the Catholic Church.

The roots of these problems are to be found in certain presuppositions of both a philosophical and theological nature, which hinder the understanding and acceptance of the revealed truth. Some of these can be mentioned: the conviction of the elusiveness and inexpressibility of divine truth, even by Christian revelation; relativistic attitudes toward truth itself, according to which what is true for some would not be true for others; the radical opposition posited between the logical mentality of the West and the symbolic mentality of the East; the subjectivism which, by regarding reason as the only source of knowledge, becomes incapable of raising its "gaze to the heights, not daring to rise to the truth of being";[8] the difficulty in understanding and accepting the presence of definitive and eschatological events in history; the metaphysical emptying of the historical incarnation of the Eternal Logos, reduced to a mere appearing of God in history; the eclecticism of those who, in theological research, uncritically absorb ideas from a variety of philosophical and theological contexts without regard for consistency, systematic connection, or compatibility with Christian truth; finally, the tendency to read and to interpret Sacred Scripture outside the Tradition and Magisterium of the Church.

8. John Paul II, Encyclical Letter *Fides et ratio* (hereafter abbreviated "FR"), 5: AAS 91 (1999), 5-88.

On the basis of such presuppositions, which may evince different nuances, certain theological proposals are developed—at times presented as assertions, and at times as hypotheses—in which Christian revelation and the mystery of Jesus Christ and the Church lose their character of absolute truth and salvific universality, or at least shadows of doubt and uncertainty are cast upon them.

I.
THE FULLNESS AND DEFINITIVENESS
OF THE REVELATION OF JESUS CHRIST

5. As a remedy for this relativistic mentality, which is becoming ever more common, it is necessary above all to reassert the definitive and complete character of the revelation of Jesus Christ. In fact, it must be *firmly believed* that, in the mystery of Jesus Christ, the Incarnate Son of God, who is "the way, the truth, and the life" (Jn 14:6), the full revelation of divine truth is given: "No one knows the Son except the Father, and no one knows the Father except the Son and anyone to whom the Son wishes to reveal him" (Mt 11:27); "No one has ever seen God; God the only Son, who is in the bosom of the Father, has revealed him" (Jn 1:18); "For in Christ the whole fullness of divinity dwells in bodily form" (Col 2:9-10).

Faithful to God's word, the Second Vatican Council teaches: "By this revelation then, the deepest truth about God and the salvation of man shines forth in Christ, who is at the same time the mediator and the fullness of all revelation."[9] Furthermore, "Jesus Christ, therefore, the Word made flesh, sent 'as a man to men,' speaks the words of God" (Jn 3:34), and completes the work of salvation which his Father gave him to do (cf. Jn 5:36; 17:4). To see Jesus is to see his Father (cf. Jn 14:9). For this reason, Jesus perfected revelation by fulfilling it through his whole work of making himself present and manifesting himself: through his words and deeds, his signs and wonders, but especially through his death and glorious resurrection from the dead and finally with the sending of the Spirit of truth, he completed and perfected revelation and confirmed it with divine testimony...The Christian dispensation, therefore, as the new and definitive covenant, will never pass away, and we now await no further new public revelation before the glorious manifestation of our Lord Jesus Christ" (cf. 1 Tim 6:14 and Tit 2:13).[10]

Thus, the encyclical *Redemptoris missio* calls the Church once again to the task of announcing the Gospel as the fullness of truth: "In this definitive Word of his revelation, God has made himself known in the fullest possible way. He has revealed to mankind who he is. This definitive self-revelation of God is the fun-

---

9. Second Vatican Council, Dogmatic Constitution *Dei verbum* (hereafter abbreviated "DV"), 2.

10. DV 4.

damental reason why the Church is missionary by her very nature. She cannot do other than proclaim the Gospel, that is, the fullness of the truth which God has enabled us to know about himself."[11] Only the revelation of Jesus Christ, therefore, "introduces into our history a universal and ultimate truth which stirs the human mind to ceaseless effort."[12]

Only (handwritten margin note)

6. Therefore, the theory of the limited, incomplete, or imperfect character of the revelation of Jesus Christ, which would be complementary to that found in other religions, is contrary to the Church's faith. Such a position would claim to be based on the notion that the truth about God cannot be grasped and manifested in its globality and completeness by any historical religion, neither by Christianity nor by Jesus Christ.

✳ My position (handwritten margin note)

Such a position is in radical contradiction with the foregoing statements of Catholic faith according to which the full and complete revelation of the salvific mystery of God is given in Jesus Christ. Therefore, the words, deeds, and entire historical event of Jesus, though limited as human realities, have nevertheless the divine Person of the Incarnate Word, "true God and true man"[13] as their subject. For this reason, they possess in themselves the definitiveness and completeness of the revelation of God's salvific ways, even if the depth of the divine mystery in itself remains transcendent and inexhaustible. The truth about God is not abolished or reduced because it is spoken in human language; rather, it is unique, full, and complete, because he who speaks and acts is the Incarnate Son of God. Thus, faith requires us to profess that the Word made flesh, in his entire mystery, who moves from incarnation to glorification, is the source, participated but real, as well as the fulfillment of every salvific revelation of God to humanity,[14] and that the Holy Spirit, who is Christ's Spirit, will teach this "entire truth" (Jn 16:13) to the Apostles and, through them, to the whole Church.

✳ (handwritten margin note)

7. The proper response to God's revelation is "*the obedience of faith* (Rom 16:26; cf. Rom 1:5; 2 Cor 10: 5-6) by which man freely entrusts his entire self to God, offering 'the full submission of intellect and will to God who reveals' and freely assenting to the revelation given by him."[15] Faith is a gift of grace: "in order to have faith, the grace of God must come first and give assistance; there must also be the interior helps of the Holy Spirit, who moves the heart and converts it to God, who opens the eyes of the mind and gives 'to everyone joy and ease in assenting to and believing in the truth.'"[16]

---

11. RM 5.
12. FR 14.
13. Council of Chalcedon, *Symbolum Chalcedonense*: DS 301; cf. St. Athanasius, *De Incarnatione*, 54, 3: SC [*Sources Chrétiennes*] 199, 458.
14. DV 4.
15. DV 5.
16. DV 5.

The obedience of faith implies acceptance of the truth of Christ's revelation, guaranteed by God, who is Truth itself:[17] "Faith is first of all a personal adherence of man to God. At the same time, and inseparably, it is a *free assent to the whole truth that God has revealed.*"[18] Faith, therefore, as "*a gift of God*" and as "*a supernatural virtue infused by him,*"[19] involves a dual adherence: to God who reveals and to the truth which he reveals, out of the trust which one has in him who speaks. Thus, "we must believe in no one but God: the Father, the Son and the Holy Spirit."[20]

For this reason, the distinction between theological faith and belief in the other religions must be firmly held. If faith is the acceptance in grace of revealed truth, which "makes it possible to penetrate the mystery in a way that allows us to understand it coherently,"[21] then belief, in the other religions, is that sum of experience and thought that constitutes the human treasury of wisdom and religious aspiration, which man in his search for truth has conceived and acted upon in his relationship to God and the Absolute.[22]

This distinction is not always borne in mind in current theological reflection. Thus, theological faith (the acceptance of the truth revealed by the One and Triune God) is often identified with belief in other religions, which is religious experience still in search of the absolute truth and still lacking assent to God who reveals himself. This is one of the reasons why the differences between Christianity and the other religions tend to be reduced at times to the point of disappearance.

8. The hypothesis of the inspired value of the sacred writings of other religions is also put forward. Certainly, it must be recognized that there are some elements in these texts which may be *de facto* instruments by which countless people throughout the centuries have been and still are able today to nourish and maintain their life-relationship with God. Thus, as noted above, the Second Vatican Council, in considering the customs, precepts, and teachings of the other religions, teaches that "although differing in many ways from her own teaching, these nevertheless often reflect a ray of that truth which enlightens all men."[23]

The Church's tradition, however, reserves the designation of *inspired texts* to the canonical books of the Old and New Testaments, since these are inspired by

17. Cf. *Catechism of the Catholic Church*, 144.
18. *Catechism of the Catholic Church,* 150.
19. *Catechism of the Catholic Church*, 153.
20. *Catechism of the Catholic Church*, 178.
21. FR 13.
22. Cf. FR 31-32.
23. NA 2; cf. AG 9, where it speaks of the elements of good present "in the particular customs and cultures of peoples"; Dogmatic Constitution *Lumen gentium* (hereafter abbreviated "LG"), 16, where it mentions the elements of good and of truth present among non-Christians, which can be considered a preparation for the reception of the Gospel.

the Holy Spirit.[24] Taking up this tradition, the Dogmatic Constitution on Divine Revelation of the Second Vatican Council states: "For Holy Mother Church, relying on the faith of the apostolic age, accepts as sacred and canonical the books of the Old and New Testaments, whole and entire, with all their parts, on the grounds that, written under the inspiration of the Holy Spirit (cf. Jn 20:31; 2 Tim 3:16; 2 Pet 1:19-21; 3:15-16), they have God as their author, and have been handed on as such to the Church herself."[25] These books "firmly, faithfully, and without error, teach that truth which God, for the sake of our salvation, wished to see confided to the Sacred Scriptures."[26]

Nevertheless, God, who desires to call all peoples to himself in Christ and to communicate to them the fullness of his revelation and love, "does not fail to make himself present in many ways, not only to individuals, but also to entire peoples through their spiritual riches, of which their religions are the main and essential expression even when they contain 'gaps, insufficiencies and errors.'"[27] Therefore, the sacred books of other religions, which in actual fact direct and nourish the existence of their followers, receive from the mystery of Christ the elements of goodness and grace which they contain.

II.
THE INCARNATE LOGOS
AND THE HOLY SPIRIT IN THE WORK OF SALVATION

9. In contemporary theological reflection there often emerges an approach to Jesus of Nazareth that considers him a particular, finite, historical figure, who reveals the divine not in an exclusive way, but in a way complementary with other revelatory and salvific figures. The Infinite, the Absolute, the Ultimate Mystery of God would thus manifest itself to humanity in many ways and in many historical figures: Jesus of Nazareth would be one of these. More concretely, for some, Jesus would be one of the many faces which the Logos has assumed in the course of time to communicate with humanity in a salvific way.

Furthermore, to justify the universality of Christian salvation as well as the fact of religious pluralism, it has been proposed that there is an economy of the eternal Word that is valid also outside the Church and is unrelated to her, in addition to an economy of the incarnate Word. The first would have a greater universal value than the second, which is limited to Christians, though God's presence would be more full in the second.

24. Cf. Council of Trent, *Decretum de libris sacris et de traditionibus recipiendis*: DS 1501; First Vatican Council, Dogmatic Constitution *Dei Filius*, Cap. 2: DS 3006.
25. DV 11.
26. DV 11.
27. RM 55; cf. RM 56 and EN 53.

10. These theses are in profound conflict with the Christian faith. The doctrine of faith must be *firmly believed* which proclaims that Jesus of Nazareth, son of Mary, and he alone, is the Son and the Word of the Father. The Word, which "was in the beginning with God" (Jn 1:2) is the same as he who "became flesh" (Jn 1:14). In Jesus, "the Christ, the Son of the living God" (Mt 16:16), "the whole fullness of divinity dwells in bodily form" (Col 2:9). He is the "only begotten Son of the Father, who is in the bosom of the Father" (Jn 1:18), his "beloved Son, in whom we have redemption... In him the fullness of God was pleased to dwell, and through him, God was pleased to reconcile all things to himself, on earth and in the heavens, making peace by the blood of his Cross" (Col 1:13-14; 19-20).

Faithful to Sacred Scripture and refuting erroneous and reductive interpretations, the First Council of Nicaea solemnly defined its faith in: "Jesus Christ, the Son of God, the only begotten generated from the Father, that is, from the being of the Father, God from God, Light from Light, true God from true God, begotten, not made, one in being with the Father, through whom all things were made, those in heaven and those on earth. For us men and for our salvation, he came down and became incarnate, was made man, suffered, and rose again on the third day. He ascended to the heavens and shall come again to judge the living and the dead."[28] Following the teachings of the Fathers of the Church, the Council of Chalcedon also professed: "the one and the same Son, our Lord Jesus Christ, the same perfect in divinity and perfect in humanity, the same truly God and truly man..., one in being with the Father according to the divinity and one in being with us according to the humanity..., begotten of the Father before the ages according to the divinity and, in these last days, for us and our salvation, of Mary, the Virgin Mother of God, according to the humanity."[29]

For this reason, the Second Vatican Council states that Christ "the new Adam... 'image of the invisible God' (Col 1:15) is himself the perfect man who has restored that likeness to God in the children of Adam which had been disfigured since the first sin... As an innocent lamb he merited life for us by his blood which he freely shed. In him God reconciled us to himself and to one another, freeing us from the bondage of the devil and of sin, so that each one of us could say with the apostle: the Son of God 'loved me and gave himself up for me' (Gal 2:20)."[30]

In this regard, John Paul II has explicitly declared: "To introduce any sort of separation between the Word and Jesus Christ is contrary to the Christian faith... Jesus is the Incarnate Word—a single and indivisible person... Christ is none other than Jesus of Nazareth; he is the Word of God made man for the salvation of all... In the process of discovering and appreciating the manifold

28. First Council of Nicaea, *Symbolum Nicaenum*: DS 125.
29. Council of Chalcedon, *Symbolum Chalcedonense:* DS 301.
30. GS 22.

gifts—especially the spiritual treasures—that God has bestowed on every people, we cannot separate those gifts from Jesus Christ, who is at the center of God's plan of salvation."[31]

It is likewise contrary to the Catholic faith to introduce a separation between the salvific action of the Word as such and that of the Word made man. With the incarnation, all the salvific actions of the Word of God are always done in unity with the human nature that he has assumed for the salvation of all people. The one subject which operates in the two natures, human and divine, is the single person of the Word.[32]

Therefore, the theory which would attribute, after the incarnation as well, a salvific activity to the Logos as such in his divinity, exercised "in addition to" or "beyond" the humanity of Christ, is not compatible with the Catholic faith.[33]

11. Similarly, the doctrine of faith regarding the unicity of the salvific economy willed by the One and Triune God must be *firmly believed*, at the source and center of which is the mystery of the incarnation of the Word, mediator of divine grace on the level of creation and redemption (cf. Col 1:15-20), he who recapitulates all things (cf. Eph 1:10), he "whom God has made our wisdom, our righteousness, and sanctification and redemption" (1 Cor 1:30). In fact, the mystery of Christ has its own intrinsic unity, which extends from the eternal choice in God to the parousia: "he [the Father] chose us in Christ before the foundation of the world to be holy and blameless before him in love" (Eph 1:4); "In Christ we are heirs, having been destined according to the purpose of him who accomplishes all things according to his counsel and will" (Eph 1:11); "For those whom he foreknew he also predestined to be conformed to the image of his Son, in order that he might be the firstborn among many brothers; those whom he predestined he also called; and those whom he called he also justified; and those whom he justified he also glorified" (Rom 8:29-30).

The Church's Magisterium, faithful to divine revelation, reasserts that Jesus Christ is the mediator and the universal redeemer: "The Word of God, through whom all things were made, was made flesh, so that as perfect man he could save all men and sum up all things in himself. The Lord . . . is he whom the Father raised from the dead, exalted and placed at his right hand, constituting him judge of the living and the dead."[34] This salvific mediation implies also the unicity of the redemptive sacrifice of Christ, eternal high priest (cf. Heb 6:20; 9:11; 10:12-14).

---

31. RM 6.
32. Cf. St. Leo the Great, *Tomus ad Flavianum*: DS 294.
33. Cf. St. Leo the Great, Letter to the Emperor Leo I, *Promisisse me memini*: DS 318: ". . . in tantam unitatem ab ipso conceptu Virginis deitate et humanitate conserta, ut nec sine homine divina, nec sine Deo agerentur humana." Cf. also DS 317.
34. GS 45; cf. also Council of Trent, *Decretum de peccato originali,* 3: DS 1513.

12. There are also those who propose the hypothesis of an economy of the Holy Spirit with a more universal breadth than that of the Incarnate Word, crucified and risen. This position also is contrary to the Catholic faith, which, on the contrary, considers the salvific incarnation of the Word as a trinitarian event. In the New Testament, the mystery of Jesus, the Incarnate Word, constitutes the place of the Holy Spirit's presence as well as the principle of the Spirit's effusion on humanity, not only in messianic times (cf. Acts 2:32-36; Jn 7:39, 20:22; 1 Cor 15:45), but also prior to his coming in history (cf. 1 Cor 10:4; 1 Pet 1:10-12).

The Second Vatican Council has recalled to the consciousness of the Church's faith this fundamental truth. In presenting the Father's salvific plan for all humanity, the Council closely links the mystery of Christ from its very beginnings with that of the Spirit.[35] The entire work of building the Church by Jesus Christ the Head, in the course of the centuries, is seen as an action which he does in communion with his Spirit.[36]

Furthermore, the salvific action of Jesus Christ, with and through his Spirit, extends beyond the visible boundaries of the Church to all humanity. Speaking of the paschal mystery, in which Christ even now associates the believer to himself in a living manner in the Spirit and gives him the hope of resurrection, the Council states: "All this holds true not only for Christians but also for all men of good will in whose hearts grace is active invisibly. For since Christ died for all, and since all men are in fact called to one and the same destiny, which is divine, we must hold that the Holy Spirit offers to all the possibility of being made partners, in a way known to God, in the paschal mystery."[37]

Hence, the connection is clear between the salvific mystery of the Incarnate Word and that of the Spirit, who actualizes the salvific efficacy of the Son made man in the lives of all people, called by God to a single goal, both those who historically preceded the Word made man, and those who live after his coming in history: the Spirit of the Father, bestowed abundantly by the Son, is the animator of all (cf. Jn 3:34).

Thus, the recent Magisterium of the Church has firmly and clearly recalled the truth of a single divine economy: "The Spirit's presence and activity affect not only individuals but also society and history, peoples, cultures and religions ... The Risen Christ 'is now at work in human hearts through the strength of his Spirit' ... Again, it is the Spirit who sows the 'seeds of the word' present in various customs and cultures, preparing them for full maturity in Christ."[38] While recognizing the historical-salvific function of the Spirit in the whole uni-

---

35. LG 3-4.
36. LG 7; cf. St. Irenaeus, who wrote that it is in the Church "that communion with Christ has been deposited, that is to say: the Holy Spirit" (*Adversus haereses* III, 24, 1; SC 211, 472).
37. GS 22.
38. RM 28. For the "seeds of the Word," cf. also St. Justin Martyr, *Second Apology* 8, 1-2; 10, 1-3; 13, 3-6: ed. E. J. Goodspeed, 84; 85; 88-89.

verse and in the entire history of humanity,[39] the Magisterium states: "This is the same Spirit who was at work in the incarnation and in the life, death, and resurrection of Jesus and who is at work in the Church. He is therefore not an alternative to Christ nor does he fill a sort of void which is sometimes suggested as existing between Christ and the Logos. Whatever the Spirit brings about in human hearts and in the history of peoples, in cultures and religions, serves as a preparation for the Gospel and can only be understood in reference to Christ, the Word who took flesh by the power of the Spirit 'so that as perfectly human he would save all human beings and sum up all things.'"[40]

In conclusion, the action of the Spirit is not outside or parallel to the action of Christ. There is only one salvific economy of the One and Triune God, realized in the mystery of the incarnation, death, and resurrection of the Son of God, actualized with the cooperation of the Holy Spirit, and extended in its salvific value to all humanity and to the entire universe: "No one, therefore, can enter into communion with God except through Christ, by the working of the Holy Spirit."[41]

III.
UNICITY AND UNIVERSALITY
OF THE SALVIFIC MYSTERY OF JESUS CHRIST

13. The thesis which denies the unicity and salvific universality of the mystery of Jesus Christ is also put forward. Such a position has no biblical foundation. In fact, the truth of Jesus Christ, Son of God, Lord and only Savior, who through the event of his incarnation, death and resurrection has brought the history of salvation to fulfillment, and which has in him its fullness and center, must be *firmly believed* as a constant element of the Church's faith.

The New Testament attests to this fact with clarity: "The Father has sent his Son as the Savior of the world" (1 Jn 4:14); "Behold the Lamb of God who takes away the sin of the world" (Jn 1:29). In his discourse before the Sanhedrin, Peter, in order to justify the healing of a man who was crippled from birth, which was done in the name of Jesus (cf. Acts 3:1-8), proclaims: "There is salvation in no one else, for there is no other name under heaven given among men by which we must be saved" (Acts 4:12). St. Paul adds, moreover, that Jesus Christ "is Lord of all," "judge of the living and the dead," and thus "whoever believes in him receives forgiveness of sins through his name" (Acts 10:36, 42, 43).

Paul, addressing himself to the community of Corinth, writes: "Indeed, even though there may be so-called gods in heaven or on earth—as in fact there are

39. RM 28-29.
40. RM 29.
41. RM 5.

many gods and many lords—yet for us there is one God, the Father, from whom
are all things and for whom we exist, and one Lord, Jesus Christ, through whom
are all things and through whom we exist" (1 Cor 8:5-6). Furthermore, John the
Apostle states: "For God so loved the world that he gave his only Son, so that
everyone who believes in him may not perish but may have eternal life. God
did not send his Son into the world to condemn the world, but in order that the
world might be saved through him" (Jn 3:16-17). In the New Testament, the
universal salvific will of God is closely connected to the sole mediation of
Christ: "[God] desires all men to be saved and to come to the knowledge of the
truth. For there is one God; there is also one mediator between God and men,
the man Jesus Christ, who gave himself as a ransom for all" (1 Tim 2:4-6).

It was in the awareness of the one universal gift of salvation offered by the Father through Jesus Christ in the Spirit (cf. Eph 1:3-14), that the first Christians
encountered the Jewish people, showing them the fulfillment of salvation that
went beyond the Law and, in the same awareness, they confronted the pagan
world of their time, which aspired to salvation through a plurality of saviors.
This inheritance of faith has been recalled recently by the Church's Magisterium: "The Church believes that Christ, who died and was raised for the sake
of all (cf. 2 Cor 5:15) can, through his Spirit, give man the light and the strength
to be able to respond to his highest calling, nor is there any other name under
heaven given among men by which they can be saved (cf. Acts 4:12). The
Church likewise believes that the key, the center, and the purpose of the whole
of man's history is to be found in its Lord and Master."[42]

14. It must therefore be *firmly believed* as a truth of Catholic faith that the universal salvific will of the One and Triune God is offered and accomplished once
for all in the mystery of the incarnation, death, and resurrection of the Son of
God.

Bearing in mind this article of faith, theology today, in its reflection on the existence of other religious experiences and on their meaning in God's salvific
plan, is invited to explore if and in what way the historical figures and positive
elements of these religions may fall within the divine plan of salvation. In this
undertaking, theological research has a vast field of work under the guidance of
the Church's Magisterium. The Second Vatican Council, in fact, has stated that:
"the unique mediation of the Redeemer does not exclude, but rather gives rise
to a manifold cooperation which is but a participation in this one source."[43] The
content of this participated mediation should be explored more deeply, but must
remain always consistent with the principle of Christ's unique mediation: "Although participated forms of mediation of different kinds and degrees are not

    42. GS 10. Cf. St. Augustine, who wrote that Christ is the way, which "has never been lack-
ing to mankind . . . and apart from this way no one has been set free, no one is being set free, no one
will be set free" (*De civitate Dei* 10, 32, 2: CCSL [Corpus Christianorum Series Latina] 47, 312).
    43. LG 62.

excluded, they acquire meaning and value only from Christ's own mediation, and they cannot be understood as parallel or complementary to his."[44] Hence, those solutions that propose a salvific action of God beyond the unique mediation of Christ would be contrary to Christian and Catholic faith.

15. Not infrequently it is proposed that theology should avoid the use of terms like "unicity," "universality," and "absoluteness," which give the impression of excessive emphasis on the significance and value of the salvific event of Jesus Christ in relation to other religions. In reality, however, such language is simply being faithful to revelation, since it represents a development of the sources of the faith themselves. From the beginning, the community of believers has recognized in Jesus a salvific value such that he alone, as Son of God made man, crucified and risen, by the mission received from the Father and in the power of the Holy Spirit, bestows revelation (cf. Mt 11:27) and divine life (cf. Jn 1:12; 5:25-26; 17:2) to all humanity and to every person.

In this sense, one can and must say that Jesus Christ has a significance and a value for the human race and its history, which are unique and singular, proper to him alone, exclusive, universal, and absolute. Jesus is, in fact, the Word of God made man for the salvation of all. In expressing this consciousness of faith, the Second Vatican Council teaches: "The Word of God, through whom all things were made, was made flesh, so that as perfect man he could save all men and sum up all things in himself. The Lord is the goal of human history, the focal point of the desires of history and civilization, the center of mankind, the joy of all hearts, and the fulfillment of all aspirations. It is he whom the Father raised from the dead, exalted and placed at his right hand, constituting him judge of the living and the dead."[45] "It is precisely this uniqueness of Christ which gives him an absolute and universal significance whereby, while belonging to history, he remains history's center and goal: 'I am the Alpha and the Omega, the first and the last, the beginning and the end' (Rev 22:13)."[46]

IV.
UNICITY AND UNITY OF THE CHURCH

16. The Lord Jesus, the only Savior, did not only establish a simple community of disciples, but constituted the Church as a *salvific mystery*: he himself is in the Church and the Church is in him (cf. Jn 15:1ff.; Gal 3:28; Eph 4:15-16; Acts

---

44. RM 5.

45. GS 45. The necessary and absolute singularity of Christ in human history is well expressed by St. Irenaeus in contemplating the preeminence of Jesus as firstborn Son: "In the heavens, as firstborn of the Father's counsel, the perfect Word governs and legislates all things; on the earth, as firstborn of the Virgin, a man just and holy, reverencing God and pleasing to God, good and perfect in every way, he saves from hell all those who follow him since he is the firstborn from the dead and Author of the life of God" (*Demonstratio apostolica*, 39: SC 406, 138).

46. RM 6.

9:5). Therefore, the fullness of Christ's salvific mystery belongs also to the Church, inseparably united to her Lord. Indeed, Jesus Christ continues his presence and his work of salvation in the Church and by means of the Church (cf. Col 1:24-27),[47] which is his body (cf. 1 Cor 12:12-13, 27; Col 1:18).[48] And thus, just as the head and members of a living body, though not identical, are inseparable, so too Christ and the Church can neither be confused nor separated, and constitute a single "whole Christ."[49] This same inseparability is also expressed in the New Testament by the analogy of the Church as the Bride of Christ (cf. 2 Cor 11:2; Eph 5:25-29; Rev 21:2, 9).[50]

Therefore, in connection with the unicity and universality of the salvific mediation of Jesus Christ, the unicity of the Church founded by him must be *firmly believed* as a truth of Catholic faith. Just as there is one Christ, so there exists a single body of Christ, a single Bride of Christ: "a single Catholic and apostolic Church."[51] Furthermore, the promises of the Lord that he would not abandon his Church (cf. Mt 16:18; 28:20) and that he would guide her by his Spirit (cf. Jn 16:13) mean, according to Catholic faith, that the unicity and the unity of the Church—like everything that belongs to the Church's integrity—will never be lacking.[52]

The Catholic faithful *are required to profess* that there is an historical continuity—rooted in the apostolic succession[53]—between the Church founded by Christ and the Catholic Church: "This is the single Church of Christ . . . which our Savior, after his resurrection, entrusted to Peter's pastoral care (cf. Jn 21:17), commissioning him and the other Apostles to extend and rule her (cf. Mt 28:18ff.), erected for all ages as 'the pillar and mainstay of the truth' (1 Tim 3:15). This Church, constituted and organized as a society in the present world, subsists in [*subsistit in*] the Catholic Church, governed by the Successor of Peter and by the Bishops in communion with him."[54] With the expression *subsistit in*, the Second Vatican Council sought to harmonize two doctrinal statements: on the one hand, that the Church of Christ, despite the divisions which exist among Christians, continues to exist fully only in the Catholic Church, and on the other

47. LG 14.

48. Cf. LG 7.

49. Cf. St. Augustine, *Enarratio in Psalmos*, Ps. 90, *Sermo* 2, 1: CCSL 39, 1266; St. Gregory the Great, *Moralia in Iob, Praefatio*, 6, 14: PL [Patrologia Latina] 75, 525; St. Thomas Aquinas, *Summa Theologiae*, III, q. 48, a. 2 ad 1.

50. LG 6.

51. *Symbolum maius Ecclesiae Armeniacae*: DS 48. Cf. Boniface VIII, *Unam sanctam*: DS 870-872; LG 8.

52. Cf. Second Vatican Council, Decree *Unitatis redintegratio* (hereafter abbreviated "UR"), 4; John Paul II, Encyclical Letter *Ut unum sint* (hereafter abbreviated "UUS"), 11: AAS 87 (1995), 927.

53. LG 20; cf. also St. Irenaeus, *Adversus haereses*, III, 3, 1-3: SC 211, 20-44; St. Cyprian, *Epist.* 33, 1: CCSL 3B, 164-165; St. Augustine, *Contra adver. legis et prophet.*, 1, 20, 39: CCSL 49, 70.

54. LG 8.

hand, that "outside of her structure, many elements can be found of sanctification and truth,"[55] that is, in those Churches and ecclesial communities which are not yet in full communion with the Catholic Church.[56] But with respect to these, it needs to be stated that "they derive their efficacy from the very fullness of grace and truth entrusted to the Catholic Church."[57]

[handwritten margin note: Prot.: only good thru Catholics ✗]

17. Therefore, there exists a single Church of Christ, which subsists in the Catholic Church, governed by the Successor of Peter and by the Bishops in communion with him.[58] The Churches which, while not existing in perfect communion with the Catholic Church, remain united to her by means of the closest bonds, that is, by apostolic succession and a valid Eucharist, are true particular Churches.[59] Therefore, the Church of Christ is present and operative also in these Churches, even though they lack full communion with the Catholic Church, since they do not accept the Catholic doctrine of the Primacy, which, according to the will of God, the Bishop of Rome objectively has and exercises over the entire Church.[60]

[handwritten margin note: Episc.]

On the other hand, the ecclesial communities which have not preserved the valid Episcopate and the genuine and integral substance of the Eucharistic mystery,[61] are not Churches in the proper sense; however, those who are baptized in these communities are, by Baptism, incorporated in Christ and thus are in a certain communion, albeit imperfect, with the Church.[62] Baptism in fact tends per se toward the full development of life in Christ, through the integral profession of faith, the Eucharist, and full communion in the Church.[63]

[handwritten margin note: Prot.: other than Episc. not Churches]

"The Christian faithful are therefore not permitted to imagine that the Church of Christ is nothing more than a collection—divided, yet in some way one—of Churches and ecclesial communities; nor are they free to hold that today the Church of Christ nowhere really exists, and must be considered only as a goal which all Churches and ecclesial communities must strive to reach."[64] In fact,

---

55. LG 8; cf. UUS 13. Cf. also LG 15 and UR 3.

56. The interpretation of those who would derive from the formula *subsistit in* the thesis that the one Church of Christ could subsist also in non-Catholic Churches and ecclesial communities is therefore contrary to the authentic meaning of *Lumen gentium*. "The Council instead chose the word *subsistit* precisely to clarify that there exists only one 'subsistence' of the true Church, while outside her visible structure there only exist *elementa Ecclesiae*, which—being elements of that same Church—tend and lead toward the Catholic Church" (Congregation for the Doctrine of the Faith [hereafter abbreviated "CDF"], Notification on the Book *Church: Charism and Power* by Father Leonardo Boff: AAS 77 [1985], 756-762).

57. UR 3.

58. Cf. CDF, Declaration *Mysterium Ecclesiae*, 1: AAS 65 (1973), 396-398.

59. Cf. UR 14 and 15; CDF, Letter *Communionis notio*, 17: AAS 85 (1993), 848.

60. Cf. First Vatican Council, Constitution *Pastor aeternus*: DS 3053-3064; LG 22.

61. UR 22.

62. UR 3.

63. UR 22.

64. CDF, *Mysterium Ecclesiae*, 1.

"the elements of this already-given Church exist, joined together in their fullness in the Catholic Church and, without this fullness, in the other communities."[65] "Therefore, these separated Churches and communities as such, though we believe they suffer from defects, have by no means been deprived of significance and importance in the mystery of salvation. For the spirit of Christ has not refrained from using them as means of salvation which derive their efficacy from the very fullness of grace and truth entrusted to the Catholic Church."[66]

The lack of unity among Christians is certainly a *wound* for the Church; not in the sense that she is deprived of her unity, but "in that it hinders the complete fulfillment of her universality in history."[67]

V.
THE CHURCH: KINGDOM OF GOD
AND KINGDOM OF CHRIST

18. The mission of the Church is "to proclaim and establish among all peoples the kingdom of Christ and of God, and she is on earth, the seed and the beginning of that kingdom."[68] On the one hand, the Church is "a sacrament—that is, sign and instrument of intimate union with God and of unity of the entire human race."[69] She is therefore the sign and instrument of the kingdom; she is called to announce and to establish the kingdom. On the other hand, the Church is the "people gathered by the unity of the Father, the Son and the Holy Spirit";[70] she is therefore "the kingdom of Christ already present in mystery"[71] and constitutes its *seed* and *beginning*. The kingdom of God, in fact, has an eschatological dimension: it is a reality present in time, but its full realization will arrive only with the completion or fulfillment of history.[72]

The meaning of the expressions *kingdom of heaven, kingdom of God*, and *kingdom of Christ* in Sacred Scripture and the Fathers of the Church, as well as in the documents of the Magisterium, is not always exactly the same, nor is their relationship to the Church, which is a mystery that cannot be totally contained by a human concept. Therefore, there can be various theological explanations of these terms. However, none of these possible explanations can deny or

---

65. UUS 14.
66. UR 3.
67. CDF, *Communionis notio*, 17; cf. UR 4.
68. LG 5.
69. LG 1.
70. LG 4. Cf. St. Cyprian, *De Dominica oratione*, 23: CCSL 3A, 105.
71. LG 3.
72. Cf. LG 9; cf. also the prayer addressed to God found in the *Didache* 9, 4: SC 248, 176: "May the Church be gathered from the ends of the earth into your kingdom" and ibid. 10, 5: SC 248, 180: "Remember, Lord, your Church...and, made holy, gather her together from the four winds into your kingdom which you have prepared for her."

empty in any way the intimate connection between Christ, the kingdom, and the Church. In fact, the kingdom of God which we know from revelation, "cannot be detached either from Christ or from the Church...If the kingdom is separated from Jesus, it is no longer the kingdom of God which he revealed. The result is a distortion of the meaning of the kingdom, which runs the risk of being transformed into a purely human or ideological goal and a distortion of the identity of Christ, who no longer appears as the Lord to whom everything must one day be subjected (cf. 1 Cor 15:27). Likewise, one may not separate the kingdom from the Church. It is true that the Church is not an end unto herself, since she is ordered toward the kingdom of God, of which she is the seed, sign and instrument. Yet, while remaining distinct from Christ and the kingdom, the Church is indissolubly united to both."[73]

19. To state the inseparable relationship between Christ and the kingdom is not to overlook the fact that the kingdom of God—even if considered in its historical phase—is not identified with the Church in her visible and social reality. In fact, "the action of Christ and the Spirit outside the Church's visible boundaries" must not be excluded.[74] Therefore, one must also bear in mind that "the kingdom is the concern of everyone: individuals, society and the world. Working for the kingdom means acknowledging and promoting God's activity, which is present in human history and transforms it. Building the kingdom means working for liberation from evil in all its forms. In a word, the kingdom of God is the manifestation and the realization of God's plan of salvation in all its fullness."[75]

In considering the relationship between the kingdom of God, the kingdom of Christ, and the Church, it is necessary to avoid one-sided accentuations, as is the case with those "conceptions which deliberately emphasize the kingdom and which describe themselves as 'kingdom centered.' They stress the image of a Church which is not concerned about herself, but which is totally concerned with bearing witness to and serving the kingdom. It is a 'Church for others,' just as Christ is the 'man for others'...Together with positive aspects, these conceptions often reveal negative aspects as well. First, they are silent about Christ: the kingdom of which they speak is 'theocentrically' based, since, according to them, Christ cannot be understood by those who lack Christian faith, whereas different peoples, cultures, and religions are capable of finding common ground in the one divine reality, by whatever name it is called. For the same reason, they put great stress on the mystery of creation, which is reflected in the diversity of cultures and beliefs, but they keep silent about the mystery of redemption. Furthermore, the kingdom, as they understand it, ends up either

---

73. RM 18; cf. John Paul II, Apostolic Exhortation *Ecclesia in Asia*, 17: *L'Osservatore Romano* (November 7, 1999). The kingdom is so inseparable from Christ that, in a certain sense, it is identified with him (cf. Origen, *In Mt. Hom.*, 14, 7: PG [Patrologia Graeca] 13, 1197; Tertullian, *Adversus Marcionem*, IV, 33, 8: CCSL 1, 634.

74. RM 18.

75. RM 15.

leaving very little room for the Church or undervaluing the Church in reaction to a presumed 'ecclesiocentrism' of the past and because they consider the Church herself only a sign, for that matter a sign not without ambiguity."[76] These theses are contrary to Catholic faith because they deny the unicity of the relationship which Christ and the Church have with the kingdom of God.

VI.
THE CHURCH AND THE OTHER RELIGIONS IN RELATION TO SALVATION

20. From what has been stated above, some points follow that are necessary for theological reflection as it explores the relationship of the Church and the other religions to salvation.

Above all else, it must be *firmly believed* that "the Church, a pilgrim now on earth, is necessary for salvation: the one Christ is the mediator and the way of salvation; he is present to us in his body which is the Church. He himself explicitly asserted the necessity of faith and baptism (cf. Mk 16:16; Jn 3:5), and thereby affirmed at the same time the necessity of the Church which men enter through baptism as through a door."[77] This doctrine must not be set against the universal salvific will of God (cf. 1 Tim 2:4); "it is necessary to keep these two truths together, namely, the real possibility of salvation in Christ for all mankind and the necessity of the Church for this salvation."[78]

The Church is the "universal sacrament of salvation,"[79] since, united always in a mysterious way to the Savior Jesus Christ, her Head, and subordinated to him, she has, in God's plan, an indispensable relationship with the salvation of every human being.[80] For those who are not formally and visibly members of the Church, "salvation in Christ is accessible by virtue of a grace which, while having a mysterious relationship to the Church, does not make them formally part of the Church, but enlightens them in a way which is accommodated to their spiritual and material situation. This grace comes from Christ; it is the result of his sacrifice and is communicated by the Holy Spirit";[81] it has a relationship with the Church, which "according to the plan of the Father, has her origin in the mission of the Son and the Holy Spirit."[82]

---

76. RM 17.

77. LG 14; cf. AG 7; UR 3.

78. RM 9; cf. *Catechism of the Catholic Church*, 846-847.

79. LG 48.

80. Cf. St. Cyprian, *De catholicae ecclesiae unitate*, 6: CCSL 3, 253-254; St. Irenaeus, *Adversus haereses*, III, 24, 1: SC 211, 472-474.

81. RM 10.

82. AG 2. The famous formula *extra Ecclesiam nullus omnino salvatur* is to be interpreted in this sense (cf. Fourth Lateran Council, Cap. 1, *De fide catholica*: DS 802). Cf. also the Letter of the Holy Office to the Archbishop of Boston: DS 3866-3872.

21. With respect to the *way* in which the salvific grace of God—which is always given by means of Christ in the Spirit and has a mysterious relationship to the Church—comes to individual non-Christians, the Second Vatican Council limited itself to the statement that God bestows it "in ways known to himself."[83] Theologians are seeking to understand this question more fully. Their work is to be encouraged, since it is certainly useful for understanding better God's salvific plan and the ways in which it is accomplished. However, from what has been stated above about the mediation of Jesus Christ and the "unique and special relationship"[84] which the Church has with the kingdom of God among men—which in substance is the universal kingdom of Christ the Savior —it is clear that it would be contrary to the faith to consider the Church as *one way* of salvation alongside those constituted by the other religions, seen as complementary to the Church or substantially equivalent to her, even if these are said to be converging with the Church toward the eschatological kingdom of God.

Certainly, the various religious traditions contain and offer religious elements which come from God,[85] and which are part of what "the Spirit brings about in human hearts and in the history of peoples, in cultures, and religions."[86] Indeed, some prayers and rituals of the other religions may assume a role of preparation for the Gospel, in that they are occasions or pedagogical helps in which the human heart is prompted to be open to the action of God.[87] One cannot attribute to these, however, a divine origin or an *ex opere operato* salvific efficacy, which is proper to the Christian sacraments.[88] Furthermore, it cannot be overlooked that other rituals, insofar as they depend on superstitions or other errors (cf. 1 Cor 10:20-21), constitute an obstacle to salvation.[89]

22. With the coming of the Savior Jesus Christ, God has willed that the Church founded by him be the instrument for the salvation of *all* humanity (cf. Acts 17:30-31).[90] This truth of faith does not lessen the sincere respect which the Church has for the religions of the world, but at the same time, it rules out, in a radical way, that mentality of indifferentism "characterized by a religious relativism which leads to the belief that 'one religion is as good as another.'"[91] If it is true that the followers of other religions can receive divine grace, it is also certain that *objectively speaking* they are in a gravely deficient situation in

83. AG 7.
84. RM 18.
85. These are the "seeds of the divine Word" (*semina Verbi*), which the Church recognizes with joy and respect (cf. AG 11; Vatican Council II Declaration *Nostra aetate* (hereafter abbreviated "NA"), 2.
86. RM 29.
87. RM 29; *Catechism of the Catholic Church*, 843.
88. Cf. Council of Trent, *Decretum de sacramentis*, can. 8, *de sacramentis in genere*: DS 1608.
89. RM 55.
90. Cf. LG, 17; RM 11.
91. RM 36.

comparison with those who, in the Church, have the fullness of the means of salvation.[92] However, "all the children of the Church should nevertheless remember that their exalted condition results, not from their own merits, but from the grace of Christ. If they fail to respond in thought, word, and deed to that grace, not only shall they not be saved, but they shall be more severely judged."[93] One understands then that, following the Lord's command (cf. Mt 28:19-20) and as a requirement of her love for all people, the Church "proclaims and is in duty bound to proclaim without fail, Christ who is the way, the truth, and the life (Jn 14:6). In him, in whom God reconciled all things to himself (cf. 2 Cor 5:18-19), men find the fullness of their religious life."[94]

In inter-religious dialogue as well, the mission *ad gentes* "today as always retains its full force and necessity."[95] "Indeed, God 'desires all men to be saved and come to the knowledge of the truth' (1 Tim 2:4); that is, God wills the salvation of everyone through the knowledge of the truth. Salvation is found in the truth. Those who obey the promptings of the Spirit of truth are already on the way of salvation. But the Church, to whom this truth has been entrusted, must go out to meet their desire, so as to bring them the truth. Because she believes in God's universal plan of salvation, the Church must be missionary."[96] Inter-religious dialogue, therefore, as part of her evangelizing mission, is just one of the actions of the Church in her mission *ad gentes*.[97] *Equality*, which is a presupposition of inter-religious dialogue, refers to the equal personal dignity of the parties in dialogue, not to doctrinal content, nor even less to the position of Jesus Christ—who is God himself made man—in relation to the founders of the other religions. Indeed, the Church, guided by charity and respect for freedom,[98] must be primarily committed to proclaiming to all people the truth definitively revealed by the Lord, and to announcing the necessity of conversion to Jesus Christ and of adherence to the Church through Baptism and the other sacraments, in order to participate fully in communion with God, the Father, Son and Holy Spirit. Thus, the certainty of the universal salvific will of God does not diminish, but rather increases the duty and urgency of the proclamation of salvation and of conversion to the Lord Jesus Christ.

CONCLUSION

23. The intention of the present *Declaration*, in reiterating and clarifying certain truths of the faith, has been to follow the example of the Apostle Paul, who wrote to the faithful of Corinth: "I handed on to you as of first importance what

92. Cf. Pius XII, Encyclical Letter *Mystici corporis*: DS 3821.
93. LG 14.
94. NA 2.
95. AG 7.
96. *Catechism of the Catholic Church*, 851; cf. also 849-856.
97. RM 55; John Paul II, Apostolic Exhortation *Ecclesia in Asia*, 31.
98. Second Vatican Council, Declaration *Dignitatis humanae* (hereafter abbreviated "DH"), 1.

I myself received" (1 Cor 15:3). Faced with certain problematic and even erroneous propositions, theological reflection is called to reconfirm the Church's faith and to give reasons for her hope in a way that is convincing and effective.

In treating the question of the true religion, the Fathers of the Second Vatican Council taught: "We believe that this one true religion continues to exist in the *one* Catholic and Apostolic Church, to which the Lord Jesus entrusted the task of *true* spreading it among all people. Thus, he said to the Apostles: 'Go therefore and *religion* make disciples of all nations baptizing them in the name of the Father and of the Son and of the Holy Spirit, teaching them to observe all that I have commanded you' (Mt 28:19-20). Especially in those things that concern God and his Church, all persons are required to seek the truth, and when they come to know it, to embrace it and hold fast to it."[99]

The revelation of Christ will continue to be "the true lodestar"[100] in history for all humanity: "The truth, which is Christ, imposes itself as an all-embracing authority."[101] The Christian mystery, in fact, overcomes all barriers of time and space, and accomplishes the unity of the human family: "From their different locations and traditions all are called in Christ to share in the unity of the family of God's children ... Jesus destroys the walls of division and creates unity in a new and unsurpassed way through our sharing in his mystery. This unity is so deep that the Church can say with Saint Paul: 'You are no longer strangers and sojourners, but you are saints and members of the household of God' (Eph 2: 19)."[102]

The Sovereign Pontiff John Paul II, at the Audience of June 16, 2000, granted to the undersigned Cardinal Prefect of the Congregation for the Doctrine of the Faith, with sure knowledge and by his apostolic authority, ratified and confirmed this Declaration, adopted in Plenary Session and ordered its publication.

Rome, from the Offices of the Congregation for the Doctrine of the Faith, August 6, 2000, the Feast of the Transfiguration of the Lord.

Joseph Card. Ratzinger   *Pope Benedict*
Prefect

Tarcisio Bertone, S.D.B.
Archbishop Emeritus of Vercelli
Secretary

99. DH 1.
100. FR 15.
101. FR 92.
102. FR 70.

PART TWO

A SAMPLING OF REACTIONS TO
DOMINUS IESUS
FROM AROUND THE WORLD

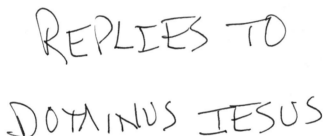

Statement of Dr. George Carey
Archbishop of Canterbury
Concerning the Roman Catholic Document
DOMINUS IESUS
5 September 2000

By restating the long-held view of the Roman Catholic Church on the position of other Christian churches, this document breaks no new ground. But neither does it fully reflect the deeper understanding that has been achieved through ecumenical dialogue and cooperation during the past thirty years. Even though the document is not part of that process, the idea that Anglican and other churches are not "proper churches" seems to question the considerable ecumenical gains we have made.

It is important that we recognize and celebrate ecumenical progress. It is a task to which I remain fully committed on behalf of both the Church of England and the world-wide Anglican Communion. It is one I shall continue to pursue with both Roman Catholic and other church leaders on the basis of deep mutual respect.

Indeed, at an important meeting of senior Anglicans and Roman Catholics in Toronto, earlier this year, which I chaired jointly with Cardinal Cassidy, we made striking advances in acknowledging substantial agreement on a range of issues and in proposing a new Joint Unity Commission to carry things forward.

Of course, the Church of England, and the world-wide Anglican Communion, does not for one moment accept that its orders of ministry and Eucharist are deficient in any way. It believes itself to be a part of the one, holy, catholic, and apostolic church of Christ, in whose name it serves and bears witness, here and round the world.

Statement of Joseph A. Fiorenza

Bishop of Houston-Galveston
President of the National Conference of Catholic Bishops
on *DOMINUS IESUS*
5 September 2000

The Congregation for the Doctrine of the Faith has once again performed a valuable service in summarizing and clarifying the teaching of the Church. In its declaration, "On the Unicity and Salvific Universality of Jesus Christ and the Church," the Congregation reiterates, mainly by recalling the teaching of the Second Vatican Council and Pope John Paul II, that Jesus Christ—the Word made flesh and Son of the Father—has an absolutely unique role in the salvation of the world.

Similarly, the Church of Christ uniquely contains the means of continuing Christ's saving mission. The Church of Christ is one, and subsists, or is found, in the Catholic Church where the fullness of the means of grace and salvation are present.

Beyond the visible boundaries of the Catholic Church, Christ's Church is also operative in those Churches which have maintained a valid episcopate, in succession to the apostles, and sacraments, above all, the Eucharist. Elements which go together to build up the life of the Church—such as Baptism, the Word of God, the virtues of faith, hope, charity—are present as well in other churches and ecclesial communities of Christians. These endowments form bonds which inspire in us a deep love and respect for them and a commitment to work with them to overcome what separates us and to achieve full communion.

The salvation offered through Jesus Christ and his Church is a gift to all humanity. We believe that Christ invites every human being to find in him "the way, the truth, and the life." Having been blessed with faith in Christ through no merit of our own, the members of the Church humbly seek to give as a gift the faith we received as a gift. Our belief in this regard in no way diminishes the sincere respect we have for the religions of the human family or our conviction that their followers can receive divine grace.

This respect—and love—goes in a special way to the Jewish community to which Christians are closely related through Christ himself and the revealed word of God in the Old Testament. Pope John Paul has witnessed to this special relationship over and over again, especially during his recent visit to the State of Israel.

The Holy Father has witnessed to the Church's respect for the other great religions during his various encounters with their leaders on his pastoral visits around the world. In his 1986 call for a Day of Prayer in Assisi, he inspired the leaders of most major religions to come together to put the power of prayer and belief behind the search for peace.

This document will be of special assistance to our theologians and theology professors, to those doing missionary work, and to all engaged in ecumenical and interfaith dialogues. We count it a blessing to live in a time marked by extensive encounters between the peoples of the world, their cultures, and their religions. One can scarcely doubt the importance of these contacts and exchanges at the religious level as they unfold in the decades ahead.

As these contacts deepen, it is not surprising that they present searching questions about how a Christian regards the relationship with other religions in light of faith in Jesus Christ as the unique and universal Savior. The answers of past centuries do not always come to terms with the reality before us. As the Congregation points out, today, facile answers do not do justice to the truth of our relationship with other religious traditions. At the same time, little good would come from contacts with other religions if those speaking on behalf of the Church were to offer an inadequate or very selective picture of the Christian faith.

Respecting the seriousness of the questions surfaced by the interreligious encounters of our time, the Congregation does not rest with pointing out the faulty answers sometimes proposed. It also invites Catholic theologians to a continuing exploration in depth and reflection on the existence of other religious experiences, on other religious traditions which also contain elements that come from God, and on their meaning in God's salvific plan.

Statement of Dr. Ishmael Noko
General Secretary of the Lutheran World Federation*
on the Vatican Document
DOMINUS IESUS
Geneva, Switzerland, 8 September 2000

The Lutheran World Federation has received news of the document *Dominus Iesus*—On the Unicity and Salvific Universality of Jesus Christ and the Church, published by the Congregation for the Doctrine of the Faith of the Roman Catholic Church on September 5, 2000.

This document pertains primarily to the inter-faith relations of the Roman Catholic Church in the wide framework of the world's religions. The Lutheran World Federation has seen this document and will want to carefully study and fully discuss it with our Roman Catholic partners.

The Lutheran World Federation has also seen a letter from the Congregation for the Doctrine of the Faith sent on June 30, 2000 to the presidents of the Roman Catholic Bishops' Conferences around the world. This letter and its accompanying document, "Note on the Expression 'Sister Churches'" says, in effect, that the word "church" should not be used by the Roman Catholic Church when addressing Protestants.

The fact that the Roman Catholic Church is ready to speak of only Orthodox churches as "sister churches" is not new to us. According to this understanding of the Roman Catholic Church, the Lutheran churches and other churches of the Reformation are not referred to as churches, but—in line with the principles now restated—as "ecclesial communities."

The document, *Dominus Iesus*, contains the observation that "ecclesial communities which have not preserved the valid Episcopate and the genuine and integral substance of the Eucharistic mystery, are not Churches in the proper sense."

Lutheran churches, together with other churches of the Reformation, are not ready to accept the categories now emphasized by the Congregation for the Doctrine of the Faith nor the definitions and criteria underlying them. We are disappointed that thirty-five years of ecumenical dialogue between Roman Catholics and Lutherans seem not to have been considered in the formulation of the letter and documents issued by the Congregation for the Doctrine of the Faith. The impact of these statements is more painful because they reflect a different spirit than that which we encounter in many other Lutheran-Roman Catholic relationships.

*The Lutheran World Federation is a global communion of 131 member churches in 72 countries representing over 59 million of the world's 63 million Lutherans. Its highest decision-making body is the Assembly, held every six or seven years. Between Assemblies, the LWF is governed by a 49-member Council, which meets annually, and its Executive Committee. The LWF secretariat is located in Geneva, Switzerland.

On October 31, 1999, the Lutheran World Federation and the Roman Catholic Church took a significant ecumenical step by signing a Joint Declaration that nullified centuries of conflict between our churches regarding the Doctrine of Justification. This was an important milestone in the history of Christian unity. In the Joint Declaration, a clarifying note states that the word "church" is used in the Declaration "to reflect the self-understanding of the particular churches, without intending to resolve all the ecclesiological issues related to them." This approach is also helpful in the wider ecumenical relationship between churches. Without it, problems arise, not only on the world level of churches and communions but also on the local level where pastors and believers are developing relationships as genuine ecumenical partners as they seek to faithfully serve God in their communities.

The Lutheran World Federation remains committed to ecumenical dialogue. We believe that ecumenism is not optional but essential to the Church. Temporary setbacks should neither be allowed to cloud or darken our vision for Christian unity as willed and prayed for by Christ himself.

Outside the Catholic Church No Salvation?

Rembert G. Weakland, O.S.B.

Archbishop of Milwaukee

14 September 2000*

After reading a newspaper article, what we remember most is the headline. This past week *The Journal Sentinel*, reporting on the document *Dominus Iesus* from the Roman Congregation for the Doctrine of the Faith, carried the headline: "Vatican insists only faithful Catholics can attain salvation." After reading carefully the full document, I can tell you this statement never occurs in the text. It does say that the Catholic Church believes it has all the means that are necessary for salvation. We Catholics are convinced of this truth. Otherwise, why would we be Catholic? (I know that members of other churches believe the same about their particular churches.)

The Asian bishops in particular, I am told, wanted a statement from Rome asserting this truth because Evangelical Christians were invading their countries in droves, preaching and disseminating literature that states that Catholics cannot be saved. I, too, am bombarded by such literature.

The first half of the document of the Congregation for the Doctrine of the Faith is directed toward those scholars engaged in theological dialogues with other great religions, especially Buddhism and Hinduism. It takes exception to those Catholic and Protestant theologians who minimize the salvific role of Jesus Christ and try to find manifestations of the presence of the second person of the Trinity (the Logos) or the salvific workings of the Holy Spirit in those other religions, while diminishing or eliminating the unique role of Jesus Christ.

Concerning members of the other great religions of the world, however, the document quotes the statement of the bishops of Vatican Council II that God can bestow salvific grace to adherents to these religions "in ways known to himself." It is impossible to reconcile that statement with the interpretation that God grants this grace only to faithful Catholics.

The second half of the document deals with the uniqueness of the Catholic Church as we Catholics understand it. The document repeats the teaching of Vatican Council II that the church founded and willed by Jesus Christ "subsists in" the Catholic Church. The bishops at that council debated at length over the right phrase to use—"subsists in," or "is the same as," or "is identified with"— and chose the first in order to acknowledge the existence of true ecclesial elements in other churches. The document admits that the bishops at Vatican Council II did not want to teach a doctrine of exclusivity, but to accept the fact that outside the structure of the Catholic Church "many elements can be found of sanctification and truth."

*From the *Catholic Herald* (14 September 2000), the newspaper of the Archdiocese of Milwaukee.

In examining what must characterize a true church, the new document cites "apostolic succession and a valid Eucharist." Without these two qualities the document does not call a Christian denomination a church. In my opinion, the documents of Vatican Council II made the role of baptism much more significant as entrance into the Body of Christ and thus into the church: "All who have been justified by faith in baptism are members of Christ's body and have a right to be called Christians, and so are deservedly recognized as sisters and brothers in the Lord by the children of the Catholic Church" (*Lumen gentium,* 3). The documents of Vatican Council II do not hesitate to use the word "churches" to characterize these communities of the Reformation (*Unitatis redintegratio*, 19). Unfortunately, *Dominus Iesus* does not take into account the enormous progress made after Vatican Council II in the mutual recognition of each other's baptisms and the ecclesial significance of such recognition.

Catholic dissent

What is disappointing about this document is that so many of our partners in ecumenical dialogues will find its tone heavy, almost arrogant and condescending. To them it is bound to seem out of keeping with the elevated and open tone of the documents of Vatican Council II. It ignores all of the ecumenical dialogues of the last thirty-five years, as if they did not exist. None of the agreed statements are cited. Has no progress in working toward convergence of theological thought occurred in these thirty-five years? Our partners have every reason to believe we may not be sincere in such dialogues. We seem to be talking out of both sides of the mouth, for example, making agreements with the Lutherans on Monday and then calling into question the validity of their ecclesial nature on Tuesday. To those involved in the ecumenical dialogues, this document will be seen as pessimistic and disheartening. It will be a burr in the side of all involved in the ecumenical movement for decades to come and will continue to promote the conviction that we Catholics are simply not sincere.

But we Catholics can all hold, without apology, as stating our position what the bishops gathered at Vatican Council II declared: "Some, and even most, of the significant elements and endowments which together go to build up and give life to the church itself, can exist outside the visible boundaries of the Catholic Church: the written word of God; the life of grace, faith, hope, and charity, with the other interior gifts of the Holy Spirit, and visible elements too. All of these, coming from Christ and leading back to Christ, properly belong to the one church of Christ" (*Unitatis redintegratio*, 3).

Statement of Pope John Paul II
at Recitation of the Angelus
1 October 2000*

With the Declaration *Dominus Iesus*—Jesus is Lord—approved by me in a special way at the height of the Jubilee Year, I wanted to invite all Christians to renew their fidelity to him in the joy of faith and to bear unanimous witness that the Son, both today and tomorrow, is "the way, and the truth, and the life" (Jn 14:6). Our confession of Christ as the only Son, through whom we ourselves see the Father's face (cf. Jn 14:8), is not arrogance that disdains other religions, but joyful gratitude that Christ has revealed himself to us without any merit on our part. At the same time, he has obliged us to continue giving what we have received and to communicate to others what we have been given, since the Truth that is has been given and the Love which is God belong to all people.

With the Apostle Peter, we confess that "there is salvation in no one else" (Acts 4:12). The Declaration *Dominus Iesus,* following the lead of the Second Vatican Council, shows us that this confession does not deny salvation to non-Christians, but points to its ultimate source in Christ, in whom man and God are united. God gives light to all in a way which is accommodated to their spiritual and material situation, granting them salvific grace in ways known to himself (*Dominus Iesus,* VI, nn. 20-21). The Document clarifies essential Christian elements, which do not hinder dialogue but show its bases, because a dialogue without foundations would be destined to degenerate into empty wordiness.

The same also applies to the ecumenical question. If the document, together with the Second Vatican Council, declares that "the single Church of Christ subsists in the Catholic Church," it does not intend thereby to express scant regard for the other Churches and Ecclesial Communities. This conviction is accompanied by the awareness that it is not due to human merit, but is a sign of God's fidelity, which is stronger than the human weaknesses and sins solemnly confessed by us before God and men at the beginning of Lent. The Catholic Church—as the Document says—suffers from the fact that true particular Churches and Ecclesial Communities with precious elements of salvation are separated from her.

The document thus expresses once again the same ecumenical passion that is the basis of my Encyclical *Ut unum sint.* I hope that this Declaration, which is close to my heart, can, after so many erroneous interpretations, finally fulfill its function both of clarification and of openness. May Mary, whom the Lord on the Cross entrusted to us as the Mother of us all, help us to grow together in our faith in Christ, the Redeemer of all mankind, in the hope of salvation offered by Christ to everyone, and in love, which is the sign of God's children.

---

*Editors' Note: When a great deal of criticism began to be raised against *Dominus Iesus*, many commentators questioned whether the Pope himself stood behind it or whether it had been published without his studying it carefully. This Angelus speech by the Pope is viewed as John Paul's seal of approval on the document.

ECUMENICAL TRENDS:
A NEW DOCUMENT AND OLD OBSTACLES*

Michael J. Champion, D.D., M.A. Th.

Archbishop of Cleveland, Ukrainian Autocephalous Orthodox Church

There is certainly much debate going on over the recent declaration of the Vatican Curia's Congregation for the Doctrine of the Faith, entitled *Dominus Iesus: On the Unicity and Salvific Universality of Jesus Christ and the Church.* Taking its name from the initial Latin words of the text: "The Lord Jesus," the declaration gives official church teaching on the centrality of Christ in the salvation of all peoples, and sees the redemptive role of Christ as the source of all salvation, including the possibility that salvation can be attained by those of other than Christian and specifically of non-Catholic faith. The publishing Congregation, that for the "Doctrine of the Faith," assists the Roman Pontiff in governing the Catholic Communion in matters of faith and morality. Referred to as the "magisterium" or "teaching office of the church," prior to the Second Vatican Council, this branch of the Roman Curia was called "The Holy Office" or "The Inquisition."

The impact of *Dominus Iesus* is being felt on the inside and on the outside of the Roman Church and from other Christians and non-Christians as well. Already, we can see the role of theology and theologians taking shape, as the document is interpreted by academic and religious leaders. The Pope himself gave a carte blanche approval of the Congregation's work in his Sunday Angelus address on October 1. John Paul used the occasion to clarify the meaning of the declaration. "Our confession of Christ as the only Son, through whom we ourselves see the face of the Father, is not arrogance that shows contempt for other religions, but the joyful recognition that Christ showed himself to us without any merit on our part," the Pope told the crowd gathered in St. Peter's Square.

Many observers believe that this particular document will cause the ecumenical movement and the church's dialogue with other world religions to regress to levels not seen since Vatican II, and that it will negate the many accomplishments in this area throughout John Paul's twenty-two-year pontificate. The Pope disagrees with this kind of interpretation, though, stating that the declaration "clarifies essential Christian elements, which do not hinder dialogue but show its bases, because a dialogue without foundations would be destined to degenerate into empty wordiness."

In fact, John Paul and the Congregation for the Doctrine of the Faith believe that *Dominus Iesus* merely continues the theology of the Second Vatican Council, which taught that there is the possibility of salvation for non-Catholics and even non-Christians, but that their salvation has its ultimate source in Christ and in the Paschal Mystery, that is, Christ's death and resur-

*First published in *Sobornopravna* (Fall 2000).

rection. "By this revelation then, the deepest truth about God and the salvation of man shines forth in Christ, who is at the same time the mediator and the fullness of all revelation ... especially through his death and glorious resurrection from the dead and finally with the sending of the Spirit of truth, he completed and perfected revelation and confirmed it with divine testimony," the document states.

Now that the fog created by the document's release is beginning to clear, it is necessary to ask whether it really will harm ecumenical dialogue and what the particular impact of *Dominus Iesus,* from the perspective of the Orthodox Church and Orthodox faithful in general, will be. No Orthodox theologian would argue with the teaching that all salvation comes in and through the person of Jesus Christ. The centrality of Christology to Orthodox liturgical and spiritual life gives firm basis to a Christological understanding of the whole cosmos, the universe, and everything and everyone created by God in his own image and likeness. While most Orthodox clergy and theologians would agree that any possibility of salvation to non-Christians, those who have not heard or accepted the message of salvation in Christ, comes in and through Jesus himself, there are many in extremist factions and even the so-called "mainline" Orthodox circles who would not permit salvation to anyone who was not Christian and more than likely any non-Orthodox Christians.

The document is much more limiting and hesitant of Protestant denominations than toward its Orthodox "sister" churches. Referring to the reformed movement, *Dominus Iesus* states that "the ecclesial communities which have not preserved the valid Episcopate and the genuine and integral substance of the Eucharistic mystery, are not Churches in the proper sense." This, expectedly, has caused a defensive response from Protestant leaders. Nevertheless, the document concedes that "those who are baptized in these communities are, by Baptism, incorporated in Christ and thus are in a certain communion, albeit imperfect, with the Church." In the bulk of Orthodox teaching also, other communities, which have separated themselves from the "true Church of Christ," the "Holy Orthodox Church," are not to be considered "real" churches, not only from the point of view of apostolic succession and valid sacraments, but because of the fact that they do not exist in communion with the "Great Church of Christ," which exists only in the worldwide alliance of selected Orthodox local churches. So actually, we can again observe that Orthodox praxis is in agreement with or even much stronger than that expressed in *Dominus Iesus.*

The different ways in which Roman Catholics and Evangelicals view the Church does not, however, totally account for the consternation provoked by *Dominus Iesus.* Nor can it be assumed that Protestants who have taken offense have not understood the document. On the contrary, the complaints may indicate that there is something to complain about. In the section on the other Christian Churches, *Dominus Iesus* suddenly reverts to an approach that once seemed outmoded. Since John XXIII and the Second Vatican Council, ecumenical dialogue has taken as its point of departure the radical equality between all Christians, based on baptism in the name of the Trinity. From there ecumenists go on to discuss the differences. But this text starts from the other end—from the necessity of bishops in the apostolic succession and a celebration of the Eucharist which has the Church's guarantee. Other Churches see this as harshly negative toward them, and they feel hurt.

The Orthodox fare much better in the declaration than do their reformed brothers and sisters. *Dominus Iesus* is specifically speaking of Orthodox Churches when it says, "The Churches which, while not existing in perfect communion with the Catholic Church, remain united to her by means of the closest bonds, that is, by apostolic succession and a valid Eucharist, are true particular Churches." This teaching affirms the progress that has been made in the ecumenical movement between the two churches since Pope Paul VI and Ecumenical Patriarch Athenagoras lifted the mutual bans of excommunication imposed by both churches against each other in 1054 CE. The Roman Church recognizes the Orthodox Church as equal in dignity to itself and really as a sister church who remains separated because of age-old disagreements on only a few matters. The document hits directly on some of these ancient sensitive points, and indeed one in particular, seen as the major obstacle to Orthodox/Catholic unity. This obstacle is the Catholic teaching, only defined since Vatican I in the last century, of Papal Infallibility or the Primacy of Peter. The declaration explains: "Therefore, the Church of Christ is present and operative also in these Churches, even though they lack full communion with the Catholic Church, since they do not accept the Catholic doctrine of the Primacy, which, according to the will of God, the Bishop of Rome objectively has and exercises over the entire Church."

This renewed emphasis on papal primacy will make it increasingly easier for Orthodox commentators to accuse the Vatican of [claiming] superiority, but, it is not a new phenomenon. The way in which Rome has dealt with Eastern Churches in communion with the Catholic Church and therefore, "real" Catholics, has been a cause [of] consternation [for] Orthodox ecumenists. As is well known, the majority of Orthodox theologians accept the role of Peter's successor as one of primacy of honor, or "presiding in love," among the other, autocephalous churches, but do not give any precedence in authority, decision, or declaration of faith to the Bishop of Rome himself.

The point of contention of the declaration *Dominus Iesus* is centered on part four, entitled *Unicity and the Unity of the Church* and the particular teaching contained therein, that "there exists a single Church of Christ, which subsists in the Catholic Church, governed by the Successor of Peter and by the Bishops in communion with him."

This idea is hard to accept for non-Catholic Christians, and especially the Orthodox, in [whom] the document suggests that there is, due to their lack of communion with Peter's successor, something essentially lacking. This imperfect condition in the one Christian Church here refers to the combined entities of those Eastern Orthodox Churches, [that], as the document testifies, possess a valid Eucharist and are therefore, true particular churches, indigenous Christian communities, which make up the entire Body of Christ. What then is lacking in the Churches of the East which are not in communion with the See of

Peter? What about real apostolic churches, where Peter had also been bishop? Is the lack of communion hindered by either side, or both, because of human frailty and pride? Again, we put forth the thesis that most any Orthodox theologian would say the same for those outside of communion with accepted world Orthodoxy, and would go further, some far enough to say that there is a lack of grace and "efficacy" of the sacraments in such churches.

This most recent piece of official church teaching joins the wealth of conciliar, papal, and patriarchal documents issued over the centuries. It is natural that much more discussion and interpretation will take place in the coming months and years. At this point, it is fair to say that for Orthodox/Catholic dialogue, the teachings in *Dominus Iesus* reflect the real state of the relationship between the two churches. It points to the all too evident situation of "stalemate" that has been attained, despite the many years of discussion, despite the mutual recognition and common prayer exercised by both parties. Without an honest attempt to redefine the role of the "Petrine ministry" on the part of the Vatican, future unity between East and West is an impossibility. Statements by John Paul II earlier this year, that he would be willing to re-examine the role that the primacy of Peter's successor plays in the universal church, must be taken seriously, without simply re-defining, regardless of an ecumenical sensitivity, the interpretations of the First Vatican Council and the recently beatified Pope Pius IX. The fact that this very Pope, who was responsible for the declaration of Papal Infallibility, the major stumbling block in Orthodox/Catholic dialogue, was recently pronounced "blessed" by John Paul, will create a further obstacle, despite any personal heroic virtues that Pius IX may have exhibited in his life. Only in a spirit of hope can the Pope's own words describing *Dominus Iesus* speak to both churches, so that "this Declaration ... can, after so many erroneous interpretations, finally fulfill its function both of clarification and of openness."

On *Dominus Iesus* and the Jews*

Dr. David Berger

Professor of History, Brooklyn College and the Graduate Center,
City University of New York

1 May 2001

The declaration *Dominus Iesus*, issued in September 2000 by the Congregation for the Doctrine of the Faith, aroused deep concern among many Jews and not a few Catholics. Let me first survey the specific areas of concern, proceed to address the question of whether or not Jews can plausibly be said to lie outside the effective scope of the document, and finally express some personal views about the propriety or impropriety of the objections that have been raised and examine the implications for Jewish-Catholic dialogue.

Jewish criticisms of *Dominus Iesus* have focused on several central points. The declaration maintains that the salvific grace of God is given only by means of Jesus and the Church. Though "individual non-Christians" can attain this grace in a manner that remains difficult to define, it is a certainty that the process cannot take place without "a mysterious relationship with the Church" (DI 20). This appears to mean that other religions, presumably including Judaism, have no independent salvific power. The text goes on to emphasize that although "followers of other religions can receive divine grace,... *objectively speaking* [emphasis in the original] they are in a gravely deficient situation in comparison with those who, in the Church, have the fullness of the means of salvation" (DI 22). Thus, Jews, if they are included in this assertion, are apparently far less likely to be saved than Catholics.

Moreover, interreligious dialogue is described as part of the "evangelizing mission" of the Church, "just one of the actions of the Church in her mission *ad gentes*" (DI 22). The declaration goes on to emphasize in this context that though "equality... is a presupposition of inter-religious dialogue, [it] refers to the equal personal dignity of the parties in dialogue, not to doctrinal content" (DI 22). For many Jews, the denial of doctrinal equality is objectionable, even deeply objectionable, in and of itself, and the ascription of evangelical intent to the dialogue appears to be a dagger thrust into its very heart.

The most comprehensive approach to neutralizing these objections is the assertion that Jews, who received the initial divine revelation and entered into a covenant with God before the rise of Christianity, are sui generis. Not only was *Dominus Iesus* not formulated with Jews in mind; Jews, we are sometimes told, are entirely excluded from the purview of its controversial assertions. I do not find this position plausible.

---

*Delivered at the 17th meeting of the International Catholic-Jewish Liaison Committee, New York, 1 May 2001.

To begin with, the declaration contains one explicit reference to Jews, and it comes in the section entitled "Unicity and Universality of the Salvific Mystery of Jesus Christ," a title almost identical with the subtitle of the document as a whole. "It was," declares *Dominus Iesus*, "in the awareness of the one universal gift of salvation offered by the Father through Jesus Christ in the Spirit (cf. Eph 1:3-14), that the first Christians encountered the Jewish people, showing them the fulfillment of salvation that went beyond the Law and, in the same awareness, they confronted the pagan world of their time, which aspired to salvation through a plurality of saviors" (DI 13). The following passages make it crystal clear that this encounter with the Jews is to be seen in the context of the firm belief that "the universal salvific will of the One and Triune God is offered and accomplished once for all in the mystery of the incarnation, death, and resurrection of the Son of God" (DI 14). It is almost superfluous to pursue the argument further. Though one short section, which declares "the canonical books of the Old and New Testament" fundamentally different from the sacred writings of other religions (DI 8), clearly places Judaism and Christianity in the same category, it needs to be stressed that the central theme of the entire declaration, underscored on virtually every page, is that salvation comes in only one essential fashion for all humanity, and that is through the triune God of Christianity and his embodied Word. To suggest that Jews, who reject belief in both trinity and incarnation, attain salvation outside this otherwise universal system is to render the document virtually incoherent.

The principal author of *Dominus Iesus* is, of course, Joseph Cardinal Ratzinger. On December 29th, the Cardinal wrote a conciliatory piece in *L'Osservatore Romano* emphasizing that "the faith witnessed by the Jewish Bible" is special to Christians because it is the foundation of their own; consequently, the dialogue with Jews takes place on a different level from all others. As a Jewish observer pointed out, the article appeals to this special relationship to assert that the Nazis "tried to strike the Christian faith at its Abrahamic roots in the Jewish people." This is a deeply objectionable effort to transform the Final Solution into a primarily anti-Christian campaign, but it is peripheral to our main concerns. The key point is that Cardinal Ratzinger's affirmation of a unique Jewish-Christian relationship, which also includes the prayer that the paths of Jews and Christians will eventually converge, in no way contradicts or even modifies the unflinching message of *Dominus Iesus*. To understand the Cardinal's position more clearly, we need to look at his other writings about Jews and Judaism, collected in a slim volume entitled *Many Religions, One Covenant*. In these essays, he speaks of reconciliation, emphasizes the ongoing role of the Jewish people, and defends the value of the Hebrew Bible. It is clear, however, that he understands these positions as a rejection of the quasi-Marcionite position that the Hebrew Bible and its God embody reprehensible moral and religious qualities. On the contrary, argues the Cardinal, the God of the Hebrew Bible is the same as that of the New Testament, and the Law of the Hebrew Bible, seen through the prism of the new covenant, does not really stand in conflict with it. But all this is simply classic, pre-modern Christian doctrine recast in a spirit of friendship.

"The Sinai covenant," writes Cardinal Ratzinger [in *Many Religions, One Covenant*], "is indeed superseded. But once what was provisional in it has been swept away we see what is truly definitive in it. The New Covenant, which becomes clearer and clearer as the history of Israel unfolds..., fulfills the dynamic expectation found in [the Sinai covenant]" (pp. 70-71). And in another formulation, "All cultic ordinances of the Old Testament are seen to be taken up into [Jesus'] death and brought to their deepest meaning...The universalizing of the Torah by Jesus...preserves the unity of cult and ethos. The entire cult is bound together in the Cross, indeed, for the first time has become fully real." Cardinal Ratzinger, then, who has also declared that despite Israel's special mission at this stage of history, "we wait for the instant in which Israel will say yes to Christ" (*National Catholic Reporter*, 6 October 2000), is a supersessionist. At this point, we need to confront the real question, to wit, is there anything objectionable about this position?

In a dialogical environment in which the term "supersessionism" has been turned into an epithet by both Jews and Christians, this may appear to be a puzzling question. We need to distinguish, however, between two forms of supersessionism, and in my view Jews have absolutely no right to object to the form endorsed by Cardinal Ratzinger. There is nothing in the core beliefs of Christianity that requires the sort of supersessionism that sees Judaism as spiritually arid, as an expression of narrow, petty legalism pursued in the service of a vengeful God and eventually replaced by a vital religion of universal love. Such a depiction is anti-Jewish, even antisemitic. But Cardinal Ratzinger never describes Judaism in such a fashion. On the contrary, he sees believing Jews as witnesses through their observance of Torah to the commitment to God's will, to the establishment of his kingdom even in the pre-messianic world, and to faith in a wholly just world after the ultimate redemption (*Many Religions, One Covenant*, pp. 104-105). This understanding of Jews as a witness people is very different from the original Augustinian version in which Jews testified to Christian truth through their validation of the Hebrew Bible and their interminable suffering in exile.

For Jews to denounce this sort of supersessionism as morally wrong and disqualifying in the context of dialogue is to turn dialogue into a novel form of religious intimidation. As Rabbi Joseph B. Soloveitchik understood very well, such a position is pragmatically dangerous for Jews, who become vulnerable to reciprocal demands for theological reform of Judaism, and it is even morally wrong. To illustrate the point from the perspective of Orthodox Judaism, I will not shrink from mobilizing the most telling illustration.

The cardinal theological sin in Judaism is *avodah zarah*, literally "foreign worship." I became embroiled in a controversy several years ago when I carelessly used the usual translation "idolatry," which is in fact sloppy and misleading in our context. Properly understood, *avodah zarah* is the formal recognition or worship as God of an entity that is in fact not God. For Jews, the worship of Jesus of Nazareth as God incarnate falls within this definition. Because of the monotheistic, non-pagan character of Christianity, many Jewish authorities denied that worship of Jesus is sinful for non-Jews, though many others did not endorse this exemption. Now, let us assume that I respect the Christian religion, as I do. Let us assume further that I respect believing Christians, as I do, for qualities that emerge precisely out of their Christian faith. But I believe that the worship of Jesus as God is a serious religious error displeasing to God even if the worshiper is a non-Jew, and that at the end of days Christians will come to recognize this. Is this belief immoral? Does it disqualify me as a participant in dialogue? Does it entitle a Christian to denounce me for adhering to a teaching of contempt? I hope the answer to these questions is "no." If it is "yes," then interfaith dialogue is destructive of traditional Judaism and must be abandoned forthwith. We would face a remarkable paradox. Precisely because of its striving for interfaith respect and understanding, dialogue would become an instrument of religious imperialism. Once I take this position, I must extend it to Christians as well. As long as Christians do not vilify Judaism and Jews in the manner that I described earlier, they have every right to assert that Judaism errs about religious questions of the most central importance, that equality in dialogue does not mean the equal standing of the parties' religious doctrines, that at the end of days Jews will recognize the divinity of Jesus, even that salvation is much more difficult for one who stands outside the Catholic Church. If I were to criticize Cardinal Ratzinger for holding these views, I would be applying an egregious double standard. I am not unmindful of the fact that these doctrines, unlike comparable ones in Judaism, have served as a basis for persecution through the centuries. Nonetheless, once a Christian has explicitly severed the link between such beliefs and anti-Jewish attitudes and behavior, one cannot legitimately demand that he or she abandon them.

We are left, however, with the profoundly troubling passage about mission as a fundamental component of inter-religious dialogue. Is it possible that at least this assertion does not apply to Jews? Once again the answer must be negative. Here too the language of the declaration is thoroughly universal. "The Church, guided by charity and respect for freedom, must be primarily committed to proclaiming to all people the truth definitively revealed by the Lord, and to announcing the necessity of conversion to Jesus Christ and of adherence to the Church through baptism and the other sacraments in order to participate fully in communion with God, the Father, Son, and Holy Spirit" (DI 22). Moreover, in an essay on dialogue dealing primarily with Jews and explicitly including them in the key passage, Cardinal Ratzinger wrote that missionary activity should not "cease and be replaced by dialogue... This would be nothing other than total lack of conviction. Rather, mission and dialogue should no longer be opposites but should mutually interpenetrate. Dialogue is not aimless conversation: it aims at conviction, at finding the truth; otherwise it is worthless." In a world where other people already know something about God, "proclamation of the gospel must be necessarily a dialogical process. We are not telling the other person something that is entirely unknown to him, rather, we are opening up the hidden depth of something with which, in his own religion, he is already in touch" (*Many Religions, One Covenant*, p. 112).

In sum, we now have an official document of the Catholic Church, "ratified and confirmed" by the Pope himself, declaring that a key purpose of inter-

faith dialogue is mission. There is overwhelming evidence that the author intended this to apply to Jews as well. Are there any considerations capable of
mitigating the impact of such a statement sufficiently to enable a self-respect-
ing Jew to continue to pursue this enterprise? The answer, I think, is yes, but it
is a highly qualified yes. First, it is very likely that a substantial majority of
Catholics involved in the dialogue disagree with this assertion in *Dominus
Iesus* despite its official standing. Second, Cardinal Ratzinger himself asserts in
his other writings that the teachings of the Church Fathers instruct us that before the end of days "the Jews must remain alongside us as a witness to the
world" (*Many Religions, One Covenant*, p. 104). And speaking about dialogue
among religions in general, he says that unification "is hardly possible within
our historical time, and perhaps it is not even desirable" (p. 109). Finally, if dialogue avoids discussion of core doctrinal issues and focuses on shared moral,
social, and political concerns, it may well be justified even with people whose
conversionary objectives are much sharper that those of *Dominus Iesus*. Many
Jews hold discussions about such issues with evangelical Protestants who conduct overt missions to the Jews, and Rabbi Soloveitchik, who did not believe
that such objectives had been abandoned by the Catholic Church, endorsed discussion of these matters with full awareness that theological content would play
a significant role.

Orthodox Jews are routinely subjected to criticism for their resistance to
theological dialogue, though the carefully formulated agenda of this meeting
demonstrates that boundaries are not altogether inflexible. The appearance of
an official Catholic assertion that a major objective of dialogue is mission is a
striking, unwelcome, and, for me at least, unexpected validation of Rabbi
Soloveitchik's much-maligned concerns. At the very least, criticism of the
avoidance of dialogue about doctrinal issues should be suspended as long as
this passage of *Dominus Iesus* remains in force without a formal assertion by
the Congregation for the Doctrine of the Faith or the Pope himself that it does
not apply to dialogue with Jews.

Many of the criticisms leveled against *Dominus Iesus* strike me as unwar-
ranted, and I greatly admire Cardinal Ratzinger's profound commitment to his
faith. Despite huge gaps in implementation, the Catholic Church as a whole and
the Pope in particular have taken steps to improve relations with the Jewish
people that merit our highest regard. Generally speaking, criticisms of these initiatives from both Jewish and Christian quarters, even when technically valid,
diminish their moral significance and sometimes cross the line into blinkered,
almost churlish petulance. For all its imperfections, I see the statement on the
Shoah as a historic act of genuine ethical stature, and the Pope's apology for
Christian antisemitism and his behavior during his trip to Israel fill me with un-
alloyed admiration. But a climactic paragraph of *Dominus Iesus* effectively expects Jews to participate in an endeavor officially described as an effort to lead
them, however gently and indirectly, to accept beliefs antithetical to the core of
their faith. Many Jews will no doubt swallow their self-respect and proceed as
if nothing has happened. But it is not clear that they should, and they should
surely not be criticized if they do not.

PART THREE

SIC ET NON:
THEOLOGICAL DISCUSSION OF
DOMINUS IESUS

1

INTRODUCTION
AND ECCLESIOLOGICAL ISSUES

Francis A. Sullivan, S.J.

INTRODUCTION

This essay will begin with a brief introduction to *Dominus Iesus* as a whole. I shall say something about its doctrinal authority, its occasion and purpose, and its principal themes. In the body of the essay I shall discuss the ecclesiological issues which it raises.

Doctrinal authority

The declaration *Dominus Iesus* was issued by the Congregation for the Doctrine of the Faith on September 5, 2000. This Congregation (CDF) has delegated authority from the Pope to exercise vigilance over the teaching of Catholic doctrine, to set forth the official positions of the church, and to condemn opinions that are judged to be contrary to Catholic faith. Official statements of the CDF are submitted to the Pope for his approval before being published. This one concludes by saying: "Pope John Paul II, with sure knowledge and his apostolic authority, ratified and confirmed this Declaration and ordered its publication." A declaration issued by the CDF with such strong papal confirmation is certainly authoritative, and must be taken seriously by all members of the Catholic Church. But it remains a document of the Congregation, not of the Pope himself, and thus has a lesser degree of authority than a papal encyclical would have. Thus, for instance, on questions regarding ecumenism, it has less authority than the papal encyclical *Ut unum sint.* In encyclicals, popes exercise their ordinary teaching authority, which as such does not oblige Catholics to give their definitive assent, but calls for an attitude of respectful listening and willingness to conform one's judgment to his teaching, as far as one is able to do so.

What response, then, does *Dominus Iesus* call for from Catholic theologians? It certainly calls for a response that respects the authority that the Pope has given it by delegation and by confirmation. It deserves careful analysis of its arguments and its conclusions. Theologians must distinguish between statements in it which are already dogmas of faith, and other statements that enjoy various lesser degrees of doctrinal weight. At the same time, a document such as this cannot be immune from respectful critique on the part of Catholic theologians. They have an indispensable critical role to play, not only with regard to what other theologians are saying but also with regard to statements issued with ordinary, non-definitive teaching authority. Much of the progress made at Vatican II would have been impossible if it had not been for the critical work done by Catholic theologians, often at great cost to themselves, in the decades prior to the Council. I am confident that any criticism of *Dominus Iesus* that will be expressed in the following essays will be respectful of the authority with which it was issued.

Occasion and purpose

In the statement which he made on the occasion of the official promulgation of this declaration, Cardinal Ratzinger, prefect of the CDF, made it clear that what prompted the Congregation to issue this document was the concern that, not only among theologians but among the Catholic faithful as well, the opinion was becoming more and more accepted that all religions are equally valid ways of salvation for their adherents. The inevitable consequence of seeing Christianity as merely one among many equally salvific religions has been to deny the uniqueness and universality of Jesus Christ as the savior of the whole of humanity, and the role of his church as the "universal sacrament of salvation." A further consequence of such thinking has been to endanger the church's missionary effort to bring the message of Christ to people who have not yet heard or accepted it. The purpose of this document, then, as the declaration itself states, is to "recall to Bishops, theologians, and all the Catholic faithful, certain indispensable elements of Christian doctrine...not to propose solutions to questions that are matters of free theological debate, but rather to set forth again the doctrine of the Catholic faith in these areas" (§3).

Principal themes

Among the "indispensable elements of Christian doctrine" which the CDF saw as being endangered by relativistic theories of religious pluralism, it listed the following:

> the definitive and complete character of the revelation in Jesus Christ, the nature of Christian faith as compared with that of belief in other religions, the inspired nature of the books of Sacred Scripture, the personal unity between the Eternal Word and Jesus of Nazareth, the unity of the economy of the Incarnate Word and the Holy Spirit, the unicity and salvific universality of the mystery of Jesus Christ, the universal salvific mediation of the Church, the inseparability—while recognizing the distinction—of the kingdom of God, the kingdom of Christ,

and the Church, and the subsistence of the one Church of Christ in the Catholic Church (§4).

These are the doctrines which constitute the principal themes of *Dominus Iesus.* The last three are the "ecclesiological issues" which will be treated in this essay.

ECCLESIOLOGICAL ISSUES

The universal salvific mediation of the church

During most of the church's history, the necessary role of the church in salvation was expressed negatively, in the axiom: "No salvation outside the church." It was commonly believed that people who were not members of the church, such as pagans, Jews, heretics, and schismatics, would justly be condemned by God for their refusal to belong to the one "ark" which offered salvation.[1] However, the discoveries of the fifteenth and sixteenth centuries made it clear that there were vast numbers of people who could not be held responsible for their being "outside the church," but were, at the same time, objects of God's universal salvific will. Catholic theologians began to apply to such people the notion which had already been used with regard to catechumens who died before actually receiving baptism: that their desire for the sacrament could suffice. Applying the view of Thomas Aquinas that an implicit desire could suffice if a person were ignorant of the need of baptism, theologians concluded that for people who were inculpably ignorant of their obligation to belong to the church, the necessary role of the church in their salvation would be satisfied by a desire which was implicit in their readiness to obey the will of God in their regard. While it took some centuries for their view to prevail and become the official teaching of the church, it was confirmed by Pope Pius XII in his encyclical on the Mystical Body (1943), and was further spelled out in the letter of the Holy Office to Archbishop Cushing (1949), which rejected the rigid interpretation of *extra ecclesiam nulla salus* being propagated by Leonard Feeney, S.J.[2]

The Second Vatican Council reaffirmed the necessity of the church for salvation, but at the same time recognized the possibility of salvation for those who were not guilty of a sinful refusal to belong to her.[3] It spoke of such people as being "related to the church in various ways," using the Latin term *ordinantur,* which suggests an orientation toward the church.[4] Vatican II did not express this in terms of an implicit desire to belong to the church, but it suggested that the necessary role of the church in the salvation of people who do not actually belong to her is explained by their relatedness to her. The distinctive contribution of Vatican II to this question is its description of the church as the "universal sacrament of salvation."[5] A sacrament is both sign and instrument of grace. To see the church as the "universal sacrament of salvation" is to see it as sign of the total work of salvation that God is accomplishing in the world, and as being used by God as an instrument in the accomplishment of that work.

This idea was expressed by the council in another context when it said of the church that "established by God as a fellowship of life, charity and truth, it is also used by him as an instrument for the redemption of all."[6] It is obvious that the church has an instrumental role in the salvation of those who belong to it. It is not so clear, nor did Vatican II offer an explanation of, how it is used by God as an instrument for the salvation of those who are not its members.

As we have seen above, *Dominus Iesus* names the "universal salvific mediation of the Church" as an indispensable element of Christian doctrine which needs to be reaffirmed, against a pluralist theory that would "consider the Church as *one way* of salvation alongside those constituted by other religions, seen as complementary to the Church or substantially equivalent to her" (§21). The first reference to the role of the church as mediating salvation is based on the Pauline notion of the church as the body of Christ: "Jesus Christ continues his presence and his work of salvation in the Church and by means of the Church which is his body" (§16). Section VI of the document, which treats this theme, begins with the doctrine of Vatican II about the necessity of the church for salvation, and its description of the church as "universal sacrament of salvation." In explaining this term, the CDF again invokes the notion of the church as body of Christ: "United always in a mysterious way to the Savior Jesus Christ, her Head, and subordinated to him, she has, in God's plan, an indispensable relationship with the salvation of every human being" (§20). Quoting John Paul II's encyclical *Redemptoris missio,* it continues: "For those who are not formally and visibly members of the Church, 'salvation in Christ is accessible by virtue of a grace which, while having a mysterious relationship to the Church, does not make them formally part of the Church, but enlightens them in a way which is accommodated to their spiritual and material situation.'"[7]

The CDF then goes on to acknowledge the fact that "with respect to the *way* in which the salvific grace of God—which is always given by means of Christ in the Spirit and has a mysterious relationship to the Church—comes to individual non-Christians, the Second Vatican Council limited itself to the statement that God bestows it 'in ways known to himself.' Theologians are seeking to understand this question more fully. Their work is to be encouraged" (§21). While the CDF does not offer any solution to this question, it does go beyond speaking of the salvation of non-Christians as having a "mysterious" or even "indispensable" relationship to the church, by saying: "With the coming of the Savior Jesus Christ, God has willed that the Church founded by him be the instrument for the salvation of *all* humanity" (§22). In the following sentence it even describes this as a "truth of faith." This raises the question whether the CDF means to describe as a "truth of faith" the proposition that the church exercises an instrumental causality in the salvation of everyone who is saved. The texts to which reference is given in support of this statement speak of Christ as the Savior of all mankind, and of the church as sent to bring his message of salvation to the whole world, but they hardly answer the question whether the church exercises instrumental causality in the salvation of people whom it does not reach with its ministry. Nor does the "universal mediation" of the church in salvation have to be understood in terms of instrumental causality.[8] I believe that the mediation of the church in the salvation of those whom it does not reach can be seen in the fact that the church offers the eucharistic sacrifice for the salvation of the whole world.[9] In my opinion it is not likely that the CDF intended to assert as a "truth of faith" that the church exercises instrumental causality in every instance of salvation. I would see that as one of the "questions that are matters of free theological debate" to which the CDF did not intend to propose solutions (§3).

Kingdom of God, kingdom of Christ, and church

The theme of section V of *Dominus Iesus* is practically identical with the theme of chapter II of the encyclical *Redemptoris missio* of Pope John Paul II: namely, that while kingdom of God, kingdom of Christ, and church are distinct realities, they are inseparable from one another. The reason which both the Pope and the CDF have had for insisting on their inseparability is that some theologians have been proposing a "kingdom-centered" theory of the divine economy of salvation, which effectively separates the kingdom of God from Christ and from the church. This is one version of a "theocentric" concept of salvation, in which God's plan of salvation and his kingdom embrace the whole world, but the role of Christ and the church are limited to the salvation of Christians.

Recognizing that there can be various theological explanations of the relationships among kingdom of God, kingdom of Christ, and church, *Dominus Iesus* insists that no explanation is admissible which would deny their intimate connection. Following the lead of *Redemptoris missio,* it declares that if the kingdom is separated from Jesus, it is no longer the kingdom of God which he revealed. Likewise, the church is not an end unto itself, but is ordered toward the kingdom of God, of which it is the seed, sign, and instrument. While remaining distinct from Christ and the kingdom, the church is indissolubly united to Christ as his body, and to the kingdom as its sacrament. The CDF concludes that theories which deny the uniqueness of the relationship which Christ and the church have with the kingdom of God are contrary to the Catholic faith.

The church of Christ subsists in the Catholic Church

Dominus Iesus is primarily concerned to reaffirm the unique role which Christ's church plays in the salvation of all of humanity, as against relativistic theories which describe other religions as equally valid ways of salvation. The reaffirmation of the teaching of Vatican II that the church of Christ "subsists in" the Catholic Church would seem to be aimed at another form of relativism, according to which all the various Christian communities would be seen as equal components of the universal church of Christ. Against this view, the CDF not only restates the doctrine of Vatican II, but also offers an interpretation of it which is different from the one it gave fifteen years ago.

To explain the language that Vatican II used, it is helpful to recall that the official Catholic doctrine prior to the council, as expressed, for instance, in the encyclical *Mystici Corporis* of Pius XII, was that the church of Christ is strictly and exclusively identified with the Catholic Church. This was still asserted in the first two drafts of Vatican II's Constitution on the Church, which said flatly: "The Church of Christ is the Catholic Church." The observation made by a number of bishops that this exclusive identification was inconsistent with the acknowledged presence of elements of the church elsewhere led the council to the decision no longer to say that the church of Christ *is* the Catholic Church, but to say, rather, that it *subsists in* it.[10] The intention clearly was to continue to make a positive statement about the Catholic Church, without the negative implication that the previous doctrine of exclusive identity had regarding the other churches. However, the Theological Commission did not spell out in detail how the term "subsists in" was to be understood.

This question was raised by Leonardo Boff, who proposed that one could say that the church of Christ subsists also in other churches. In its critical "Notification" of 1985 concerning Boff's book, *Church, Charism and Power*,[11] the CDF rejected this opinion as contrary to the authentic meaning of Vatican II. It added: "The Council instead chose the word *subsistit* precisely to clarify that there exists only one 'subsistence' of the true Church, while outside of her visible structure there only exist *elementa Ecclesiae*, which—being elements of that same Church—tend and lead toward the Catholic Church."[12]

In an article published in 1986,[13] I criticized this statement by the CDF, noting that Vatican II had not said that outside the Catholic Church there exist *only* elements of the church. I observed that if that were what the council had meant, it would hardly have been consistent with itself when it recognized that there were not only elements, but churches and ecclesial communities outside the Catholic Church. I also argued that the meaning of *subsistit* which best corresponds to its meaning in classical Latin, and to its context in the passage where it occurs, is "continues to exist." I further argued that in the light of the Decree on Ecumenism, one can conclude that the council meant to affirm that the church which Christ founded continues to exist in the Catholic Church with a fullness of the means of grace and of unity that is not found in any other church.

It is gratifying to see that this is how the term is now explained in *Dominus Iesus*, which says: "With the expression *subsistit in*, the Second Vatican Council sought to harmonize two doctrinal statements: on the one hand, that the Church of Christ, despite the divisions which exist among Christians, continues to exist fully only in the Catholic Church, and on the other hand, that 'outside of her structure, many elements can be found of sanctification and truth'" (§16). Here the word "fully" plays a key role; it is only if "subsists" means "continues to exist fully" that one can say that the church of Christ subsists *only* in the Catholic Church. It is crucial to keep this in mind when one reads footnote 56 of *Dominus Iesus*, which says: "The interpretation of those who would derive from the formula *subsistit in* the thesis that the one Church of Christ could subsist also in non-Catholic Churches and ecclesial communities is therefore contrary to the authentic meaning of *Lumen gentium*." I would insist that this is true only if *subsistit* means what the CDF now agrees that it means. To be noted also is the fact that in its recent document the CDF does not say that outside the visible structure of the Catholic Church there exist *only* elements of the church (even though in footnote 56 it quotes its 1985 statement which did say that).

Other churches and ecclesial communities

In *Dominus Iesus* the CDF has followed Vatican II in recognizing that outside the Catholic Church there are not only elements of the church, but Christian communities which are used by the Holy Spirit as means of salvation for their members. In speaking of them, the Council consistently distinguished between those which it called "churches" and those which it called "ecclesial communities." While there is no explicit explanation of this language in the conciliar documents, its meaning can be inferred from a passage in the Decree on Ecumenism which says, speaking of "the ecclesial communities separated from us": "We believe that especially because of the lack of the sacrament of orders they have not preserved the genuine and total reality of the Eucharistic mystery."[14] On the other hand, in a report to the bishops, the commission responsible for this text mentioned the Old Catholics, saying that their communities, like the Orthodox, should be called churches "in view of the valid sacrament of orders and valid Eucharist which they possess."[15] From these texts it is evident that the council judged the presence of "the genuine and total reality of the Eucharistic mystery" so essential to the full reality of a church that it preferred not to use this term of communities which, "because of the lack of the sacrament of orders," had not preserved it. The council never specified which those communities were, but it was well known that Pope Leo XIII had declared Anglican orders invalid, and that orders in most Protestant communities were not conferred by episcopal ordination in the historic apostolic succession, on which Catholics believe their validity to depend.

In its recent document, then, the CDF has followed Vatican II in distinguishing between "churches" and "ecclesial communities," and in limiting the term "churches" to those in which the Catholic Church recognizes the presence of valid orders. Speaking of them it says:

> The Churches which, while not existing in perfect communion with the Catholic Church, remain united to her by means of the closest bonds, that is, by apostolic succession and a valid Eucharist, are true particular Churches. Therefore the Church of Christ is present and operative also in these Churches, even though they lack full communion with the Catholic Church, since they do not accept the Catholic doctrine of the Primacy, which, according to the will of God, the Bishop of Rome objectively has and exercises over the entire Church (§17).

It is obvious that here such churches as the Orthodox are being recognized as "true particular Churches." This was explicitly noted by Fernando Ocáriz, a member of Opus Dei and a regular consultor to the CDF, who took part with Cardinal Ratzinger in the presentation of *Dominus Iesus* to the press, giving a summary of the ecclesiological contents of the declaration. He explained that to speak of "true particular Churches" means to say that they are portions of the one People of God, and that the one, holy, catholic, and apostolic church is present and operative in them. He went on to say: "Therefore there exists only one Church (subsisting in the Catholic Church) and at the same time there exist true particular Churches which are not Catholic. This is not a paradox: there exists only one Church of which all the true particular Churches are portions, even though in some of them (those that are not Catholic) there is not the fullness of church, since their union with the whole is not perfect because of their lack of full communion with . . . the Successor of Peter."

Given the fact that Ocáriz is a consultor of the CDF, and was called upon to present the ecclesiology of *Dominus Iesus* to the press, it is safe to say that it is now the mind of this official body that the church of Christ is more extensive than the Roman Catholic Church, and that it includes all "true particular churches," that is, those which have preserved a valid episcopate, and in which the church of Christ is present and operative. Vatican II explained that the universal church exists "in and from" the particular churches.[16] It would seem, therefore, to be the mind of the CDF that the church of Christ consists of all and only those which it calls "true particular Churches." While not all of these are "fully" churches, they all have the essential gifts of episcopate and Eucharist, and while not all are in full communion, their actual unity is seen as sufficient to justify speaking of all of them together as constituting the one church of Christ. This corresponds to a statement made by John Paul II in his apostolic letter *Orientale lumen.* In a context in which he was referring to the effort to restore full communion between the Catholic Church and the separated Eastern churches, he said: "The church of Christ is one. If divisions exist, that is one thing; they must be overcome, but the church is one, the church of Christ between East and West can only be one, one and united."[17]

This positive assessment of the non-Catholic churches which have preserved valid episcopal orders is followed by a negative assessment of those which are judged to lack them. As is well known, Vatican II had spoken of these as "ecclesial communities," rather than as "churches." On the other hand, the council never flatly declared that the ecclesial communities are "not churches in the proper sense." This the CDF has now done in *Dominus Iesus,* saying: "The ecclesial communities which have not preserved the valid Episcopate and the genuine and integral substance of the Eucharistic mystery, are not Churches in the proper sense" (§17). The strongly critical comments which have been expressed by a number of Anglicans and Protestants have understandably focused on this statement.

Negative reaction to Dominus Iesus

I suggest that the strength of this reaction can be explained in the light of hope that had been raised during more than thirty years of productive dialogues in which the Catholic Church had been engaged with the Anglican and Protestant churches, and the sense that a dash of cold water has been thrown on this hope by the recent document. The hope I refer to was that the Catholic Church might be moving toward a more favorable evaluation of the ecclesial status of these communities with which it has been in dialogue. The dialogues had shown that there was broad agreement not only between Catholics and Anglicans but also between Catholics and Lutherans on Eucharist and ministry, as well as on the doctrine of justification. Many on both sides have thought that the recognition of common faith on such important matters would justify a more positive evaluation of the churches involved.

In what way has the CDF in its recent document disappointed this hope? As we have seen, it has spoken in a more negative fashion than Vatican II in saying that such communities "are not churches in the proper sense." It makes no mention of the agreements which Catholics have reached in dialogues with Anglicans and Protestants during the past three decades, and thus gives no encouragement to the idea that those agreements could justify a more positive evaluation of their churches than was expressed at Vatican II. Finally, the CDF has ignored a positive statement that was made about the ecclesial communities at the council, and which was repeated by John Paul II in his encyclical *Ut unum sint*. Let us consider these points in a bit more detail.

Perhaps one might justify the silence of the CDF regarding agreements reached in dialogues with Anglicans and Protestants on the grounds that *Dominus Iesus* was principally concerned with the other religions. However, the disappointing fact remains that it spoke more negatively than Vatican II had about Christian communities with which the Catholic Church has been in prolonged and productive dialogue, with no hint that judgments being made in Rome concerning those communities might reflect the progress made in the recognition of the extent to which we share common faith.

In *Dominus Iesus* it is only with regard to the Orthodox Churches and others having valid episcopal orders that the statement is made that "the Church of Christ is present and operative in them." However, that this can be said, although with some qualifications, also of the other Christian communities, was affirmed at Vatican II by its Theological Commission, which explained and justified the council's use of the expression "ecclesial communities," in the following way:

> It must not be overlooked that the communities that have their origin in the separation that took place in the West are not merely a sum or collection of individual Christians, but they are constituted by social ecclesiastical elements which they have preserved from our common patrimony, and which confer on them a truly ecclesial character. In these communities the one sole church of Christ is present, albeit imperfectly, in a way that is somewhat like its presence in particular churches, and by means of their ecclesiastical elements the church of Christ is in some way operative in them.[18]

This positive assessment of the "ecclesial communities" that was expressed at Vatican II was recently confirmed by John Paul II, when he said: "Indeed, the

elements of sanctification and truth present in the other Christian communities
…constitutes the objective basis of the communion, albeit imperfect, which
exists between them and the Catholic Church. To the extent that these elements
are found in other Christian communities, the one church of Christ is effectively present in them."[19]

Despite what both Vatican II and the Pope have said, the recent document
of the CDF would give one the impression that the church of Christ is present
and operative only in those which it calls "true particular Churches." More than
thirty years of productive dialogue would surely have warranted a more positive appreciation of the ecclesial character of the Anglican and Protestant communities than one finds in *Dominus Iesus*.

One way to arrive at a more positive appreciation would be to balance the
one-sided emphasis that has been put on the question of the validity of ministry
in those communities by giving the proper emphasis to its evident fruitfulness.
Whatever deficiency there may be with regard to their orders, there can be no
doubt about the life of grace and salvation which has been communicated for
centuries through the preaching of the word of God and other Christian ministry in the Anglican and Protestant churches. We have to keep in mind that the
"fullness" which Vatican II and *Dominus Iesus* attribute to the Catholic Church
is a matter of institutional integrity: a fullness of the *means* of grace, which is
not the same thing as the fullness of grace itself. There is no question of denying that other Christian communities, perhaps lacking something in the order of
means, can achieve a higher degree of communion with Christ in faith, hope,
and love than many a Catholic community. Means of grace have to be used well
to achieve their effect, and the possession of a fullness of means is no guarantee of how well they will be used.

2

A RAHNERIAN RESPONSE

Harvey D. Egan, S.J.

Given the current inter-religious climate at Boston College and in many places in the wider church, I welcome the Vatican declaration *Dominus Iesus* because it rightly eschews "that mentality of indifferentism characterized by a religious relativism which leads to the belief that 'one religion is as good as another'" (§22), while at the same time rejecting "nothing of what is true and holy in these religions" (§2). Moreover, the declaration "seeks to recall to Bishops, theologians, and all the Catholic faithful, certain indispensable elements of Christian doctrine" (§3), namely, that Jesus Christ is the *one* mediator between God and humanity, that Jesus Christ died and rose for *all,* that Jesus Christ is the definitive and full revelation of God, that the Holy Spirit always was and is the Spirit of Jesus Christ, that the salvific work of the Logos and the Spirit can never be dissociated from Christ, and that the "Church of Christ . . . continues to exist *fully only* in the Catholic Church, and on the other hand, that outside of her structure, many elements can be found of sanctification and truth" (§16, emphasis added).

Thus, the declaration strives to speak to a Roman Catholic audience about truths of the faith which should be self-evident. Some critics of the declaration accuse the magisterium of bad faith because of the somewhat public nature of its promulgation. However, these critics might be the same people who would be the first to brand church authorities as "secretive," had they chosen a more private forum.

The torrent of negative responses to this document prompted the media to proclaim it a "public relations disaster."[1] But after several careful readings of this admirable declaration—a document which in fact says little beyond what one reads in the documents of the Second Vatican Council and the two encyclical letters of Pope John Paul II, *Redemptoris missio* and *Fides et ratio*—I concluded that both the negative responses to it and the contemporary theological and pastoral scene prove convincingly just how necessary and timely this declaration is. Now even the apex in the "hierarchy of truths" must be defended.

Two concerns immediately sprang to mind as I read *Dominus Iesus.* The first is represented by an event that occurred a few years ago when emergency surgery prompted a colleague to ask me to replace him at an international, inter-religious symposium on mysticism that was to be held in Israel. Given the short notice, I requested a brief description of his planned lectures. When I asked why they focused almost exclusively on the negative way[2] in Christian mysticism, he replied that believers in other religions do not like to hear about Jesus Christ. However, I went to Israel as a member of the Society of *Jesus*—in no way hesitant to speak about the riches of a tradition that has penetrated to the heart of the mystery of the Triune God in Christ. In fact, these talks were well received.

The second concern has to do with the passion for inter-religious dialogue, which sometimes leads scholars to encourage students to participate in various forms of non-Christian worship. For these scholars, one must promote non-Christian religions—not only tolerate them. I would maintain, however, that most Catholic students do not know their own tradition. Helping to promote non-Christian religions does not aid Christian students to deepen their own identity by coming to terms with the *internal* criteria by which they can measure their fidelity to the Christian tradition. If one truly *worships* the crucified and risen Christ, the *only* Son of God, then this indeed casts a different light on how one ought to approach religious pluralism. The question early Christians put to the heretical Arians remains apposite: "Why do you worship a creature?" If one truly worships Jesus Christ as the God-Man, pluralism must give way to singularity.

The declaration urges theologians to seek to understand "the *way* in which the salvific grace of God—which is always given by means of Christ in the Spirit and has a mysterious relationship to the Church—comes to individual non-Christians" (§21). No theologian has struggled harder to find a theological explanation of this "way" than Karl Rahner.

DOMINUS IESUS—A CRITICISM OF RAHNER'S THEOLOGY?

Some theologians read *Dominus Iesus* as a veiled attack on the great German theologian, Karl Rahner, S.J., who died in 1984. In part, I was invited to respond to *Dominus Iesus* because of my work on this theological titan. Let me say right off that Rahner's theology definitely agrees with *almost* everything in this document, especially its self-evident high Christology and its Christocentric pneumatology and ecclesiology. Moreover, Rahner took to heart what Ignatius of Loyola wrote in his *Spiritual Exercises:* "It is necessary to suppose that every good Christian is more ready to put a good interpretation on another's statement than to condemn it as false."[3] Rahner never demonized or patronized his theological or ecclesiastical opponents. Critical reverence for church authority and tradition flowed from what he called his "indissoluble relationship" to the church.

Perhaps the secret of Rahner's appeal is his synthesis of three elements: an awesome respect for the Roman Catholic tradition, an indefatigable effort to bring about Christian unity, and a deep respect for non-Christian religions. He would have applauded the declaration's desire to hold together both inter-religious dialogue and "the *missio ad gentes,* directed toward that 'mystery of unity,' from which 'it follows that all men and women who are saved share, though differently, in the same mystery of salvation in Jesus Christ through his

Spirit'" (§2). Still, he would have undoubtedly recommended reading *Dominus Iesus* along with the more ecumenically directed encyclical, *Ut unum sint.*

A reading of Rahner's monumental *Foundations of Christian Faith*[4] and various articles in the twenty-three English volumes of his *Theological Investigations* evinces his profound Christocentrism, his unabashed Roman Catholic identity, and his ecumenical and inter-religious openness. He stated repeatedly that Jesus Christ is the absolute, eschatological expression and offer of God's own self, without which Christology is not Christian.[5]

Toward the end of his life Rahner said: "Despite my ecumenical openness . . . the fact remains that I must be and want to be a Catholic, a Roman Catholic . . . Even today I consider religious indifference as something completely erroneous, despite my conviction that the Christian confessions can and must do more than they have done to unite in the one Church of Christ."[6] The question posed by some disgruntled Catholics—"Shall I stay in the Church?"— made Rahner almost physically ill.[7] Still, his last book, *Unity of the Churches: A Real Possibility,*[8] and the prayer composed on his death bed, "Prayer for the Reunion of All Christians,"[9] demonstrate his theological daring in matters ecumenical. Also, his article (to cite but one), "On the Importance of Non-Christian Religions for Salvation,"[10] witnesses to his genuine openness to non-Christian religions.

Rahner understood that because of sin, one aspect of God's loving self-communication—which reached its high point in Jesus crucified and risen—is the forgiveness and healing of sins now required to make us partakers of the divine life. However, like Duns Scotus, he also maintained that even if Adam had not sinned, the incarnation would have still taken place because God creates in order to communicate self. Covenant, our deification—not redemption from sin—is God's *primary* purpose for creation and the Incarnation. From the very beginning, all creation, the one human race, the one history of revelation and salvation, and the whole of world history are all oriented to the incarnate Word.

Rahner often cited 1 Timothy 2:3-5: "This is right and is acceptable in the sight of God our Savior, who desires everyone to be saved and to come to the knowledge of the truth. For there is one God; there is also one mediator between God and humankind, Christ Jesus, himself human, who gave himself as ransom for all." He insisted, moreover, that God desires *efficaciously* "everyone to be saved" because God's self-offer in Christ stamps the being of every single person—even of those who lived prior to the Incarnation. "Antecedently to justification by grace, received sacramentally or extra-sacramentally," Rahner wrote that

> man is already subject to the universal salvific will of God, he *is* already redeemed and absolutely obliged to tend to his supernatural end. This "situation" is not merely an external one; it is inclusively and inalienably precedent to man's free action, and determines that action; it does not only exist in God's thoughts and intentions, but is a real modification of man, added indeed to his nature by God's grace and therefore supernatural, but in fact never lacking in the real order.[11]

Therefore, everyone comes into this world—even before the actual birth of
Jesus Christ—already redeemed *objectively,* that is, graced by the Spirit of
Jesus Christ. No time or place ever existed in which people were not offered
Christ's Spirit. Even those born before Jesus are predestined in Christ, a pre-
destination which must freely either be accepted or rejected.

REVELATION IN NON-CHRISTIAN RELIGIONS?

God's self-communication in Christ also transforms every person's consciousness, which Rahner understood as an infinite, multi-dimensional sphere. He
spoke of marginal consciousness and of explicit consciousness, of implicit and
explicit awareness, of a transcendental and implicit knowing embedded in the
subjective pole of consciousness, of a preconceptual knowledge and of a direct,
conceptual knowledge. Knowledge may be of a connatural kind or of a kind expressed in propositions. Both repressed and unrepressed knowledge exist. One
must also distinguish between the spiritual activities of consciousness itself and
the interpretations of these activities. Finally, Rahner emphasized the difference
between direct, conceptual knowledge and the implicit, unthematic knowledge
of the horizon in which explicit knowledge takes place. In short, both a poste-
riori conceptual knowledge and a priori unthematic knowledge exist.
    Because God's self-offer in Christ alters every person's consciousness,
God truly reveals himself to everyone. In every person's graced consciousness,
God's self-offer is marginally, preconceptually, connaturally, and unthemati-
cally known as the graced "eyeglasses" through which everything else is
known. This implicit but real knowledge of God's self-offer in Christ enables
every person to respond freely to it in true supernatural faith—without which
salvation is impossible. Since revelation is universal, the possibility of genuine
faith is universal. The purely natural person, the person to whom God has not
revealed himself, the uninspired person, to Rahner, does not exist.
    Rahner also emphasized the *social* and *historical* dimensions of the human
person. Thus, God's self-communication and self-revelation penetrate not only
the hidden depths of every person's being and consciousness. They also incarnate and interpret themselves—with varying degrees of success—in diverse societies throughout history. To Rahner, non-Christian religions are the more or
less successful historical, social incarnations and interpretation of God's self-
communion and revelation. However, the one history of the one human race is
directed by Christ's Spirit to reach its full incarnation and revelation in the person of Jesus Christ and his church.
    Dominus Iesus distinguishes sharply between "*theological faith*" in the
Judeo-Christian tradition and "*belief* in other religions" (§7). It focuses on the
error which occurs when "theological faith (the acceptance of the truth revealed
by the One and Triune God) is . . . identified with belief in other religions, which
is religious experience still in search of the absolute truth and still lacking assent
to God who reveals himself" (§7). Thus, only in the Judeo-Christian tradition
can one find *divine revelation* without which theological faith is impossible.

Outside of this tradition, one finds only the *human* striving for God which underpins belief—"that sum of experience and thought that constitutes the human treasury of wisdom and religious aspiration, which man in his search for truth has conceived and acted upon in his relationship to God and the Absolute" (§7).

However, the declaration affirms with previous documents that one can be saved even in non-Christian religions (§§2, 21). It states further that the "various religious traditions contain and offer religious elements which come *from God,* and which are part of what 'the Spirit brings about in human hearts and in the history of peoples, in cultures, and religions'" (§21, emphasis added). Can these statements be reconciled with the passages just quoted concerning "belief" as only the "human" striving for God? The church teaches explicitly that a person is saved through *faith.* Mere belief never suffices. For faith to exist, *revelation* must exist—not merely a "religious experience still in search of the absolute truth." Has not Rahner offered the real theological grounds for maintaining that both revelation and faith can be found in people outside the Judeo-Christian tradition?

Thus, he defended the view that non-Christian salvation in faith, hope, and love exists. And if a non-Christian attains salvation, then non-Christian religions must play a *positive* role in its attainment. The social-historical nature of the human person demands that even the most interior of decisions be somehow mediated by the concreteness of one's social and historical life—in this case, a person's non-Christian religion.

Nonetheless, Rahner always upheld Christianity's absolute claim to be *the* religion intended for all humankind. He even spoke of a possible "depravity" in non-Christian religions, called attention to their "provisional character," and said that they might even have a "negative effect" on the event of a non-Christian's salvation. Thus, he would have agreed with the declaration that: "If it is true that followers of other religions can receive divine grace, it is also certain that *objectively speaking* they are in a gravely deficient[12] situation in comparison with those who, in the Church, have the fullness of the means of salvation" (§22).

Many critics stress what they consider to be the insulting tone of this section of the declaration. One might ask, however, if most adherents of non-Christian religions judge their religions any differently. To nearly all believers of non-Christian religions, are not those outside of their religion at a serious disadvantage with respect to life's ultimate goal? Most—if not all—religions eschew indifferentism and religious relativism.[13]

THE CHRISTOLOGICAL CHARACTER OF THE ACT OF FAITH

Rahner argued that the act of faith itself—which is always and everywhere possible—has a *Christological* character. Thus, no time or place existed in which Jesus Christ was not present and operative in non-Christian believers and religions. People were, are, and will be saved only through faith in *Jesus Christ.* Thus, the salvific revelation and faith found in non-Christian religions cannot be dissociated from the person of the Lord Jesus Christ.

Even prior to the crucifixion and resurrection, Jesus Christ was present and operative through his Spirit in non-Christian believers and their religions. Only Jesus' Spirit makes faith possible. Catholic theology has long maintained that the Spirit is given "in view of Christ's merits." The crucified and risen Word— and no other—is the reason the Spirit is given. Thus, a real, intrinsic connection exists between the person of Jesus Christ and the grace of the Spirit present always and everywhere. From the initial creation of the world, the Spirit of Jesus Christ has been the inner dynamism of a revelation and salvation always mediated historically and socially. The Spirit directs this one history of revelation and salvation to its high point: the crucified and risen Christ. Only Jesus Christ is the absolute savior, the fullness of God's revelation and salvation. No theologian has shown so clearly the *intrinsic* relationship between the Holy Spirit and the crucified and risen One as Karl Rahner, or why pluralism must bow before the singularity of God's revealing and saving activity in Jesus Christ.

This is consonant with the view in the declaration which instructs us that "there are also those who propose the hypothesis of an economy of the Holy Spirit with a more universal breadth than that of the Incarnate Word, crucified and risen. This position also is contrary to the Catholic faith, which, on the contrary, considers the salvific incarnation of the Word as a trinitarian event. In the New Testament, the mystery of Jesus, the Incarnate Word, constitutes the place of the Holy Spirit's presence as well as the principle of the Spirit's effusion on humanity, not only in messianic times, . . . but also prior to his coming in history" (§12).

Rahner's warm, passionate love for Jesus Christ refused to reduce the real flesh-and-blood person of Jesus of Nazareth either to an abstract religious ideal or to just another charismatic human being, prophet, wise man, or enlightened one of history, or to a "cosmic Christ," a cosmotheandric principle which asks no one to renounce his or her religion for the sake of accepting this universal Christ. Only Jesus of Nazareth is the absolute savior, the God-Man, the *one* mediator between God and humanity—in short, the one ultimately sought by the "seeking Christology" written into every person's being and consciousness by the grace of God's Christocentric self-communication. Of course, this "seeking Christology" may objectify itself in myths or be projected onto historical savior figures. "Savior figures in this history of religion," Rahner wrote, "can readily be regarded as an indication of the fact that humanity, moved always and everywhere by grace, anticipates and looks for that event in which its absolute hope becomes irreversible in history, and becomes manifest in its irreversibility."[14] This event, to Rahner, is none other than Jesus crucified and risen. Christianity's superiority resides not in Christians themselves but in Jesus' person, his message, and his salvific work. Only Jesus of Nazareth is that which nothing greater can be thought because God himself can do nothing greater.

Moreover, only Jesus of Nazareth is the absolute savior, because only Jesus of Nazareth was raised bodily from the dead. The New Testament interprets everything concerning Jesus in the light of his resurrection. To Rahner, the resurrected Jesus is neither a resuscitated corpse called back to ordinary life nor the charismatic impression made on his disciples during his life, nor a God-given revelation given to the disciples after his death. The bodily resurrection happened to Jesus of Nazareth, not to his disciples. Through the resurrection, God communicates himself to the world in the Son whom the resurrection has definitely identified. Christians must take seriously that resurrection has not been predicated of *any* historical figure with any degree of credibility other than Jesus of Nazareth. Exclusive and singular indeed is this salvific activity of God in which one finds the Father's "yes" to the human situation. Christianity without a bodily resurrection is a deceitful oxymoron.

One finds a similar theology expressed in the declaration. For example, it states that "in contemporary theological reflection there often emerges an approach to Jesus of Nazareth that considers him a particular, finite, historical figure, who reveals the divine not in an exclusive way, but in a way complementary with other revelatory and salvific figures . . . More concretely, for some, Jesus would be one of the many faces which the Logos has assumed in the course of time to communicate with humanity in a salvific way . . . The doctrine of faith must be *firmly believed* which proclaims that Jesus of Nazareth, son of Mary, and he alone, is the Son and the Word of the Father" (§§9-10). *Dominus Iesus* further teaches that "it is likewise contrary to the Catholic faith to introduce a separation between the salvific action of the Word as such and that of the Word made man . . . Therefore, the theory which would attribute, after the incarnation as well, a salvific activity to the Logos as such in his divinity, exercised 'in addition to' or 'beyond' the humanity of Christ, is not compatible with the Catholic faith" (§10).

ONE MEDIATOR BUT MANY MEDIATIONS

Rahner stressed both Jesus Christ as the one mediator between God and humanity and the many mediations of Christ's grace: the church, the sacraments, the Blessed Virgin, and the saints. However, to Rahner, non-Christian religions and their various savior figures also participate—to some extent—in the mediation of the grace of God's self-communication in *Jesus Christ.* This is consonant with what one finds in the declaration where it quotes both *Lumen gentium* and *Redemptoris missio* as follows: "The unique mediation of the Redeemer does not exclude, but rather gives rise to a manifold cooperation which is but a participation in this one source . . . Although participated forms of mediation of different kinds and degrees are not excluded, they acquire meaning and value only from Christ's own mediation, and they cannot be understood as parallel or complementary to his" (§14).

THE ANONYMOUS CHRISTIAN

Rahner daringly called a non-Christian—even an agnostic or an atheist—an "anonymous Christian," if that person has surrendered to the deepest depths of his or her being. The person who follows his or her conscience lives a life of

salvific faith, a faith—not mere belief—made possible by God's self-offer in
Christ. To be sure, a person may not be able to or will not so name it. None
other than Jesus' Spirit efficaciously enlightens and inspires people everywhere
and always. Everyone is called to be a Christian—and nothing less. Insofar as
the faith of the anonymous Christian has not fully flowered into explicit Christian life, objectively speaking, the non-Christian lives in a "disadvantaged" situation with respect to salvation, as pointed out in the declaration (§22). Thus,
Rahner considers missionary activity essential—not because non-Christians do
not already know in a hidden way something about the mystery of God's love
in Christ—but because they must be awakened to what they really are in the
depths of their being and consciousness: namely, those graced by God's self-
communication in Christ.

Rahner's controversial anonymous Christian theory, moreover, offers to
Christians a *"way"* requested by the declaration (§21) to understand how truly
saving faith is possible outside of explicit Christianity and how this grace is always based on Christ's grace. He never wanted this theory to be used to pa-
tronize virtuous non-Christians by telling them that they are Christians without
knowing it. In fact, Rahner allowed himself to be called an "anonymous Zen
Buddhist" by Nishitani, an eminent Japanese philosopher. Rahner asked if the
Buddha nature was everywhere and if Nishitani found him to be even a bit enlightened. Of course, Nishitani replied "yes." According to Zen Buddhist principles, therefore, Rahner was indeed an "anonymous Zen Buddhist."

NON-CHRISTIAN RELIGIONS: A PREPARATION FOR THE GOSPEL

The Second Vatican Council's document on Divine Revelation says: "God
... wisely arranged that the New Testament be hidden in the Old and the Old be
made manifest in the New. For, though Christ established the New Covenant in
His blood..., still the books of the Old Testament with all their parts, caught
up into the proclamation of the gospel, acquire and show forth their full meaning in the New Testament... and in turn shed light on it and explain it."[15] Jesus
is a Jew and understood himself and his mission in terms of the Old Testament.
The early Christians interpreted Jesus and themselves in the light of the Old
Testament. The intrinsic relationship between the Old and New Testaments
means that Christians cannot and do not regard Judaism as simply another
world religion. "Salvation is from the Jews," Jesus said (Jn 4:22); Paul saw Israel as the "rich root" (Rom 11:17) onto which all other people are grafted. The
singularity of God's salvific action toward his chosen people offers yet another
reason for rejecting the relativism of pluralism.

In their missions to the Gentile world, the early Christians found "seeds of
the Word" there and praised Greek culture as a "preparation for the Gospel." If
one correctly understands Christ as the fullness of God's revelation, is it not
true that Christianity deepened its own understanding of that fullness through
its encounter with the Greek world? And will not contemporary Christianity

further deepen its own understanding of the mystery of Christ through its encounter with non-Christian religions?

Rahner would have unhesitatingly maintained that the "seeds of the Word"
can be found in these religions and that they, too, in some sense, are a "preparation for the Gospel." If the New Testament is hidden in the Old Testament,
then it is likewise hidden in *differing degrees* in non-Christian religions. And
the sacred texts of other world religions in *differing degrees* will likewise "acquire and show forth their full meaning in the New Testament . . . and in turn
shed light on it and explain it."

A Christian reads and interprets the Old Testament in the light of the New
Testament. Rahner also maintained that the holy scriptures of other religions
were to be read and interpreted in the light of Jesus Christ because they also—
to some extent—may be inspired. Thus, without denying the normative status
of the Christian Bible or that Christ is the hermeneutical principle for interpreting both the Hebrew scriptures and those of non-Christian religions, Rahner would have therefore qualified the declaration's statement that "the
Church's tradition . . . reserves the designation of *inspired texts* to the canonical
books of the Old and New Testaments" (§8).

The declaration states that "some prayers and rituals of the other religions
may assume a role of preparation for the Gospel, in that they are occasions or
pedagogical helps in which the human heart is prompted to be open to the action
of God. One cannot attribute to these, however, a divine origin or an *ex opere
operato* salvific efficacy, which is proper to the Christian sacraments. Furthermore, it cannot be overlooked that other rituals, insofar as they depend on superstition or other errors . . . , constitute an obstacle to salvation" (§21). Rahner
held that the Christian sacraments caused grace by "signifying" it. He spoke of
them as the "outbursts" or "epiphanizations" of God's self-communication in
Christ. Moreover, Aquinas's use of the term "natural sacraments" for the rites
and rituals found in the Hebrew tradition fascinated Rahner. Consequently, without denying the normative status of the Christian sacraments, he argued for
sacraments—and not merely natural ones—in an analogous way in non-Christian religions because God's universal self-communication in Christ attains social-historical manifestations in these religions and in their rites and rituals.[16]

Rahner understood well that the Christian view of Jesus Christ as the God-
Man posed one of the greatest difficulties in inter-religious dialogue. However,
serious and honest inter-religious dialogue demands that no side water down its
position. And, admitting that European theology had traditionally treated Christology before theologizing about the Holy Spirit and grace, Rahner added:
"Perhaps an Eastern theology will one day reverse this perspective. Because of
God's universal salvific will and in legitimate respect for all the major world
religions outside of Christianity, perhaps an Eastern theology will one day
make pneumatology, a teaching of the inmost, divinizing gift of grace for all
human beings (as an offer to their freedom) the fundamental point of departure
for its entire theology, and then attempt from this point—and this is something
that might be achieved only with considerable effort—to gain a real and radi-

cal understanding of Christology."[17] Thus, for the sake of genuine dialogue with non-Christian religions, Rahner suggested, tentatively, that one begin with the Holy Spirit and the primordial experience of God and from this perspective come to a deeper understanding of *Jesus Christ.*

Proponents of religious pluralism often quote this text to buttress their own view of the Holy Spirit. However, Rahner's text clearly states that starting with the Holy Spirit and with the primordial experience of God leads one more deeply into the mystery of *Jesus Christ.* To Rahner, the Holy Spirit always was, is, and will be the Spirit of Jesus Christ. Responding to an interviewer's query, Rahner once said,

> The center of my theology? Good Lord, that can't be anything else but God as mystery and Jesus Christ, the crucified and risen one, as the historical event in which this God turns irreversibly toward us in self-communication ... We have to remember that humanity is unconditionally directed toward God, a God which we ourselves are not. And yet, with this God, who in every respect infinitely surpasses us, with this God himself, we do have something to do; God is indeed not only the absolutely distant one, but also the absolutely near one, absolutely near, also, in his history. It is precisely because of this that God—the center of our existence—simultaneously makes Jesus Christ also the center.[18]

SINGULARITY—NOT PLURALISM

It has been suggested that a respect for religious pluralism renders both the theology of the declaration and of Karl Rahner moot. I do not share this position. In fact, both the declaration and Rahner rightly emphasize the immense *singularity* of many of God's mighty deeds: the one order of creation, the one human race, the one history of revelation and salvation, the one incarnation, the one crucifixion and resurrection, the one mediator between God and humanity, the one triune God, and the one God and Father of our Lord Jesus Christ.

Moreover, the Catholic Church has become a *world* church. Jesuits from six continents now work or study at Boston College. Should one urge them to preach a soft gospel when they return to their respective countries, or a gospel which definitely emphasizes the singularity of the triune God and of this God's salvific work? Should pluralism or *inculturation* of the gospel be uppermost in their minds? The early Christians *re*interpreted and *transformed* Judaism. Should not the same process of reinterpretation and transformation occur through Christianity's encounter with world religions? Still, genuine inter-religious dialogue and service mean neither unfeeling tolerance nor the promotion of non-Christian religions. One must preach *the* gospel of Jesus Christ—the way the early Christians did in their encounter with Greek culture. These Christians found seeds of the gospel and a ray of truth among the Greeks. However, they never backed down from preaching Jesus Christ as *the* way, the truth, and the light.

Finally, Rahner once said of Thomas Aquinas that his "theology is his spiritual life and his spiritual life is his theology."[19] This can certainly be said of Rahner, whose theological thinking definitely flowed from his spiritual life and whose spiritual life was nurtured by his powerful Christian thinking. His theology flowed from and into prayer. This was brought home to me at the end of a particularly difficult theological evening, when Rahner reminded his graduate students that theological problems always remain. However, he said that, before going to bed, he would throw his arms around Christ and worship: "My Lord and my God, *Dominus Iesus*."

3

A PROTESTANT REFLECTION ON ECUMENISM AND INTERFAITH ISSUES

S. Mark Heim

I read this declaration with two particular interests. As a Protestant, I am one of those Christian outsiders to the Roman Catholic Church who look with some interest to see how they are characterized in the document. As a theologian with special interest in the Christian theology of religions, I read the document to see how it treats the relationship between Christianity, Christ, and salvation on the one hand, and the religions, their teachings, practices, and their ends on the other. The two major sections of this article thus deal, first, with some Christian ecumenical reflections on *Dominus Iesus* and, second, with some comment on its counsel to Christians in their theological apprehension of religious pluralism.

It is hard not to develop some sympathy with the declaration in light of the willful misreading and condemnations to which it has been subjected. Those firmly convinced of the wrong-headedness or wickedness of what its writers must have meant have often paid little attention to what it says. This is the case with those commentators who insist the declaration would deny salvation to those of other religions or of other Christian communions, when it explicitly says the opposite, in conformity with long-standing teaching. I must also say that I admire and respect the impulse toward consistency this statement represents. The declaration tries to bring together what the church is saying out of the missionary and evangelistic side of its mouth with what it is saying out of the inter-religious dialogue side of its mouth. Those of us in other Christian communions must honestly acknowledge how difficult it might be to offer an equivalent effort in our communities, often lacking either the means or the fortitude to seek this kind of clarity.

However, this effort at integration is not the primary focus of the document. The primary focus is an internal teaching for Roman Catholics, and especially teachers and theologians: a reminder that the uniqueness of Christ as savior, the universality of that saving work, and the fullness of the Roman communion as Christ's true church must be upheld. To underline this central point, the document offers an authentic if somewhat one-sided reading of its own immediate prior tradition on both ecumenical and interfaith relations. I say that this reading is authentic, because when many defenders of *Dominus Iesus* maintain that nothing said here has not been said before they are quite accurate. But the reading is one-sided because much that has been said before, including

things said in formal agreements with other Christians, is not said. This selection may be based on the fact that in addressing certain errors, one marshals
only the material needed for that purpose. But even this end would be better
served with a more nuanced memory.

I believe *Dominus Iesus* is an example of a church document we are likely
to see with increasing frequency in our communions in times ahead. It is essentially an instruction to those inside a communion, designed to forestall
members from drawing certain conclusions from the church's own teaching and
actions bearing on ecumenism and interfaith relations. Although the developments at issue may be influenced by currents in the culture outside the church,
and although the ostensible targets may be theologians who are "giving away
the store," much of the impetus comes from altered tone and emphasis if not
substance in the church's own practice. We may engage in religious dialogue at
the highest level and gather for prayer at Assisi with leaders of other traditions.
We may have unprecedented experiences of common worship and theological
agreement with other Christian communions. We may even ask humbly for forgiveness for our sins against those of other faith communities and regularly
speak of a new day in ecumenical or interfaith relations. But, says this document, don't draw the wrong conclusions from all this. This should rightly be
seen as a new way of expressing the basic truths of the faith, not a change in
them. Some of the outrage or perplexity in response to *Dominus Iesus* comes
from people who, having observed these many events and developments, drew
an implicit inference that somewhere, somehow, there must have been a revision of basics. When the declaration plainly says there has not been, some feel
themselves the victims of a kind of "bait and switch" approach.

In some respects, this is similar to the phenomenon that has been noted
among Protestant churches, specifically within those denominations in the United
States (Reformed, Lutheran, and Episcopal) that recently concluded full communion agreements with each other.[1] In many of these there has been a coordinate
upsurge in efforts, catechetical and educational, to reinforce and define "brand
name" confessional identity. Having taught so emphatically, by word and example, that at least many major Protestant churches could be regarded as one with
their own, those in these communions felt an equal if not entirely opposite impetus to reclaim their own unique identity. A similar dynamic was much in evidence
when after Vatican II the Roman Catholic Church moved dramatically into ecumenical discussion, particularly into bilateral dialogues with other Christian
groups. This proved to be a dramatic catalyst for those groups to dust off and
reappropriate their denominational identities as the ground for conversation.

ECUMENICAL ISSUES

No doubt the feature of *Dominus Iesus* that has attracted the most comment is
the line that says of followers of other religions "*objectively speaking* they are
in a gravely deficient situation in comparison with those who, in the Church,
have the fullness of the means of salvation" (§22). This is said of the faithful in

other religious traditions, not of other Christians. But I think it is consistent with *Dominus Iesus* to say that it holds that non-Eastern Orthodox Christians, those who belong to what are "not Churches in the proper sense" (§17), are also objectively speaking in a deficient situation (if not so gravely deficient). The dividing line between these two deficient situations is marked by the fact that those in other Christian communions seek the same end (salvation) as the Catholic Church, preserve the same scriptures, and have at the least the intent and capacity to incorporate persons into Christ by baptism. None of this can be said of other religions.

Dominus Iesus is quite clear that in either case this deficiency does not bear on the *possibility* or even the likelihood of salvation, but on relative access to and understanding of the "fullness of the means of salvation." So, for instance, there is no alteration in this document of the teaching that those outside the church may be saved. This is true even though, as has been pointed out, in its liberal quotations from Vatican II it does not explicitly reference article 16 in *Lumen gentium* where this point is made most emphatically about other religions. Nor is its concern even to caution against undue dogmatism regarding the hope of universal salvation. The primary emphasis is to teach Roman Catholic Christians that they are to firmly believe that whoever is saved (up to everyone) is saved through the action of God in Christ, which action is (a) most fully presented in the Christian church and (b) within the Christian church most fully presented within the Roman church.

Protestants, like other non-Roman Christians, disagree with (b). They hold either that some Protestant churches, at least, offer fuller depth of the means of salvation than the Roman church or that some Protestant churches, at least, are no worse and no better. As someone involved in Faith and Order discussions in the World Council of Churches and the National Council of Churches for nearly twenty years, I must say the vehemence of the reaction to the phrase in *Dominus Iesus* that speaks of communions like my own as "not Churches in the proper sense" is rather surprising. This position (and a similar one advanced if anything more emphatically by the Orthodox) has been constantly and firmly maintained in ecumenical discussion during all that time. It could hardly come as a shock to those familiar with the dialogues. However, over that same time period it is true that ecumenical theological dialogue has purposely steered away from addressing the question directly. The "Toronto Statement" of the World Council of Churches central committee in 1950 stipulated that participation in the Council and in its Faith and Order dialogue did not commit any church to recognition of its interlocutors as true churches. Membership "does not imply that each church must regard the other member churches as churches in the true and full sense of the word."[2] In this declaration, member churches of the World Council allow for precisely the attitude toward each other that *Dominus Iesus* expresses on behalf of the Roman Catholic Church.

Although half a century has passed and ecumenical dialogue has made dramatic strides, the Toronto Statement still stands. It provides the umbrella under which progress like the document *Baptism, Eucharist and Ministry* has been possible, while the most vexing questions of the status of the parties to the discussion have been bracketed. Suggestions to revisit or revise this principle have come to naught. Of course, many members of the World Council would recognize each other as churches "in the true and full sense of the word," even apart from those who have adopted formal agreements on full communion. I simply observe that however liberally this recognition may be granted in fact, it is not expected as a matter of principle. *Dominus Iesus* indicates that other communions generally are not in fact to be seen as churches in the proper sense, but through the example of the Orthodox churches it also indicates that this recognition is not in principle excluded for non-Roman communions.

The Faith and Order movement identified three minimal dimensions of Christian unity. The first was a resolution of the church's divisions over baptism, eucharist, and ministry. The second was common confession of the apostolic faith. The third was some common means of teaching and decision-making together. To these was eventually added a fourth: solidarity in action for justice. The first two have been the subject of intensive ecumenical dialogue, and they have been addressed in a rough chronological order.[3] Only the first study has so far produced a document (*Baptism, Eucharist and Ministry*) sent to the churches for their formal responses "at the highest appropriate level of authority." It is hoped that the study on common confession of the apostolic faith might reach a similar point in another decade or so. In fact, it is only since the Fifth World Conference on Faith and Order in 1993 that the "toxic" topics in the third heading of ecclesiology proper (including church authority, order, and primacy)—long shelved as automatic deal-breakers—were placed on the agenda for intensive study in the same manner.[4] It is unfair, therefore, to accuse *Dominus Iesus* of backtracking with its assertion that the authentic church subsists in the Roman Catholic communion. If this claim has not constantly echoed in ecumenical discussion, that is not because it was abandoned and now is reasserted, but because other questions have held center stage.

Francis Sullivan's elegant review of the issue makes it clear that when *Dominus Iesus* says that Protestants are "not Churches in the proper sense," this must be understood in quite narrow terms. What "subsists" *only* in the Roman Catholic Church is the historical continuity of the one church and the fullness of the means of grace. This teaching does not mean that the church does not exist—is not instantiated—in Protestant communions, but that it has not continually existed there and does not exist there in all its fullness, according to Roman criteria. Subsistence becomes a technical term to refer to this "fullness." Protestant communions are not churches in this "proper sense," but one might also say that they are churches in all but this proper sense. As Sullivan shows, the "truly ecclesial character" that Vatican II attributed to Protestant communions has been given more weight in other recent documents than in *Dominus Iesus.*

There is a deeper issue, however, that has to do with the understanding of ecclesiology itself. *Dominus Iesus* reiterates that it is necessary for Catholics to believe that the true and single church of Christ subsists in the Roman Catholic Church. I see two parts to that statement—the first says that it is necessary to the very nature of the church that it should always be present in history as one visible, concrete, historical society ("as tangible as the Republic of Venice" I believe one earlier exponent put it). Protestants have not generally shared this principle of ecclesiology, though believing that the church indeed must always be manifest in history as a tangible reality. They have held that this reality could be manifest in "societies" without the same kind of organic structure as is presumed in *Dominus Iesus* and in Catholic thought generally, or that the church may be manifest more as a continuous event of proclamation and response to the gospel, with the "society" of the church visible only to God. Prior to asking in *which* historical community the Church (with the capital C) subsists, the key question is whether it is essential to be able to make such an identification (and, if so, what the nature of that community must be). This document says that Catholics must believe firmly in the necessity of making this determination, and believe likewise that structural unity and Roman primacy are essential criteria for it. Protestants are not without the means for making their own similar "exclusive" statements on ecclesiology, but they frame the problem differently. The characteristic form of this statement would be to say that the true church subsists where *this* gospel is preached, believed, and practiced, with a specification of the "this" providing a confessional definition of the church. Protestants would differ among themselves about the extent to which this confession, in which the church subsists, must have coordinate structural expression.

The modern ecumenical movement has had a significant impact on this intra-Protestant conversation, at least for those denominations that have taken an active part. Continual reflection on the goal of the ecumenical movement, and the repeated reformulation of "the nature of the unity we seek" have drawn many toward an acknowledgment that the unity of the church requires a more extensive "visible unity" than free churches and some other Protestants would have granted previously. To be truly united, the church must be tangibly, visibly one in a real historical sense. It must be one eucharistic fellowship. It must be able to confess and teach and act as one. This dialogue about the nature of a future united Church has prompted some reassessment of current Protestant ecclesiologies, and a new openness to some themes in ecclesiology that one may regard as characteristically Roman Catholic emphases.

Many Protestant ecumenists (I speak particularly in terms of the response from the Faith and Order Commission in the United States) believed that the encyclical *Ut unum sint* represented an analogous development on the side of the Vatican. If dialogue had enhanced some Protestant communions' respect for the need of a tangible historical body for the church, they saw this encyclical as declaring in turn from the Roman Catholic side an openness to reconceiving the nature of that tangibility. Specifically, that document seemed to consider new ways in which a universal ministry of the bishop of Rome might serve and represent the "one society" in which the church subsists. At least indirectly, it opened the question of what it might mean to be "in communion" with that see. Without changing the fundamental principle of a visible Body of Christ enunciated in *Dominus Iesus,* might it be possible by links less than organic union to regard the "separated brethren" as part of that body? This document does not flatly rule out the exploration that *Ut unum sint* seemed to invite, but does seem to dampen it.

As other contributors to this discussion know much better than I, these matters also bear on internal discussions in Roman Catholic ecclesiology. Visions of the church itself as a sign of the kingdom of God or as a sacrament of Christ's presence have been developed alongside, if not in place of, a more traditional emphasis on the church as vehicle of the kingdom. Such theologies emphatically retain stress upon the *visibility* and *tangibility* of the church as essential to its mission of representation as sign and witness. But they may not see a need to stress that this historical particularity subsumes the fullness of the means of salvation. *Dominus Iesus* explicitly cautions against a tendency for kingdom-centered or "theocentric" ecclesiologies to make the church instrumental to and not constitutive of the realization of God's saving purpose for humanity (§19). Just how wide-ranging this criticism is meant to be is unclear, but it invites a fuller discussion among scholars. If *Ut unum sint* expressed a willingness to engage with reflections from Christians outside the Catholic communion, even on the cardinal topics of Catholic ecclesiology, it would seem that there ought to be a coordinate interest in ecclesiological thought within the Catholic tradition that tries to build bridges for such common conversation.

INTERFAITH MATTERS

I have applied the passage in article 22 to non-Roman Christians only by inference. It speaks directly of followers of other religions and their "gravely deficient situation in comparison with those who, in the Church, have the fullness of the means of salvation." This is the feature of the document that has elicited the most emphatic criticism from those in other traditions and from many Christians. This statement comes virtually at the end of the document, after *Dominus Iesus* has rehearsed essential points that Christians must firmly hold (for the purposes of this discussion, I leave aside essential points that Roman Catholic Christians must firmly hold regarding the nature of the Roman Church). The points underlined with the injunction that they must be "firmly believed" are:

(1) that in the mystery of Jesus Christ "the full revelation of divine truth is given" (§5),

(2) that a clear distinction must be maintained between faith (as the acceptance of the truth of Christ's revelation) and belief in other religions, which is "that sum of experience and thought that constitutes the human treasury of wisdom and religious aspiration, which man in his search for truth has conceived and acted upon in his relationship to God and the Absolute" (§7),

(3) that Jesus of Nazareth alone is the "Son and the Word of the Father" (§10), the only savior who has brought the history of salvation to fulfillment (§13),

(4) that there is one economy of salvation and that the universal salvific will of God is accomplished once for all in Christ's incarnation, death, and resurrection (§14), and

(5) that the church is necessary for salvation and that it is possible for
all humanity to be saved (§20).

The document affirms "the salvific universality of Jesus Christ," the conviction that Christ is constitutive of the condition of salvation: not only a
unique instrument to open the possibility for it but the one with whom communion is an inextricable dimension of salvation for all who participate in it.
Dominus Iesus says this is part of the formative grammar of Christian faith. A
state for which relation with Christ (and through Christ communion with God
and others) is optional or superfluous is not what Christians understand by salvation. Critical reactions to this aspect of *Dominus Iesus* from Christians tend
to divide in two types. There are those who affirm this foundation but who
question what they see as imperious or hasty inferences drawn from it. And, as
Robert Imbelli points out in his essay, there are those who seem pained to find
this foundation in place at all, who view its reassertion as an act of reactionary
petulance. They suggest that such confession is by its very nature an inter-religious injury, fatal to dialogue and mutual respect, to be avoided at all costs by
a person of good will. No doubt the authors of *Dominus Iesus* intended this second group, or those inclined to be instructed by them, as the primary audience
for its injunctions.

I agree with the positive, confessional points that *Dominus Iesus* affirms.
The fact that they are themselves so much at issue in the controversy over the
document is testimony enough that a question crucial to the church's self-understanding has been addressed. This agreement is not only an expression of
Christian commitment on my part (though it is that). It also reflects a conviction that something similar to the affirmation expressed in *Dominus Iesus* is integral to virtually every religious faith and tradition. Acknowledgment of this
is necessary if we are to be able to register true pluralism and if authentic dialogue is to take place. We can test or at least explore this assertion by putting
the shoe on the other foot. That is, we may ask whether internal Christian dis-
satisfaction with this document is rooted in a principle regarding the proper attitude of any religious believer toward his or her own confession—whether,
that is, it expresses distress that Christians privilege their tradition in a way that
none should and others do not. Or is it more a special case, seeking a change in
one's own religion that one would not expect of another? Some who disagree
with the substance of this text believe that it is nevertheless an expression of the
proper generic self-understanding of a tradition. So Muzammil Siddiqi (president of the Islamic Society of North America) said that *Dominus Iesus* spells
out the Catholic position that other religions are deficient, but "our position is
the same thing: that the Catholic position is deficient."[5]

Gavin D'Costa, in a new book, *The Meeting of Religions and the Trinity,*
has a chapter in which he offers an extensive consideration of the Dalai Lama's
perspective on religious pluralism, representing a particular strand of Tibetan
Buddhism.[6] I think it is instructive to review this example briefly to see comparison and contrast with the case of *Dominus Iesus,* and also to judge the extent to which we as Christians apply different formal principles to other religious traditions than our own case.

D'Costa titles his chapter "The Near Triumph of Tibetan Buddhist Plural-ist-Exclusivism." The title intimates D'Costa's judgment that of the primary so-called "pluralistic" theologies of religion that he reviews, notably those of John Hick and Paul Knitter (to which *Dominus Iesus* would appear to intend to take exception), this is the most serious and cogent precisely because of its honest confessional exclusivism, not in spite of it. That is to say, he finds more in common between the Dalai Lama's approach (one we might presume most critics of *Dominus Iesus* would applaud) and that reflected in the Congregation for the Doctrine of the Faith document than might first appear.

That is, the Dalai Lama's outlook on religious pluralism is founded on the conviction that only within one particular brand of Tibetan Buddhism—the dGe lugs tradition—are the "fullness of the means of attaining liberation or bud-dhahood" to be found. This is essentially an exclusivist claim that "all religions and all forms of Buddhism will eventually come to the insight of truth held by and practiced by the dGe lugs. Consequently all religions, including rival forms of Buddhism, are ontologically false and erroneous."[7] The lesson to be drawn from this tradition-specific truth is a pragmatic tolerance for all religions that serve in some measure as instruments of compassion. Objectively speaking, those in such traditions are in a gravely deficient situation in comparison with those who have the fullness of the means of enlightenment. The only way to remedy this deficiency is to eventually change location (most likely in some fu-ture life).

Though this is the substructure of the tradition's conviction, it is rarely laid out quite so baldly as D'Costa's summary puts it. This is because the tradition also believes in instruction and spiritual advance as taking place through levels or layers of skillful means, in which people work with lesser or fuller approxi-mations of truth that are appropriate to their stage of development. Having tra-ditionally understood parallel or competing Buddhist sects in terms of lesser vehicles for those at lower stages of development, this group has expanded this spectrum to include other religious traditions, which may be located some-where below other Buddhist traditions. The Dalai Lama says often that it is im-portant for seekers to choose the religion that is most suitable for them, that in essence all religions have the same aim of human betterment and compassion, that devout practice in any faith can advance one toward that aim, and that it is an intrinsically good thing to have religious variety. And he says as well that Buddhists feel no compulsion to convert others but only to contribute to soci-ety in their own way and to respond to those who come to a point of interest in Buddhism. As D'Costa points out, none of these statements conflict with the exclusivism that actually grounds them. People who hear these statements are apt to take them in another sense, as statements of equality between religions, for instance. But when read through the "doctrinal" suppositions of this tradi-tion, they have rather different meaning, affirming the tributary value of reli-gions in a structure defined and crowned by dGe lugs Buddhism.

How might a Christian regard such a position, one in which we can see confessional universal claims reflected back at us, as it were? In this perspec-tive, Christians are known to be in a gravely deficient situation with regard to both the knowledge and the practice that lead to the one highest end. In fact, they will never attain that end until and unless they come to acknowledge and adopt this knowledge and practice, present only in dGe lugs Buddhism. Other religions contain certain limited and lower truths, teachings appropriate to help people make true progress, but only to levels that would fit them eventually for better teaching and practice. The texts and practices of Christianity are seen to have true value, because of their capacity to foster some of the compassion and some measure of the insight available in fullest form in the one, privileged religion. They are interpreted, that is, within the categories of this particular Buddhist tradition.

It seems to me that this is an eminently honorable religious outlook—one I can admire and endorse formally, while I cannot accept it substantively. Is it possible for Christians to have fruitful dialogue with persons who hold such a view of the status of the Christian tradition? My limited experience suggests that it is. Plainly, there is a difference between the partner tradition as it is grasped by a Christian through Christian categories, and that tradition as it understands itself (and through whose categories it grasps Christian tradition). Therefore there can be no substitute for attentive study of another tradition's self-presentation. This is not because it is finally "unfair" for someone to view that tradition from his or her own religious perspective, but because we owe every effort to assure that *what* we are viewing is the distinctive, living reality actually known by its adherents. This tension is the primary challenge for those who engage in comparative religious reflection. How may my understanding of the other be an act that arises out of my own integral religious identity while at the same time retaining for the "other" that is known the integrity of its own identity and not reducing it to an abstraction in my categories? But that tension is the source of the fruitfulness of dialogue.

And it is also a shared bond, uniting the partners in the modality of their religious life if not in their convictions. Thus, if people find the Dalai Lama treats all specific religious traditions equally as vehicles of compassion and therefore privileges no tradition, they have it rather backwards. It is the privileging of one tradition as true and effective that provides the basis for an attitude of pragmatic tolerance to all religion. It is for this reason that D'Costa lauds the Dalai Lama's as the most cogent and consistent form of so-called religious pluralism: because it is clear (if publicly reticent) about its root in a specific tradition, and other versions of pluralism deny or evade this truth about themselves.

But would the Dalai Lama ever issue such a document as *Dominus Iesus*? Probably not! Its public form (presupposing a situation different from that of an exiled minority community dependent on the goodwill of a majority tradition around it), and its different assumptions about the teaching role in a religious community (stressing a univocal common voice more than the application of varying explanations to different kinds of hearers), as well as the substance of its confessional convictions, reflect particularities of the Christian (and, as indicated in our earlier discussion, the Roman) tradition. However, D'Costa points out that in literature directed internally to the core teachers of his own community

—a famously scholastic one—the Dalai Lama undertakes a task that seems closely analogous to that in *Dominus Iesus.* Such instruction trains and reminds dGe lugs Buddhists not to lose track of the unique truth (in which all other religions are deficient) upon which rests (among other things) the relatively positive view of dGe lugs toward those religions. I do not know if the Dalai Lama or his circle face any concerns regarding groups in their community advocating abolition of dGe lugs exclusivism such as we have described and arguing it has no place in today's Tibetan Buddhism. But if there were such a movement, and if a generic Western form of pluralism were to drive out the Dalai Lama's particularist and exclusivist kind, I am not convinced that this would be a triumph for religious diversity or a boon to dialogue.

If Christians respect and value such an outlook in another religious tradition (and D'Costa's discussion is an example of both), then they are not inconsistent in practicing it themselves. Though these comments represent a certain defense of *Dominus Iesus,* the document fails in one important respect to merit that defense. The outlook I have described presumes a deep respect for the specificity of religious traditions. And this is notably missing in the document, not so much in the substance of what it says in general statements about other traditions as in the lack of acknowledgment that such statements are insufficient. They have meaning only when developed in close study of particular traditions and expressed in interaction with the vocabulary and understanding within those traditions. And this needs to go hand in hand with recognition that the particularity of religions includes their capacity to interpret our tradition in their categories. If it could not exemplify this in limited space, the declaration was still obliged to state it.

Let me give one example that reflects the point I have been making. *Dominus Iesus* is addressed primarily to Catholic teachers of the faith, and only secondarily to other Christians and those of other religious traditions. But it might have communicated more effectively with all (without changing its aim) if it had not focused on the salvific universality of Christ so exclusively in terms of the fullness of the *means* of salvation but had put more emphasis on it as constitutive of salvation. One critic of the document writes: "It instructs that God saves in only one way, which is through Christ."[8] This is a conviction which the critic rejects and I accept. But it would be helpful if *Dominus Iesus* noted or stressed a coordinate idea: salvation is only one thing, which is communion with Christ. To move so quickly and emphatically to Christ as the only way suggests to many if not most hearers of other faiths that their own traditions are being dismissed as the paths to *any* religious good (since they are not "the way") and ignored as offering distinctive ultimate ends against which *Christianity* may be found wanting. "Salvation," in this perception, stands for *all* or *any* highest good. If we make clear that what Christians mean by salvation, by definition, is Christocentric, we acknowledge that what is "gravely deficient" in the situation of other religious traditions is their insufficient Christocentrism and their lack of orientation toward communion with God through Christ.

I am not aware of religious traditions disturbed because they fail at being the church, or offended to have others notice they are not Christians. Their aim is to succeed at being something else. Christians do not compromise their affirmations about Christ or salvation to recognize that in living from such affirmations Christians place themselves in a "gravely deficient" situation from the perspective of most other religious traditions. *Dominus Iesus* plainly says that those in other faiths can be saved. It insists the only *way* in which they are saved is through Christ. The most wholesale critics of *Dominus Iesus* maintain that what ought to be said is that people of other faiths are saved through the substance of their own traditions, without any relation with Christ. The first stresses the universal exclusivity of the Christian means; the second stresses the universal exclusivity of the Christian end. It would be more helpful to maintain the distinctive way that relation with Christ constitutes the specific Christian end of salvation—open in principle to those of all religious traditions, while recognizing that other religious traditions constitute distinctive ends of their own, whose particularity Christians can respect even if they must regard them as penultimate. In other words, just as the document would be strengthened with greater attention to specificity in the other religious traditions, it would benefit from greater attention to the specificity of the Christian understanding of salvation.

CONCLUSION

I return, last, to one of my first points. I admire the effort in *Dominus Iesus* to express the consistency in the Roman Church's approach to its tasks of mission and dialogue. But this cannot be done simply by assertion. It will be done much more effectively in the long run by explanations of how the two relate to each other. A document that quoted its own tradition in a less one-sided way would highlight the resources for just such interaction. Though a cautionary word may be in order, it will be fruitless if it serves to stifle the very theological work that is needed. That work requires detailed understanding of each religion's particularity as a basis for learning how to interpret that particularity in Christian theological terms and to respect another tradition's interpretation of Christian particularity. This work will make the confession of Christ that is rightly so dear to the heart of this document more credible, not less. Faithful persistence in this task will be a profound witness that Christian respect for other faiths is ultimately *rooted in* commitment to Christ, not competitive with it.

Roman Catholic theologians have in many cases been pioneers for the entire Christian community in engagement with religious pluralism. It is hard for me to imagine my own work in this area without the stimulus and example of major contemporary Catholic thinkers in this field. Therefore I confess to something more than an observer's concern with the character of this declaration as an intra-Catholic communication, one part of that church signaling to other parts of that church about the limits to theological exploration. I agree with *Dominus Iesus* in its criticism of theological relativism and indifferentism, and respect its injunction to Roman Catholic scholars to maintain key Christian convictions. However, I am concerned that the way it frames the issue seems to be poised to cut off necessary theological exploration. Christian theologians can work from a grounding in the confession that the document commends, and still face an extraordinary sweep of possible ways to understand the specific relation of other faith traditions to God, Christ, and salvation. That Christ is the sole redemptive mediator for all humanity does not mean that the full extent and nature of that saving work is known to Christians or understood by them— nor that the uniqueness and decisiveness of Christ's mediation rules out providential roles for other traditions in relation to God, roles not only tributary to salvation but also perhaps constitutive in their own right of ends other than salvation. It would be a loss to the entire Christian family if the conclusion drawn from this document were to err on the side of restriction rather than patience with the investigations of Catholic scholarship in this area. In the Congregation for the Doctrine of the Faith and the teaching office of the bishops the Roman church has an organ that most of the rest of the Christian world lacks. A primary gift of such a situation, to this outsider, is that when this office is vigorously exercised, as it is in this document, there should be a commensurate capacity for the church to encompass wide investigation and experimentation. This breadth would prove much more threatening to the identity and unity of Christian communions who lack the capacity to speak so clearly alongside and above the voices of its individual members.

4

NEW TESTAMENT ESCHATOLOGY
AND *DOMINUS IESUS*

Pheme Perkins

TRUMPETING THE MISSION: TRIUMPHALISM OR ANXIETY?

Dominus Iesus recalls those foundation stories from the New Testament which
first-century Christians told to explain how it was that followers of a Jewish
messianic figure, a miracle-worker, prophet, and teacher, began to preach salvation in his name for all people. It rightly affirms that evangelization to the nations (*missio ad gentes*) remains part of the non-negotiable identity of those
faithful to that tradition. So it is quite reasonable to ask, as the document does,
how the twenty-first century dialogue between Christianity and other religious
traditions impacts the identity of the church. Have certain theological, religious, or cultural assumptions eroded the fundamental truth that God revealed
a path of salvation for all peoples in Jesus? That the one who died on the cross
and was raised from the dead under Pontius Pilate was not just an enlightened
Jewish teacher, but in a real sense God-self? That the God who created all
things has called all humanity to a single "body of Christ," so that no path of
salvation can attain its goal without passing in some sense through Christ?
These are all essential propositions of Christian belief which can easily be
grounded in the New Testament witness.[1] Nor is it wrong for theologians to ask
whether the new forms of encounter have called an end to understanding the
other as a search for the entry point to preach the gospel. Is it not true that the
old *missio ad gentes* which understood the "other" in biblical terms as the immoral idolater, ignorant of God, not only generated horrendous forms of religious intolerance and persecution but is false to the gospel?[2] Yet at this point
Dominus Iesus begins to sound defensive. It confuses centuries of faithful testimony to the gospel of Jesus Christ with never being wrong in what one says
that "good news" implies in the concrete situations of history.[3]

Dominus Iesus treats texts of scripture in the same way as warrants for
dogmatic assertions that exist without context, whether that be within the texts
that make up the canon, as representative of developments in which the people
of God were addressing concrete situations, or as texts that have had a check-
ered "post-history" in Jewish and Christian circles. To those who might protest
that such a use of scripture is little short of theological malpractice, the docu-

ment has a ready answer. Anyone who differs is either an "outsider" or subject to ecclesiastical condemnation for engaging in "the tendency to read and to interpret Sacred Scripture outside the Tradition and Magisterium of the Church" (§4). If one were to take *Dominus Iesus* as a model for how to read scripture, one would have to conclude that the meaning of biblical texts derives from how they have been used (and misused) as evidence for a series of dogmatic hypotheses. That is, one's commentaries would have to contain a series of quotations from other church documents as in the following concatenation:

> The Church's Magisterium, faithful to divine revelation, reasserts that Jesus Christ is the mediator and the universal redeemer: "The Word of God, through whom all things were made, was made flesh, so that as perfect man he could save all men and sum up all things in himself. The Lord . . . is he whom the Father raised from the dead, exalted and placed at his right hand, constituting him judge of the living and the dead" [GS 45; cf. also Council of Trent, *Decretum de peccato originali,* 3: DS 1513]. This salvific mediation implies also the unicity of the redemptive sacrifice of Christ, eternal high priest (cf. Heb 6:20; 9:11; 10:12-14) (§11).

A patchwork of New Testament affirmations derived from a Vatican II document, which the footnote equates to a decree from Trent, is further expanded by a dogmatic statement concerning the understanding of Christ as eternal high priest in Hebrews. There is not a hint of the polemical context of that language in Hebrews. The assertion of that "once for all" sacrifice in Hebrews 9:11-12 initiates an argument that the sacrifices of the Jewish cult are inferior copies and, worse, that Jewish liturgy cannot set the conscience right with God (Heb 9:11-14), for example. Exegetes agree that Hebrews intends to affirm a superior and permanent efficacy to the sacrifice of Christ on the cross that was unlike the competing sacrifices of the day, especially the Jewish feast of Yom Kippur and the red heifer of Numbers 19:3.[4] But they also recognize that the author is employing language which depends upon convictions not widely shared in the twenty-first century: that blood serves as a cleansing agent for offenses against God, and that a Platonic metaphysic of eternal, heavenly realities as superior to the corruptible material world can be found in the Bible. Patristic authors provide a wide variety of allegorical readings to explain the "tabernacle" into which Christ is said to enter. Harold Attridge's commentary lists the following: Christ's human body, his whole human life, his glorified body, the liturgy of the new covenant, or the church.[5] Thus the impression that reading scripture on the basis of tradition will yield the univocal, dogmatic assertions attached to particular passages can be shown to be false.

Neither scripture nor tradition are permitted a voice except as they are employed by the magisterium, which to this untrained eye appears to be found in church documents that are also treated as though they enunciated universal, univocal propositions that have no need of context or argument. So even the exegete who agrees that much of what *Dominus Iesus* wishes to affirm is crucial to our Catholic identity, and even that it can be discovered in scripture and tradition, comes away feeling that she or he has been hit with a sucker punch. No surprise that many non-Catholics are not reassured by being told that this document is an internal matter or addressed to those responsible for the public teaching of the church.

One might be tempted to consider the tone of *Dominus Iesus* just another case of Roman Catholic triumphalism: outside the church (= full communion with Rome), no salvation. Have all the efforts of scholars, theologians, episcopal conferences, Vatican II, and even popes for the past century come to naught? Or is this document evidence of a deeper, unacknowledged anxiety? Are its authors afraid that we will not be able to find a faithful and credible witness for the so-called postmodern world? Sociologist David Lyons describes several elements of postmodern belief and practice that should be unsettling to an institution which projects the monolithic identity of doctrinal belief and practice advocated in *Dominus Iesus*. Institutions can no longer guard their boundaries as they once did. Nor can they treat the coalescence of elements from divergent traditions as an isolated phenomenon. Lyon writes: "Beliefs and practices once sealed within institutional form now flow freely over formerly policed boundaries . . . Syncretism, previously a problem peculiar to certain intellectual and theological settings, is now generalized and popularized in practice as in belief."[6] It is easy to see the anxieties over porous boundaries and the syncretistic nature of popular beliefs throughout this document. Yet its authors are insensitive to the postmodern cultural dynamic. They blame a rationalism which cannot accept the supernatural and "the eclecticism of those who, in theological research, uncritically absorb ideas from a variety of philosophical and theological contexts without regard for consistency, systematic connection, or compatibility with Christian truth" (§4). Shooting the messengers does not speak to the problem. Yet *Dominus Iesus* has only one category for interpreting the religious dynamic of the twenty-first century—a "relativisitc mentality"—and that, it asserts, is incompatible with Christian faith (§5).

"HE CAST THE POWERFUL FROM THEIR THRONES . . ." (LK 1:52) A VOICE TO EVANGELIZE

"He cast down the mighty from their thrones, and exalted the lowly," Mary sings in the Magnificat (Lk 1:52). In so doing, she echoes a fundamental theme in the Jewish piety which shaped Jesus and his followers.[7] Lyon discusses another trend which brings the postmodern context into contact with the world in which Christianity emerged. There is a growing socio-cultural and religious divide in the global village between the elite with access to education, technology, the ability to move easily across national boundaries, and the like, and the "choiceless," those who cannot change their harsh situation. If they cross national boundaries it is as refugees or illegal immigrants. Lyon refers to such persons as the socioeconomic "alter-egos" of the elites. The "gospel" is part of their armor against the elites—as are other forms of religious fundamentalism

in non-Christian settings.[8] Though we have our disagreements over which social models best describe the followers of Jesus in the first century, since the
considerable mobility of tradespersons in the Roman empire was crucial to the
spread of Christianity, nonetheless Christians are the "alter-egos," not the powerful.[9] When these *humiliores* of the first century sing of God's powerful inter-
vention lifting them up and casting down the mighty, they know an experience
of faith in God's promise to carry out in the end what God is beginning in their
midst. The key, "carry out in the end," highlights the fact that for the first Christians all language of exaltation, peace, victory is what we call "eschatological."
It speaks to God's disposition of salvation, not to what human institutions may
accomplish.

Dominus Iesus has no ear whatsoever for the eschatological tonality of
New Testament texts. The consequences are painful to hear. Consider the opening of article 2: "In the course of the centuries, the Church has proclaimed and
witnessed with fidelity to the Gospel of Jesus. At the close of the second millennium, however, this mission is still far from complete." Who is the judge of
"far from" or "complete"? This is a no-brainer for the New Testament authors.
God is the judge of "complete." When Jesus comes again, then the faithful servants get their reward. But the "when" is permanently unknown (for example,
Mark 13:32).[10] How does the document consistently "get it wrong"? While admitting that the "kingdom of God" announced by Jesus is an eschatological reality that awaits the end-time for its fulfillment (§18), *Dominus Iesus* insists
upon an indissoluble unity between the church and both Christ and the kingdom. This unity guarantees the mediation of divine grace through the sacraments. In fact, the document is highly suspicious of too much of a "kingdom-
centered" ecclesiology as detached from Christ and undervaluing the role of the
church in mediating salvation (§19). As usual, these broad-brushed condemnations are backed up only with references to church documents—in this case a
papal encyclical and the *Catechism of the Catholic Church*.[11] And to pretend
that tradition also authorizes this move, footnote 73 supports the statement,
"The kingdom is so inseparable from Christ that, in a certain sense, it is identified with him," by referring to Origen (*Hom. Matt* 14, 7: PG 13, 1197) and Tertullian (*Adversus Marcionem,* IV, 33, 8: CCSL 1, 634). But *Dominus Iesus* is no
better at reading patristic texts than at reading the New Testament. Origen provides an elaborate allegory of the "keys of the Kingdom of Heaven" given to
Peter (Mt 16:19) as descriptions of virtues. When he comes to the ecclesiastical use of the "power of the keys"—which is distributed among bishops as a
group, not attached to the bishop of Rome—he concludes that only those bishops with the virtues of Peter can authentically exercise the power of binding
and loosing.[12]

Such reservations about how to apply the text show an ability to distinguish the divine grace given through the church from particular persons and circumstances that have been entrusted with ecclesial authority. The former is
never separated from Christ. The latter always stand under God's judgment.
Dominus Iesus speaks with the voice of the elites in the twenty-first century
global village, not with the voice of the pious, humble ones like Mary or

Peter—not even with the voice of the divided, persecuted, yet growing church
of the pre-Constantinian centuries. These Christians knew that but for God's
sustaining power, they could be wiped out. They hoped for the coming of the
Lord precisely because existence was so fragile.

When the New Testament church speaks of evangelization, it does so from
the margins, not from a center of power. From that perspective, the resurrection
scenes in which Jesus sends his disciples with a message to the nations (Acts
1:8; Lk 24:46-48; Mt 28:16-20) sound very different. The sustaining presence
of the Lord has been given to uphold the disciples in the face of a task which
will often meet with failure. Within the New Testament itself we find a regular
pattern of rejection and readjustment. Consider the problem of evangelizing
Jewish communities which prove resistant to belief in Jesus. Many contemporary exegetes read Romans 9–11 as Paul's conclusion that the mission to Israel
is finished, at least until God brings about an end-time change of heart to re-
unite what the gospel has divided (Rom 11:25-36).[13] Similarly, one of the key
texts in *Dominus Iesus,* Matthew 28:16-20, may intend the phrase "going therefore teach all the nations..." (v. 19a) as a shift from the original limitation to
Israel (Mt 10:5). If the Greek *ta ethnê* ("the nations") is used as it often is for
"the Gentiles," then Israel is excluded.[14] Even if Matthew envisages an ongoing mission among Jews even as Christians move beyond the limits of Jesus'
own activity, he never infers that massive conversions will occur prior to the
end-time. Two striking passages instruct readers that non-believers will be
counted among God's elect on the basis of deeds of righteousness.[15] Matthew
10:40-42 describes the missionaries as "little ones" who are stand-ins for Jesus.
Jesus' mission instructions have left them radically dependent upon those to
whom they speak. Some will recognize Jesus in his emissaries, and in receiving Jesus also receive God. Others will not. Yet persons who assist the "little
ones" or show even the small kindness of a cup of water will be rewarded. Thus
one sees a transition from a statement which could be construed in an exclu-
sionary manner: to receive or reject a missionary is to receive or reject Jesus
(and in him God)[16] to a more expansive possibility of salvation. Matthew 10:42
assumes persons who might admire the "name," Jesus, which the "little ones"
bear and so be moved to provide a drink of water.[17]

Matthew concludes the final sermon on the judgment with an even more
direct example of the same point in the parable of the sheep and the goats (Mt
25:31-46). This parable opens with Jesus/Son of Man seated on the divine
throne to judge all the nations assembled before him. Neither the elect ("the just
people," v. 37) nor the condemned saw Jesus in the suffering "least of these my
brothers" (v. 39). The criterion of distinguishing the elect or "just ones" from
those condemned has no reference to explicit faith in Jesus or even mild admiration. Its requirements are fundamental to Jewish traditions from the Hebrew
Bible through rabbinic texts in which deeds of mercy are done to God or in im-
itation of God's presence.[18] For Matthew there is no contradiction in combining
the call to evangelize the nations with the affirmation that most of those in the
"kingdom prepared for you from the foundation of the world" (v. 34) will accept Jesus for who he is only in this final moment of judgment.

"IF I PREACH, IT IS NOT MY BOAST…" (1 COR 9:16)
EVANGELIZING FROM THE CROSS

Dominus Iesus tries to clothe its understanding of mission in divine authority by appeals to sections of the New Testament which use liturgical phrasing (Jn 1:1-18; Col 1:15-20; Eph 1:3-14; 1 Cor 8:5-6). Such passages do speak as though all that really matters in salvation has been realized in the cross and resurrection, the exaltation of Jesus. Yet early Christian liturgy was never without its reminders that the Lord is to come in glory. Even the Eucharist as a celebration of the Lord's death is only "until he comes again" (1 Cor 11:26). Faith, hope, and love are directed toward what we cannot know fully now (1 Cor 13:12-13). Paul's retention of the Aramaic *maranatha* ("our Lord come!") in 1 Corinthians 16:22 shows that prayer for the Lord's return was an expression of Christian hope from the earliest days of the church.[19] The reader gets the impression that identifying the church with Christ and the preference for hymnic formulae misled the authors of *Dominus Iesus* into assuming that New Testament authors equate their experiences of salvation in the community with the eschatological reality of salvation when the Lord returns. They do not. Paul spends considerable time arguing against just such tendencies at Corinth. *Dominus Iesus* likes the apostolic tone of authority, citing Paul's statement about handing on a received tradition (1 Cor 15:3) as its own (§23) without acknowledging that Paul uses this formula only in setting forth fixed liturgical or creedal statements.[20] Just as the document is unable to hear the sound of the New Testament authors speaking from the margins, so it fails to hear Paul's central case against the triumphalist, over-realized eschatology at Corinth: its lack of fidelity to God's revelation on the cross.

Dominus Iesus adopts phrases in which Paul affirms his own unwavering commitment to the gospel that God entrusted to him without attending to the context within which Paul is speaking. Had its author(s) paid attention to the actual testimony of the apostle, they might have noticed the cross-centered nature of apostolic authority. When Paul says, "If I preach it is not my boast, for necessity is laid on me…" (1 Cor 9:16), he wishes to use the lowliness and humility of his example, a setting aside of "rights" to demand support or lord it over the faith of the Corinthians, against persons who seek to use their theological insight to compel the conscience of "weak Christians" (1 Cor 8:1–9:2).[21] Paul does enunciate a mission strategy in this context, but one quite dissimilar in tone from that for which his words have been hijacked (§2). Paul will burden himself with what was culturally a slave-like existence, working at his trade, in order to preach the gospel free of charge and free of indebtedness to wealthy patrons.[22] As he goes on to say, "for being free from all, I have enslaved myself to all so that I might win over more" (v. 19). Paul cannot claim to give his apostolic work "freely" insofar as God has laid the necessity on him.[23] But he can demonstrate that he is acting freely, out of the same love which moved Jesus to the cross, by enslaving himself to the conditions of being a leatherworker in the commercial agora. In short, Paul deliberately moves to a position which identifies him with the weaker, not the stronger members of the Corinthian church.[24] Genuine evangelization occurs only when its apostles enact in the concrete circumstances of their own time the exchange modeled on the cross, setting aside power, authority, rights, and wages for the constraints of those not in control even of their own destiny.

Dominus Iesus is fond of Pauline expressions which refer to his apostleship as part of God's plan, the "mystery" of calling the Gentiles to salvation (Col 1:24-27; Eph 2:19; 4:15-16; §16). It shifts the "mystery" from its Pauline meaning, an insight into God's eschatological plan of salvation, to the church and substitutes "Church" for apostle. Yet one wonders how that reinterpretation would sound if the author(s) had included Paul's personal reflection that introduces this section of Colossians. He writes, "Now I rejoice in my sufferings on your behalf and I am filling up the 'lacks' in the afflictions of Christ in my flesh on behalf of his body which is the church" (Col 1:24). The apostle is not the church, but one who suffers on her behalf just as Christ did on the cross. Nor does Paul think metaphorically. When he refers to his "sufferings in the flesh" or the "slave brands (*stigmata*) of Jesus on his body" (Gal 6:17), Paul means the very physical sufferings that have been part of his decades-long service preaching the gospel. He holds that sharing in Christ's death is essential to the well-being of his converts (see 2 Cor 4:10-12).[25] But Paul's understanding is misunderstood if its relationship to eschatology is neglected. Such sufferings are characteristic of the end-times. As long as the final reconciliation of all things to God is not complete,[26] sufferings remain the lot of the righteous.[27] Paul does not claim that there is some imperfection in Christ's self-offering on the cross. But for Paul the end of the ages has begun with the coming of the messiah Jesus. The pattern of the suffering servant continues to be enacted until the end. Christians live in the tension between the new age which is effectively present in "the present evil age" (Gal 1:4) and the eschatological transformation of all things in Christ.[28]

"CHRIST LOVED THE CHURCH AND GAVE HIMSELF..." (EPH 5:25) CHURCH AS HOLY

Dominus Iesus stresses the unity and holiness of the church in support of the conclusion that "the fullness of Christ's salvific mystery belongs also to the Church, inseparably united to her Lord" (§16). New Testament metaphors which speak of the church as "bride of Christ" are pressed into service as evidence (2 Cor 11:2; Eph 5:25-29; Rev 21:2, 9). Here too attention to the context would modify the apparent claim to have transferred the eschatological perfection of God's people into the church as she lives out the time prior to the end. In the first instance (2 Cor 11:2) Paul introduces the metaphor to castigate the Corinthians for taking in false apostles. He is not speaking about the church as a whole but about accusations against his ministry in establishing a specific community, that in Corinth. Paul considers himself "father" to the churches he founded (1 Cor 4:14-15). The metaphor contrasts Paul, the father who preserves his daughter's honor and purity for her wedding, with the opponents, who are compared to the serpent who deceived Eve.[29] Paul in no way asserts that the particular church in question retains the perfection of its origins. Rather, he puts the future into question using a metaphorical antithesis loaded with emotional overtones for his first-century audience.[30] In the end, they must decide whether or not to safeguard the apostle's teaching. Thus 2 Corinthians 11:2-3 does speak to a concern voiced in *Dominus Iesus:* that more popular forms of piety can be created by alleged teachers at the expense of the true gospel. But because Paul evangelizes from a position of weakness, from the cross, he must awaken a consent to the gospel that is born of love.

Similarly, Ephesians 5:25-26 draws a striking picture of the love of Christ in dying for the church. But the church so depicted as the bride, bathed and spotless, does not refer to the social reality found in the cities of the Pauline mission. It refers to the cosmic, heavenly church with Christ as its head. Ephesians 5:32 signals the presence of an eschatological image for God's universal plan of salvation by using the term "mystery" to describe the image of Christ and the church. For Ephesians this reality is already made present through the death and exaltation of Christ.[31] At this point, the heavy metaphors have been introduced to order relationships not within the community but between first-century husbands and their wives. And the Pauline commitment to cruciform depictions of what it means for the socially advantaged, in this case husbands, to imitate Christ's love is still intact.

While the Pauline tradition agrees that one can take clues from the image of church as "bride of Christ" to describe how Christians ought to act, the imagery employed in Revelation 21:2, 9 has no link to the church or her members in the present age. It is entirely eschatological. The bride is the new Jerusalem. Revelation 21:2 weaves together a complex of images derived from Isaiah to depict the fulfillment of God's promises once the old creation has passed away and the new come into being.[32] The new Jerusalem of the prophet's vision in Revelation 21:9–22:9 is an elaborate antitype for the ruling world power, imperial Rome, the great whore of Revelation 17:1–19:10.[33] In no case does Revelation imply that the "bride of the Lamb" refers to the present reality of the church. In fact, the "bride" provides only a transient metaphor in the larger complex of images devoted to the new Jerusalem.[34] These include aspects of the traditional Jewish view of Eden: the throne of God, the rivers, and the tree of life.[35] With its interim millennial rule of Christ (Rev 20:4) along with the 144,000, Revelation envisages a considerable expanse of time before all things are as the creator intended, and the servants of God dwell in face-to-face communion with the Lord (Rev 22:3-5). Those who have remained faithful witnesses through the trials of the present age have this great promise held out to them (Rev 3:21). Certainly, the prophet John agrees that only those Christians who remain faithful and resist the socio-cultural and religious allurements of the cities in which they live are to be citizens of this glorious city. Scholars acknowledge that the desire to avoid persecution by assimilating to civic pressures to honor the emperor and the like are behind the crisis Revelation addresses.[36] The Christian prophet John, whose visions make up Revelation, could easily agree with *Dominus Iesus* that there is no salvation apart from the church.[37] But Revelation does not collapse the new Jerusalem into the church as she exists in the present age. The church as an empirical, human reality stands under two signs: the sign of the cross evident in the faithful suffering of her martyr-witnesses, and the sign of the Son of Man who is to come in judgment, evident in the call for reform among the churches of Asia Minor.

Dominus Iesus presumes that Catholics draw their faith neither from scripture nor from tradition but from ecclesial documents in which catch-phrases and references from the former are passed through as rhetorical ornaments. The consequence of such disregard for the sources of revelation is alienation between those in control of such documents and the rest of the faithful, so the church's legitimate concern about retaining basic concepts of Christian faith appears to be no more than a power play. Yet much of what *Dominus Iesus* would like to preserve can be found in scripture. And perhaps, more importantly, the first generations of Christians knew how to evangelize a world full of competing religious traditions. It is easy to assume that speaking from the margins, incarnating the cross in the life of the apostle, and even deferring claims to perfection and holiness to the end-time were strategies born of necessity. But Paul makes a deliberate missionary strategy of doing so in circumstances which did not require it of him. Therefore one must ask whether the wholesale rejection of an eschatological perspective evident in the ecclesiology of *Dominus Iesus* has not undermined its perception of how Christ intended his disciples to bring his teaching to all nations. Perhaps Luke has a better idea in the introduction to the sending out of the seventy. The task of evangelization is not a huge cattle drive in which the church has "succeeded" if she can get everyone into the corral and branded. Perhaps the task is a bit more modest: to prepare the nations for the Coming of the Lord. As Luke puts it so simply: "The Lord . . . sent them in pairs before him to every city and place he was intending to visit" (Lk 10:1). Because of their eschatological perspective, the New Testament churches understood themselves as God's advance team.

5

"THERE'S A WIDENESS IN GOD'S MERCY"

Frederick Lawrence

INTRODUCTION

Dominus Iesus is intended to support the mission to the nations and inter-religious dialogue and to promote theological exploration. The provocation of current relativism, and of the flattening-out effect of many views about religious pluralism, is real and serious. The document assumes a *kairos* for bishops and pastors to be given the guidance of traditional teaching, excluding erroneous opinions. As the provocation is great, so the document is defensively expository, reasserting what it considers "home truths" in order to stop the erosion of the absolute truth concerning salvific universality. It does not state much that is new, but it gives the overall impression of a narrowing in perspective. I shall focus on five aspects of narrowing, each containing subsidiary points.

1. Trinitarian creed and Abrahamic faith

The document begins with the Greek version of the Symbol of the First Council of Constantinople (381). It speaks of the Spirit as proceeding only *ek patrou,* from the Father, and does not mention the old Latin liturgy; even Denzinger-Schönmetzer's Latin version of this passage uses the *filioque.*[1] This could be construed as a conciliatory gesture to the Orthodox, but I am told this happens to be the trinitarian theology favored by John Paul II and Cardinal Ratzinger.

My sense is that those who reject the formulation of the *filioque* have not understood its core meaning—that the *ho theos* identified with *agapê* at 1 John 4:8, 16 expresses itself in its Word, its Logos, which is (according to Thomas Aquinas) a *verbum spirans amorem.* As a judgment of value this Word grounds a Proceeding Love identified with the Holy Spirit.[2] I believe the procession of the Holy Spirit from the Father and the Son is both true and more consonant with important points the document wants to make later on.

However promising and fundamental, this creedal starting point, by itself and without any prelude, misses an opportunity to call to mind the dangerous memory that Christ Jesus decisively culminates *Israel's* faith in the promises given to Abraham, Isaac, Moses, and David. As John Paul II made clear in the

Holy Land, the church today has to manifest a clear intention of amendment for its anti-Jewish words and deeds. The issue of Christian anti-Jewishness was addressed some years ago by Ben Meyer, who wrote:

> When a Gentile Christianity took root after the Church had achieved political legitimacy in the fourth century, it would combine the inheritances of Mediterranean Jewish-Christian polemic and the old Roman anti-Semitism, thus perpetuating for a millennium and a half a dark mythology that would poison the soul of Europe with the gangrene of anti-Jewish hatred. A thread running through the whole of Christian history, it was also a classic case of collective amnesia.[3]

Today we need to remedy this "collective amnesia" in the light of contemporary biblical scholarship's salutary reminder that Jesus was not a Christian but a Jew. With scholars such as Ben Meyer, E. P. Sanders, N. T. Wright, Francesco Rossi de Gasperis, Carlo Maria Cardinal Martini, and a host of others, our Christian understanding of the Old and New Testaments can be enriched by understanding Jesus in the context of first-century Palestinian Judaism.[4] In its pedagogical intent, the document should encourage Christians to appreciate how the earliest understanding of Jesus' message and of his announcement in word and deed of the definitive arrival of God's kingdom grows out of and transforms the chief Jewish symbols of Torah and Temple, of ethnicity and the land.

I believe that since the *Shoah* (the German attempt to extinguish the Jews) and in view of world-historical events, the church's authoritative doctrinal pronouncements should use every opportunity to highlight the Christian church's intimate relationship to the "Abrahamic faiths" of Judaism and Islam.

2. Ambiguities regarding church as institution: "People of God, Body of the Lord, and Temple of the Holy Spirit" or "Perfect Society"?

> The Church is no *universale ante rem:* she is entirely embodied in each man, even if not all the members give expression to the Church's nature in the same way...Because the Church (also in her social being) is always present where there is a genuine Christian, and the more purely his Christian existence shines forth and becomes incarnated, the more purely the idea of the Church shines forth—as is especially the case of Mary, the mother of Jesus.[5]

The document's use of the expression "a single Church of Christ, which subsists in the Catholic Church, governed by the Successor of Peter and by the Bishops in communion with him" (§17) confuses *Lumen gentium*'s teaching. Vatican II taught that the *means* of salvation are to be found most fully in the sacraments of the Roman Catholic Church, *not* that salvation is to be found fully only in that church. This confusion is perhaps a function of an overemphasis on the "institutional" dimension of the church.

This document does not allude to the changes in the pilgrim church's self-understanding in its epoch-making transition from a Jewish church, awaiting the imminent return of Christ, to a lasting world-church.[6] The whole point of the church is participation in the eschatological mission of the Palestinian Jew, Jesus. His words, deeds, suffering, death, and resurrection fulfill God's promise to deliver his people from exile and evil because he is the Word incarnate, the Son of God become man. If God becomes man in Jesus of Nazareth, the true claim that Jesus intended a church must imply that the mystery of the church over time is located in people. The church is the People of God, the Body of the Lord, and the Temple of the Holy Spirit,[7] and if its genesis is portrayed in an ahistorical way, the beauty of the church's complicated development is kept hidden.

During the age of martyrs from Paul to Constantine, the Gnostic crisis spurred the emergence of the authoritative interpretive role of bishops, led by the bishop of Rome, and of the canon, in the recognition that the Word of God is revealed in the sacred scriptures.[8] In the era of Christendom from the Constantinian Reversal until the Enlightenment, the church had to face the dilemmas arising from the new relationship between church and state and between Athens and Jerusalem, bringing about the great distinction between *imperium, sacerdotium,* and *studium* that is constitutive of Western civilization.[9] According to Joseph Komonchak, from the eleventh to the fifteenth centuries "the 'institutionalization' of the Church was carried out more as a sociological necessity than as a reflexively conscious decision."[10] This does not diminish the theological reality of the church's nature, but is integral to it.

Dominus Iesus seems to invoke once again the Christian self-understanding that shaped the church until Vatican II. It arose in the modern era from the Enlightenment to the present,[11] and tended to overstress the institutional dimension of the church. It linked this institutional self-understanding rather one-sidedly to the divine dimension of the church.

Both Hermann J. Pottmeyer[12] and Komonchak have shown that this imbalance was "reinforced by the centralization of the Tridentine Reform in Rome." This overemphasis became centrally important "in a series of retreats" in which "the Church would feel itself obliged to preserve its own unique and privileged social order before the threats of the Enlightenment, the political revolutions of the eighteenth and nineteenth centuries, and the general secularization of modern European life." At the same time, "the Church ceased to be in creative contact with the forces shaping the modern world and sought to preserve its identity by insisting upon its uniqueness and by making the transcendence of its origin, center, and goal apply to its nearly every feature."

Redolent of Pius XII's *Mystici Corporis* (1943), *Dominus Iesus* seems to express the idea of the church as a "perfect society," which underpinned the original preparatory scheme drafted by the Roman Curia in preparation for Vatican II. J. Neuner and H. Roos characterize this conception as follows:

> The Church possesses all the properties of a true society... The Church
> is not a member or a part of another society, nor is it to be somehow

grouped with any other. In itself it is so perfect that it is elevated above all human communities, ranging far beyond them. The Church in its constitution is so completely set apart and distinct that no society which is separated from the unity of faith or from the community of this body can in any way be called a part or member of the Church. The Church is also not dispersed and divided by the various societies that call themselves Christian; it is completely gathered into itself and enclosed into a unity.[13]

Bernard Lonergan tells us that:

On an ancient and traditional view, society is conceived as the orga-nized collaboration of individuals for the pursuit of a common aim or aims. On the basis of this very general definition various kinds of so-ciety are distinguished and, among them, the church and the state which are named "perfect" societies on that ground that each in its own sphere possesses ultimate authority.[14]

Does the document's approach to ecclesiology presuppose this concept of a "perfect society"? For Lonergan, such a conception is rooted in a classicist, normative, and juridical approach to human reality. Thus, during the Counter-Reformation, ecclesiologists spontaneously appealed to legal categories and *Denkformen,* perhaps because the first of the human sciences to emerge and mature were based on codified Roman Law, in contrast to the more empirical, and possibly more prudential, common-law approach in Anglo-Saxon coun-tries. Ecclesiology became what Komonchak calls "hierarchology" in the guise of a treatise on public law[15]—a perfect match for the contemporaneous moral theology's synthesis of Stoicism and probabilism.

As a "perfect society" the church is conceived as independent of external influences; it always remains one and the same and has its identity centered in papal sovereignty, alongside yet above all other temporal rulers.[16] In apparent contrast to the present document, the council fathers rejected this schema.[17]

3. Church: Full, particular, and ecclesial communities

As I have already suggested, when Vatican II's *Lumen gentium* also spoke of the church of Christ subsisting in the Catholic Church, it did not thematize the qualifications to other denominations' membership in the church. The faithful were free to suppose that the one church of Christ subsists in the Orthodox, An-glican, and Protestant churches as well. The present document's interpretation of the phrase "the Church of Christ subsists in the Catholic Church" distin-guishes between the Catholic Church *simpliciter,* "particular churches," and "ecclesial communities." Fortunately, the document (§18) also cites another conciliar definition of the church as "the people gathered by the unity of the Fa-ther, the Son and the Holy Spirit," which is open to a more concrete and em-pirical treatment of the church's reality. This is not to depreciate centrally constitutive Catholic realities of the Eucharist, apostolicity, and orders, or to imply that sacraments and church order are matters of indifference. On the contrary.

Still, more than thirty years of ecumenical dialogue have underscored what an old seminary teacher of mine used to say: "Confidence is the feeling you have before you really understand the situation." Christians divided are still in the process of understanding each other, exploring areas of agreement and disagreement in friendly conversation, praying and working together in common causes. During this process, is it helpful to use differences of conviction respectfully held in an invidious manner against the sincere listening and service in the Spirit to the Word which we share?[18]

4. What about holiness?

The Congregation for the Doctrine of the Faith document places an almost exclusive stress upon the unity, catholicity, and apostolicity of the church, giving short shrift to the mark of holiness. Mary, the mother of Jesus, is the exception to prove the rule that the church as human comes under judgment as sinful. Read in contrast to articles 39-42 of *Lumen gentium,* the document does not give one the deep impression that the church is what Paul in Romans 5 describes as a solidarity in Christ Jesus moving from sin through death to eternal life.

In contrast to the leadership, actions, and words of John Paul II, the document scarcely alludes to the demand that the sinfulness of the church in its members must always be openly acknowledged and humbly repented. Instead, the first sentence in article 2 states: "In the course of the centuries, the Church has proclaimed and witnessed with fidelity to the Gospel of Jesus." This is true, but the rhetoric of the statement seems to betray a lack of humility and an insouciance about the historic church's sinful record highlighted by the Holy Father during this Jubilee Year of Reconciliation.

5. Understanding the missions of Word and Spirit

In a manner that is faithful to the texts of Vatican II and of John Paul II, the document is Christocentric in its elaboration of the economy of salvation established by the Three-personed God in whom Christians believe. It neither presents nor presupposes an adequate analogical understanding of God's ways of sending both his Son and his Spirit. This may be why it neglects mentioning the passage in *Lumen gentium* which teaches that "those who, through no fault of their own, do not know the gospel of Christ or his church, but who nevertheless seek God with a sincere heart, and, moved by grace, try in their actions to do his will as they know it through the dictates of their conscience—these too may attain eternal salvation" (§16). The document is ambiguous about whether those members of the great world religions who have not explicitly known and accepted Jesus truly receive the Spirit.

A more adequate theological understanding of what Bernard Lonergan calls "the threefold giving that is the gift of the Holy Spirit . . . the gift of the divine Word..., the final gift of union with the Father"[19] would enable us, with Lonergan and Frederick Crowe, to "interpret the religions of mankind, in their positive moment, as the fruit of the gift of the Spirit."[20] It would conceive the unity of the economy of Son and Spirit in the world in terms of their two clearly distinct personal foci, which are, as Crowe says, "as clearly related in equality and complementarity as they are themselves related to one another in their divine being and their temporal mission."[21] Such an understanding of the revealed sources, of tradition, and of Christian experience, in prayer and in action, can acknowledge that the positive moment in the non-Christian religions of humankind is, in Crowe's words, "God's love, not yet fully avowed due to the 'notable anonymity to this gift of the Spirit.'"[22]

The mission of the Holy Spirit to all humankind from the beginning allows us to affirm with Crowe

> our religious community with the world religions in some true and basic sense of the word, community, if not in the full sense of a common confession of faith, a common worship, and a common expression of hope in the eschaton. The community is effected by our common religious conversion, which, in Lonergan's view, is our common orientation to the mystery of love and awe through the indwelling Holy Spirit who is given to us. We do not, therefore, go to the world religions as strangers, as to heathens, pagans, enemies of God. For we are one with them in the Spirit, and expect to find in them the fruits of the Spirit. If these fruits seem too often to be lacking, we will reflect that they are far too often lacking in ourselves also, though we have the outer word of doctrine and the sacraments deriving from the Son.[23]

This recognition of an incognito sending and gift of the Holy Spirit to all of humanity in no way compromises or dispenses with the mission of the Son, or with the fact that the church is constituted by the continuation of the missions of the Word and Spirit. The Father's sending of the Spirit is due to and correlative with the salvific work of the Son, who is, as Crowe says, "God's full avowal of his love."[24]

As Lonergan put it: "Without the visible mission of the Word, the gift of the Spirit is a being-in-love without a proper object; it remains simply an orientation to mystery that awaits its interpretation. Without the invisible mission of the Spirit, the Word enters into its own, but his own receive it not."[25] This teaching harmonizes with Thomas Aquinas's opinion in the *Summa theologiae* that Christ is the head, not only of a historically limited *corpus mysticum,* but of all human beings from the creation of the world to the end.[26]

Catholic Christians will want—indeed are compelled—to do everything they can to share their personal, eucharistic life in Christ Jesus, because the obscurity and anonymity of the gift of the Spirit is removed only by

> the fact that the Father has spoken to us of old through the prophets and in this final age through the Son (Heb. 1.1-2). His communication

is twofold: it is both by linguistic meaning and by incarnate meaning. By linguistic meaning he rebuked those that give scandal, announced redemption for sinners, provided for the forgiveness of sin, established the bond of the Eucharist, promised the gift of the Spirit, and set before men the destiny of the eternal life. But all such linguistic meaning was endlessly reinforced by the incarnate meaning to be contemplated in the life and ministry and, above all, in the suffering, death, and resurrection of Christ.[27]

CONCLUSION

My basic unease with the declaration is that it does not make two things sufficiently clear. First, it does not sufficiently reaffirm what Paul VI said in article 38 of *Ecclesiam suam* (1964): "The Church must enter into dialogue with the world in which it finds itself living. The Church makes itself a word. The Church makes itself a message. The Church makes itself a conversation."[28] To make itself a conversation it must embody not only the mission of the Word but also the mission of the Holy Spirit of contemplation and listening. And, second, rather than render luminous it obscures what the line from an old hymn by Frederick Faber makes loud and clear: "There's a wideness in God's mercy!"

6

THE REAFFIRMATION OF THE CHRISTIC CENTER

Robert Imbelli

PRELIMINARY OBSERVATIONS

The controversy engendered by the declaration of the Congregation for the Doctrine of the Faith, *Dominus Iesus,* deserves three preliminary comments before moving to some observations concerning the Christological substance of the document. First, one would be hard pressed to discover another official document from any source, Catholic or non-Catholic, that has been so misrepresented as has *Dominus Iesus.* One egregious example was the report published in the *Boston Globe* on Sunday, September 10, 2000. The writer declared that the document "bars [other believers] from the gates of heaven, despite their most sincere intentions and good lives." There is absolutely no warrant in the text of *Dominus Iesus* for so mischievous a claim; indeed, the document explicitly affirms the opposite.[1] As Mark Heim acknowledges in his insightful contribution to this volume, the declaration has been subject to "willful misreading." One can only wonder how a supposedly responsible press could be complicit in the propagation of such disinformation. It represents another instance of "the kind of Manichaean journalism from which Catholics suffer so much today."[2]

Second, amidst the consternation voiced in certain ecumenical circles, there was nonetheless heard, from the more informed, the grudging admission that in reality the document contained "nothing new." Why then the widespread dismay? Kilian McDonnell offers an interesting conjecture. He states that, though the claims articulated in the declaration faithfully reflect the teaching of Vatican II, "the shock comes from having them all gathered in one place."[3] As I shall suggest below, at least part of the problem stems from the rather selective appeal to Vatican II that has characterized Catholic and non-Catholic theological and ecumenical discussion over the past thirty-five years. In this sense there is some merit in the assertion that what is ultimately at stake in Catholic circles is the authentic interpretation of the meaning and import of Vatican II.

Third, one can vigorously defend the crucial importance of the declaration without having to justify every aspect of the document. Some have lamented what they consider a too imperious tone. Others, while affirming all that was said, would have wished that other things might have been said as well. Thus

Richard John Neuhaus writes: "*Dominus Iesus* is nothing more than a clear restatement of long-established Catholic teaching, and I agree with every word of it. But one may be forgiven for thinking it is missing other words that might have avoided misunderstandings and would have made it more difficult for those bent on misrepresenting Catholic teaching."[4]

Nevertheless, despite reservations concerning tone and omission, the reaffirmation by *Dominus Iesus* of the Christic center of Catholicism is urgently needed, not least for clarifying the fundamental principles that Catholics must bring to ecumenical dialogue, if they are faithfully to represent Catholic tradition. As Pope John Paul II said subsequent to the issuance of the declaration and the serious concerns it raised in some quarters: "The Document clarifies essential Christian elements, which do not hinder dialogue but show its bases, because a dialogue without foundations would be destined to degenerate into empty wordiness."[5]

THEOLOGICAL CONTEXT

On November 18, 1965 the dogmatic constitution on divine revelation, *Dei verbum,* was promulgated by the Second Vatican Council. *Dei verbum* is a remarkable—indeed revolutionary—document. The rejection of the preliminary draft of the constitution three years earlier had marked the effective beginning of Pope John's Council and the beginning of the end of post-Tridentine Catholicism with its undeniable beauties and banalities. *Dei verbum* was justly celebrated for recovering a more vibrant, personalist understanding of God's revelation, whose fullness is given in the person of Jesus Christ. I say "recover" because such an understanding is, in fact, more in keeping with the orientation of the New Testament and patristic understanding than was the one-sided "propositional" approach to revelation that characterized post-Tridentine scholasticism.

Yet, thirty-five years later, the robust Christocentrism of *Dei verbum* seems to evoke embarrassment in certain theological and missionary circles of contemporary Catholicism. Hence the benign neglect and, at times, outright repudiation of the constitution on revelation. This anomalous situation, I contend, forms a considerable part of the context that the declaration *Dominus Iesus* is addressing. Though the ecclesiological teaching of *Dominus Iesus* certainly merits attention and discussion, I shall in the following remarks limit myself to the Christological teaching, both because ecclesiological issues are treated in other essays in this volume, and also, more importantly, because, as the title of the declaration itself suggests, the profession of faith in Jesus Christ constitutes the very heart of the matter.

The declaration is directed, in the first instance, not to ecumenical dialogue partners of the Catholic Church, nor to all people of good will, but to the bishops of the Catholic Church, to be communicated in particular to theological faculties and missionary congregations.[6] It is important to underscore this, even as one may legitimately raise the question whether, in the Internet age, such a limitation of audience is any longer possible.

The intent of *Dominus Iesus* is to recapitulate the church's faith in the uniqueness and universal salvific significance of Jesus Christ, the incarnate Word of God: the article of faith upon which the church itself stands or falls. What is crucial about this document is that this article of faith, everywhere professed and presumed by Vatican II and the guarantee of the council's legitimacy and continuity with the great tradition, can no longer be taken for granted as in "pacific possession." Thus, the contemporary theological context differs greatly from that which prevailed at Vatican II. Put bluntly: there is abroad today a measure of innocent and, sometimes, quite intentional apostasy.

Faced with this situation of covert and overt relativizing of Christological normativity, the document seeks not to mount a theological argument but to set forth a profession of faith, drawing in particular upon the New Testament, the documents of Vatican II, and the papal magisterium of John Paul II. It is of utmost significance that the first number of the declaration and its very first quotation is the creed of the Council of Constantinople in its original articulation (without the later Western addition of the *filioque*): the common trinitarian faith of the undivided church. Thus the declaration is "dogmatic," not in the invidious sense of arbitrary or unenlightened, but in the precise sense of what ultimately binds believers and constitutes their identity as Catholic Christians.[7]

It comes as no surprise, then, that *Dominus Iesus* cites *Dei verbum,* the dogmatic constitution on divine revelation, seven times in its first section on "The Fullness and Definitiveness of the Revelation of Jesus Christ." Perhaps the climactic teaching of Vatican II's constitution is the following affirmation: "By this revelation then, the deepest truth about God and the salvation of man shines forth in Christ, who is at the same time the mediator and the fullness of all revelation" (DV 2; DI 5).

Now, lest it be thought that this perspective of *Dei verbum* is somehow displaced by other documents of Vatican II, let me briefly suggest, with *Dominus Iesus,* that it is, on the contrary, everywhere presupposed. The ample citations from the documents of Vatican II in the declaration do not represent an exercise in proof-texting, but an exercise of spiritual discernment, re-echoing the Christo-logic of the council in a new context in which it can no longer, alas, be taken for granted.

Thus the very first words of the dogmatic constitution on the church, *Lumen gentium* (another conciliar document often cited selectively in both "traditionalist" and "progressive" quarters), confesses that Christ is "the light of all peoples" and that all (not only Christians) are called to union with Christ. Hence the council's recognition that God's grace is operative outside the visible boundaries of the Catholic Church in no way lessens the missionary imperative incumbent upon the church by the Lord's own command, as an attentive reading of *Lumen gentium* articles 16 and 17 makes abundantly clear.[8]

Indeed, the council's epoch-making declaration on the relationship of the church to non-Christian religions, *Nostra aetate,* explicitly professes both respect and evangelical responsibility—for both are mandated by the Christocentric vision that characterizes *Dei verbum* and *Lumen gentium.* It states (in a passage several times referred to by the recent declaration):

The Catholic Church rejects nothing of what is true and holy in these religions ... Yet she proclaims, and is in duty bound to proclaim without fail, Christ who is the way, the truth, and the life (Jn 14:6). In him, in whom God reconciled all things to himself (2 Cor 5:18-19), men and women find the fullness of religious life (NA 2).

Further, the equally celebrated declaration on religious liberty, *Dignitatis humanae* (also quoted by the declaration, despite reports to the contrary in an often adversarial secular press), affirms this same tensive *both/and.* It certainly acknowledges the right of men and women to be free from coercion in fulfilling their duty to worship God. At the same time it "professes its belief that God himself has made known to the human race the way in which men and women are to serve him, and thus be saved in Christ and come to blessedness" (DH 1).

Finally, the pastoral constitution on the church in the modern world, *Gaudium et spes,* which many believe to be the most distinctively original of the council's documents, reflects, as it must, this same Christological vision and faith. *Gaudium et spes* is indeed a pastoral constitution, but one set on a solid dogmatic foundation. It confesses, in striking fashion, the incarnational faith of the gospel and the Catholic tradition:

The Word of God, through whom all things were made, was made flesh, so that as perfect man he could save all men and women and sum up all things in himself. The Lord is the goal of human history, the focal point of the desires of history and civilization, the center of mankind, the joy of all hearts, and the fulfillment of all aspirations. It is he whom the Father raised from the dead, exalted and placed at his right hand, constituting him judge of the living and the dead (GS 45; DI 15).

Clearly, Christological normativity, the uniqueness and salvific universality of Jesus Christ, was not invented by the Congregation for the Doctrine of the Faith. It is simply the doctrine of the faith.

In the thirty-five years since the close of the council, there has been frequent appeal, especially in "progressive" theological circles, to the "hierarchy of truths." At one time or another the claim is put forward that birth control or even papal infallibility do not "rank high" in the hierarchy of truths. Well, we now stand at the summit. For if the doctrine of the unique Incarnation of Jesus Christ and the doctrine of the Trinity which flows from that confession of faith do not form the apex of the hierarchy of truths, then there is no such thing; and simple honesty prohibits pretending otherwise.

The declaration addresses, therefore, a contemporary context of Christological drift and ambiguity in which some are suggesting "multiple incarnations" of the Christ, or that Jesus is Savior only for Christians, or that the salvific role of the Spirit is more universal than that of Jesus Christ, or that Trinity is but one "model" for speaking of the incomprehensible mystery of God. Such "unitarianism of the Spirit" is no figment of some over-heated Roman imagination. It appears in print, both at a popular and a more sophisticated theological level. If the church's magisterium cannot authoritatively declare that such is *not* "the faith delivered once and for all to the saints" (Jude 3), then there is no legitimate role for the magisterium. It is simply otiose.

The declaration's reaffirmation of this faith by no means precludes further theological exploration. *Dominus Iesus* several times encourages precisely such reflection (see §14 and §21). Indeed, in a paragraph that has received insufficient attention, the declaration frames its own purpose in the context of the need to address new questions that have arisen in the course of inter-religious dialogue. These clearly require "pursuing new paths of research, advancing proposals, and suggesting ways of acting that call for attentive discernment" (§3). This difficult and indispensable task is part of the ecclesial vocation of theologians. But such theological investigation must be faithful to the distinctive content of revelation, if it is truly to be theology: faith, the response to divine revelation, seeking further understanding of the Mystery, whose fullness is given in Jesus Christ. "In this task, the present Declaration seeks to recall ... certain indispensable elements of Christian doctrine, which may help theological reflection in developing solutions consistent with the contents of the faith and responsive to the pressing needs of contemporary culture" (§3).

CHRISTOLOGICAL PARAMETERS AND PERSPECTIVES

As just noted, *Dominus Iesus* expressly encourages further theological reflection. It states, for example, that

> theology today, in its reflection on the existence of other religious experiences and on their meaning in God's salvific plan, is invited to explore if and in what way the historical figures and positive elements of these religions may fall within the divine plan of salvation. In this undertaking, theological research has a vast field of work under the guidance of the Church's Magisterium (§14).

In dialogue with observations and criticisms which the declaration has elicited, including some offered in this volume, I would like to ponder three Christological issues concerning which Catholic theology is called today to creative fidelity.

1. Jesus Christ: The Word made flesh

Not seldom, in inter-religious discussions, one hears the claim that Judaism, Christianity, and Islam are united by being each a "religion of the Book." As an attempt to indicate some commonality and to suggest some common ground for respectful dialogue, there is much to recommend the assertion. But it also risks neglecting real differences. Primary among them is that Christianity is much more a religion of the Person than of the book. At the heart of the gospel is the good news who is Jesus Christ. Jesus, for the Christian community and for the

individual believer, is more than prophet, more than messenger: he is the kingdom in person. In the phrase of Origen, the early Greek father of the church,
Jesus Christ is the *autobasileia*. As Pope John Paul stated in his encyclical, *Redemptoris missio* (of which *Dominus Iesus* is, in many respects, a résumé):
"The kingdom of God is not a concept, a doctrine or a program subject to free
interpretation, but is before all else a person with the face and name of Jesus of
Nazareth, the image of the invisible God."[9]

Already in the earliest writings of the New Testament, astonishing and un-
paralleled claims are made concerning one who had been executed as blasphe-
mer and revolutionary a scant twenty-five years previously. These claims unite
in tensive and transcendent synthesis both the personal and the cosmic, the particular and the universal. Thus Paul in Galatians speaks personally and with
tender affection of "the Son of God who loved me and gave himself for me"
(2:20). Yet he has no hesitation to extend the same grace to all: "In Christ Jesus
you are all sons of God through faith" (3:26); indeed, "there is neither Jew nor
Greek, there is neither slave nor free, there is neither male nor female; for you
are all one in Christ Jesus" (3:28).

The human universality that the passages from Galatians stress further unfolds in other New Testament texts to disclose a cosmic universality. Thus, in
an almost matter-of-fact way, Paul reminds the Corinthians that "for us there is
one God, the Father, from whom are all things and for whom we exist, and one
Lord, Jesus Christ, through whom are all things and through whom we exist"
(1 Cor 8:6). With this confession we verge upon the extraordinary claims embodied in the Christological hymn of Colossians where the Lord Jesus Christ is
celebrated as "the firstborn of all creation," the one in whom "all things were
created," and in whom "all things hold together" (Col 1:15-17).

In the early church, before the content of the scriptural canon was firmly
established, appeal was made to "the rule of faith": the normative and defining
Christian confession. Perhaps its shortest and most fundamental formulation in
the New Testament is found in Paul: *Kurios Iesous* (1 Cor 12:3; Phil 2:11). Its
Latin translation is, of course, *Dominus Iesus*. Thus the Catholic New Testament scholar, Luke Timothy Johnson, writes that

> as early as Paul . . . the community's experience of the risen and living
> Jesus was so powerful as to demand some propositional expression of
> who Jesus must be in order to have altered reality so fundamentally.
> The earliest of such confessions may well have been "Jesus is Lord"
> (see 1 Cor 12:3; Rom 10:9; Phil 2:11; Acts 2:36). This simple yet pow-
> erful confession bears within itself implicitly all the later creedal de-
> velopment, for it poses the question of what it means to call both the
> God of Israel and Jesus of Nazareth "Lord."[10]

Rather than betraying a scriptural naiveté, as some suggest, *Dominus Iesus*
powerfully re-echoes and confesses this rule of faith which itself underlies and
generates the New Testament canon—a canon which, of course, includes the
"longer ending" of Mark's gospel (appealed to not only by the declaration, but

by Vatican II). For the New Testament is "scripture," authoritative writing, only within the believing and worshipping community which, in the Spirit, acclaims Jesus as Lord to the glory of the Father. Otherwise it is merely ancient Near-Eastern literature, of interest only to an academic guild.

Moreover, as the quotation from Johnson well suggests, it is a fundamental principle of Catholic theology that the conciliar creeds do not represent a "hellenization of the gospel," a misreading or falsification of its meaning and intent. Rather, the creeds draw out the truth of the gospel in the more differentiated language that new questions and contexts require. Thus, as we have seen, *Dominus Iesus* begins with the profession of the creed of the Councils of Nicaea and Constantinople. In so doing it aligns itself with the church's millennial dogmatic tradition. In effect, it refuses to succumb to what Johnson has elsewhere called "the academic captivity of the church," whether in its liberal Protestant form of the beginning of the twentieth century or its Jesus Seminar form of that century's close. Instead, the declaration promotes the agenda Johnson himself proposed as imperative: "A church that has lost a sense of its boundaries—that is, a grasp of its self-definition—can only recover it by reasserting its character as a community of faith with a canon of Scripture and a creed."[11]

Now, with respect to the creed of the undivided church, one must frankly admit that some today advocate a return to an *ante*-Nicaea stage of doctrinal development, which is, for all practical purposes, often *anti*-Nicaea. In such a climate Jesus becomes reduced to the status of a moral teacher, a wisdom figure, even a prophet. But to stop there is only to revert to the answers elicited by the question: "Who do *others* say I am?" (Mk 8:27); it is not to advance to the question that evokes the faith of the church: "Who do *you* say I am?" (Mk 8:29). A Jesus who is fully, but only, human may be an impressive moral exemplar. He can scarcely be "the way, the truth, and the life" (Jn 14:6), the vine of which we are the branches (Jn 15:5).

At the heart of Christian experience is mystical relation to the person of Jesus Christ. This is the transcendent reality the conciliar dogmas of Nicaea and Chalcedon seek to safeguard. Borrowing Karl Rahner's insight, dogma is mystagogic: it leads to the Mystery in whom alone we find life. I am in full accord, then, with the view of Frans Jozef van Beeck in his programmatic study, *Catholic Identity After Vatican II*. He writes: "Christian identity is fundamentally a matter of *mystical* experience." And he makes clear that such mystical experience is fundamentally Christic: *"The person of Jesus Christ alive in the Spirit is the source of Christian identity-experience as well as the Christian experience of openness to the world."*[12] If Karl Rahner is correct that the Christian of the future will be a mystic or will not be,[13] then clearly the mysticism in question must be Christocentric, as must be the theology that reflects upon this primal and transformative experience.[14]

Hence I am not persuaded by Charles Hefling's contention in this volume concerning a tension running through *Dominus Iesus*. Hefling locates this in particular in the declaration's alleged support for "foundations conceived in the classicist manner." May I suggest, instead, that *Dominus Iesus* forcefully reminds us that *the* foundational event is the person of Jesus Christ and the conversion to which disciples are summoned. If theological foundations in the new context of religious pluralism entail reflection upon conversion, as Lonergan proposes,[15] then the declaration proclaims the one foundation upon which all Christian theologians must build if their writings are to be anything more than straw. In effect, *Dominus Iesus* echoes Paul: "For no one can lay any foundation other than the one that has been laid; that foundation is Jesus Christ" (1 Cor 3:11).

Saying this, one sometimes hears anguished cries of "Christomonism," the complaint of an exclusive focus upon the person of Jesus Christ to the neglect of the full mystery of the Trinity. The charge has sometimes been leveled against the theology of Karl Barth, the greatest Protestant theologian of the last century. It seems a strange accusation, given that Barth has developed one of the most profound trinitarian visions in the history of Christian theology. But let me merely insist that we have absolutely no access to trinitarian faith save through Christology. If our claims regarding Jesus are exclusively within the familiar ambit of human categories, there is no reason to posit a God who is Trinity. Only through the narrow way of the unique Christological claim, that the eternal Word of God has become flesh in Jesus Christ, is there basis and reason for (admittedly always) halting speech about the God who is Triune.

2. The Word and the Spirit: The two hands of God

Though themselves acknowledging the uniqueness of Jesus Christ and the trinitarian faith to which it gives rise, some yet fault *Dominus Iesus* for insufficient attention to the Holy Spirit. While not pretending that the declaration has said all that needs to be said regarding the Holy Spirit, it is important to stress the theological context that the text is addressing. In the very first sentence of the important article 12 of *Dominus Iesus* we find a clear statement of its concern: "There are also those who propose the hypothesis of an economy of the Holy Spirit with a more universal breadth than that of the incarnate Word, crucified and risen."

However, notwithstanding the declaration's Christic focus, I do not find warranted Frederick Lawrence's assertion that the document is "ambiguous about whether those members of the great world religions who have not explicitly known and accepted Jesus truly receive the Spirit." *Dominus Iesus* affirms clearly that those who "are not formally and visibly members of the Church" may attain salvation in Christ; and, quoting *Redemptoris missio,* it confesses: "This grace comes from Christ; it is the result of his sacrifice and is communicated by the Holy Spirit" (§20).

The declaration's teaching, rather, is to insist upon the inseparability of the workings of the incarnate Word and the Holy Spirit. In the memorable metaphor of Irenaeus, the second-century father of the church, God accomplishes all God's works through the joint operation of God's "two hands": the Son and the Spirit.[16] Any attempt to separate them dissolves the one economy of salvation. In more conceptual language, the two "missions" of Christ and Spirit must never be disjoined. The presumed ecumenical gain would be at the price of the incalculable loss of Christian identity.

One is repeatedly struck by the "Irenaean tenor" of *Dominus Iesus*. Not
only is Irenaeus explicitly invoked four times in the notes to the declaration
(see notes 36, 45, 53, and 80), but the conclusion to article 12 sounds the fundamental theme of Irenaeus' theology. "There is only one salvific economy of
the One and Triune God, realized in the mystery of the incarnation, death, and
resurrection of the Son of God, actualized with the cooperation of the Holy
Spirit, and extended in its salvific value to all humanity and to the entire universe" (§12).

Thus I must demur at Hefling's view that "the Word's role and mission in
that economy begins with his taking on a human nature," while "the role and
mission of the Spirit does not." This seems to imply that the Word was not active in Israel or that "seeds of the Word" were not present in the religious aspirations and intimations of the ancient world. With Harvey Egan (and Karl
Rahner!), I hold, as a principle of Catholic theology, that "even prior to the
crucifixion and resurrection, Jesus Christ was present and operative through
his Spirit in non-Christian believers and non-Christian religions... The crucified and risen Word—and no other—is the reason the Spirit is given."

It is worth recalling, in this connection, the work of the great theologian,
Yves Congar. His three-volume study, *I Believe in the Holy Spirit,* marks a significant recovery of a theology of the Holy Spirit for Catholic thought in our
time. Nonetheless, in a volume published as a sequel to this study, Congar
writes: "If I were to draw but one conclusion from the whole of my work on the
Holy Spirit, I would express it in these words: no Christology without pneumatology and no pneumatology without Christology."[17] One simply cannot separate Christ and the Spirit; God always uses "two hands." And, in a sentence
quite apposite to the present discussion, Congar further states: "The Spirit dis-
plays something that is new, in the novelty of history and the variety of cultures,
but it is a new thing that comes from the fullness that has been given once and
for all by God in Christ."[18]

What is required, then, is a true synthesis of Christology and pneumatology. Interestingly, though many in the Christian West make appeal at this point
to the tradition of the Christian East, which purportedly has a greater pneuma-
tological sensitivity, one of the foremost theologians of the Orthodox Church,
Bishop John Zizioulas, frankly admits that "Orthodox theology has not yet
worked out the proper synthesis between Christology and Pneumatology." Indeed, he suggests that, due to the West's distinctive sensitivities and concerns,
it will, understandably, always give "a certain priority" to Christology over
pneumatology. And he makes a striking concession: "There are reasons to suppose that this could be spiritually expedient, especially in our time."[19] Such, I
think, is also the considered spiritual discernment of *Dominus Iesus*.

3. Re-imaging the Transfiguration

Toward the end of his sympathetic reflection on *Dominus Iesus* in this volume,
Mark Heim suggests the need to give "greater attention to the specificity of the
Christian understanding of salvation." And Philip Cunningham, at the conclu-

sion of his own more critical assessment, sounds a similar note. Cunningham rightly cites article 21 of *Dominus Iesus,* which calls for theologians to seek to understand more fully how God's salvific grace, given in Christ, is mediated to non-Christians. While concurring with the need for further theological investigation of this crucial issue, I would offer two observations. First, the issue of salvation receives more extensive treatment in Pope John Paul's encyclical, *Redemptoris missio.* I have already stated my belief that, in many respects, the Congregation for the Doctrine of the Faith document is a résumé of the Pope's earlier encyclical. Thus it is important that the two be read in tandem. I recommend, in particular, articles 3, 7, 10, 11, 14, 16, and 44 of *Redemptoris missio* for their more ample soteriological teaching. Second, *Dominus Iesus* itself does provide some indication of the direction that reflection on the constitutive nature of salvation in Christ should pursue. Let me briefly highlight several passages.

Early in the declaration a summary statement of its teaching is given: "In the mystery of Jesus Christ, the Incarnate Son of God . . . the full revelation of divine truth is given" (§5). Later in the same paragraph, a fuller exegesis of the affirmation is given by quoting *Dei verbum:* "Through his words and deeds, his signs and wonders, but especially through his death and glorious resurrection from the dead and finally with the sending of the Spirit of truth, [Jesus Christ] completed and perfected revelation." For the declaration, as for the New Testament itself and the church's liturgical tradition, the heart of Christian salvation is founded in the paschal mystery of Jesus Christ.

Later the declaration clearly teaches that Christ's salvific action transcends the visible boundaries of the church to embrace all humanity. It again turns to Vatican II to substantiate its claim.

> Speaking of the paschal mystery, in which Christ even now associates the believer to himself in a living manner in the Spirit and gives him the hope of resurrection, the Council states: "All this holds true not only for Christians but also for all men of good will in whose hearts grace is active invisibly. For since Christ died for all, and since all men are in fact called to one and the same destiny, which is divine, we must hold that the Holy Spirit offers to all the possibility of being made partners, in a way known to God, in the paschal mystery" (§12, quoting GS 22).

Once again: constitutive of salvation is participation in the paschal mystery of Christ.

Finally, in article 20, in a passage I have already cited, *Dominus Iesus* reiterates that the followers of other religions can indeed receive divine grace and attain salvation in Christ. But it insists, with *Redemptoris missio,* that "this grace comes from Christ; it is the result of his sacrifice and is communicated by the Holy Spirit."[20] The sacrifice of Jesus Christ is singled out as the universal source of salvific grace; and it is this paschal grace that is actualized in the Holy Spirit.[21]

From these statements I think the following thesis is consonant with the teaching of *Dominus Iesus:* to speak of salvation in Christ is to speak especially of the paschal pattern of salvation. Wherever salvation is truly taking place, its form is Christic and paschal: the transformation of sin and death, in their myriad forms, into new life. This is what Christians mean by salvation. The "grammar" of salvation in Christian speech is always paschal. Salvation's "logic" is Christo-logic. One can and should say many other things regarding Christian salvation, particularly in the new context of inter-religious dialogue. But whatever one says must be according to its paschal depth grammar, if one is not to utter theological nonsense.[22]

Of course, one ought not restrict theological language to the conceptual. Dante's poetry and Bach's music figure among the greatest creations of the Christian theological tradition. In almost every respect their power exceeds many ponderous *summas,* for they succeed in engaging the affections as well as the mind. Pictorial representation also can offer rich and imaginative theological insight. I think in particular of the iconographic tradition of Eastern Christianity. Let me close these reflections, then, by setting before our mind's eye the icon of the transfiguration of the Lord.

The synoptic gospels place the account of the transfiguration of Jesus at their very center; while the entire gospel of John is bathed in transfigured light: "We have seen his glory, the glory as of the Father's only Son, full of grace and truth" (Jn 1:14).

In the synoptics the account of the transfiguration follows close upon Peter's confession of Jesus' messiahship and the subsequent prediction by Jesus of his rejection, passion, and vindication by God. As the evangelists narrate the scene, Moses and Elijah are presented conversing with the transfigured Jesus. Luke specifies further that "they spoke of his exodus that he was going to accomplish in Jerusalem" (Lk 9:31). And each of the synoptics records the climax of the scene when the voice speaks from the overshadowing cloud of glory and declares: "This is my beloved Son; listen to him."

The common interpretation of the event may be summed up by the New American Bible's note on Mark 9:5. "Moses and Elijah represent respectively law and prophecy in the Old Testament...They now appear with Jesus as witnesses to the fulfillment of the law and the prophets taking place in the person of Jesus as he appears in glory." But the way to glory is the paschal way, the enduring scandal of the cross: the exodus of death that leads to resurrected life.

All this and more is communicated beyond words in the icon of the transfiguration. The challenge to the Christian theological imagination is to depict the salvific fulfillment in Christ in the new context of the world religions. How might the transfiguration be painted today? Who are the dialogue partners of the Lord Jesus? How represent symbolically the Christic center? It may be providential, then, that *Dominus Iesus* is dated August 6, 2000, the Solemnity of the Transfiguration of the Lord. For, to adapt a line from T. S. Eliot: "The hint half guessed, the gift half understood" is transfiguration.

7

METHOD AND MEANING IN *DOMINUS IESUS*

Charles Hefling

My reflections on *Dominus Iesus* are those of an Anglican and a systematic theologian—mostly the latter.[1] Pretty much all that needs to be said about the document from an Anglican point of view was said by the Archbishop of Canterbury when it was first issued. In a brief official statement, the Archbishop observed that *Dominus Iesus* breaks no new ground. He regretted that it seems to call into question the achievements of ecumenical dialogue during the last thirty years. And he firmly rejected the one point that was bound to touch Anglicans on the raw, averring that our communion "does not for one moment accept that its orders of ministry and Eucharist are deficient in any way."[2]

Dominus Iesus has elicited many reactions of the same sort, within the Roman Catholic Church as well as from outside. On the one hand, there seems to be agreement that the document says nothing which has not been said before. Yet, on the other hand, its statements have in many quarters met with disappointment, if not dismay. Perhaps then it is not so much what *Dominus Iesus* says that has occasioned consternation, as *how* it says what it does. Complaints about the "tone" of the document move in that direction, and arguably there is something to complain about. Even the Pope felt called upon to amplify, as the source and motivation of its assertions, a theme which is not very prominent in *Dominus Iesus* itself—"joyful gratitude that Christ has revealed himself to us without any merit on our part."[3] Similarly, complaints about "balance," or lack of it, have noted that besides what the document does say there is much that it could and perhaps should have said as well.

My comments will be concerned with the "how" of *Dominus Iesus* in yet another sense: its methodology. By using that term I do not mean to imply that the document was produced by carrying out a recipe. I mean that it has a logic, that it pursues its ends by identifiable means and for identifiable reasons, that it makes some moves and not others, that it follows certain procedures and adheres to certain criteria, implicitly and sometimes explicitly. Nor does investigating the document from a methodological standpoint mean leaving out its substantive points. "Manner" can never be separated from "matter." But they are not the same, either; that is why it is possible to say the right thing not only in the wrong way but for the wrong reasons. Conversely, it is also why one may agree wholeheartedly with much, even most, of *what* is said in *Dominus*

Iesus—as I do—and at the same time regard its procedural strategy and tactics with reservations—as I also do.

My investigation has four parts. The first is an overview; it analyzes *Dominus Iesus* from a methodological standpoint, presents the basis on which the analysis is conducted, and adumbrates certain difficulties that are developed later. The second part offers a comparison between this document and one that can claim all but universal acknowledgment and acceptance among Christians. The similarities and the differences that are pointed out lead, in the third section, to an assessment of the methodological characteristics that were described in the first, stated in a pair of reservations about the document. The final section takes a wider view by proposing what I conclude is the religious axis around which everything in *Dominus Iesus* turns.

1. THREE METHODOLOGICAL CHARACTERISTICS

To borrow an apt phrase from Robert Imbelli's contribution to this volume, the overall aim of *Dominus Iesus* is to correct "Christological drift." We are given to understand that propositions have been put forward which veer away from the mainland of what may acceptably be said about the Lord Jesus. On the negative side, *Dominus Iesus* calls attention to this trend, and warns that it is headed for danger. More positively, the document proposes to tow the bark of Christology back to shore and anchor it on solid ground.

The way in which *Dominus Iesus* sets out to achieve this aim gives the document as a whole three characteristics that evince its methodological strategy. All three are fairly conspicuous, two by their presence, one by its absence. Since all three are more or less explicitly acknowledged, it is safe to regard their deployment as in some measure deliberate.

First characteristic. The document states. It is what it says it is: a declaration. It is consistently, almost exclusively, assertional, propositional, and, in a neutral and descriptive sense of the word, "dogmatic."

Second characteristic. The document states and what it states it does not explain. It prescinds largely if not entirely from spelling out the meaning of its terms and concepts,[4] from showing how its assertions are related to each other, and from articulating the way its own statements might bear on other statements or *vice versa*.

Third characteristic. The document states and its statements are restatements. It is a text mostly made up of other texts, transcribed from existing documents. Since these excerpts include nearly all its most significant assertions, the declaration could be described as a fabric of quotations arranged and connected by transitional passages and summaries.

None of these characteristics is fortuitous. A compact announcement of them appears near the beginning, in the declaration's self-description. The discourse to follow, it notes, will be "expository" (first characteristic). The matters treated will not be treated in a "systematic manner" (second characteristic), nor will they effect innovation: the document will simply present what has previ-

ously been taught, so as to "reiterate certain truths" that have already been it-
erated (third characteristic). The three characteristics, then, go together. The
second and third specify the first, so that as an ensemble they give a functional
definition of what a dogmatic declaration, this one at least, is.

We may therefore begin with the elementary point that *Dominus Iesus* aims
to say something, to make statements. The first thing to ask is: What sort of
question do these statements answer?—for statements, regarded methodologically, are never statements only. They are always answers to questions too. And
since questions are of different kinds, the particular kind of question that a
given statement answers, whether explicitly or not, is part of what the statement
means.

Plainly enough, the sort of question to which *Dominus Iesus,* taken on the
whole, corresponds as an answer is the question, What is to be believed? Again
and again the document says that "it must be *firmly believed* that...," or "it
must be held that..." or something equivalent. This is only a different way of
saying it is a dogmatic document: it asserts propositions, asserts them as true,
and asserts them as to-be-assented-to. Assenting to such propositions is what
Dominus Iesus means by believing.[5] Hence the general form of the question
that its assertions answer is what I shall call a *whether*-question. Such questions
ask, Is it so? Is it true?

The significance of relating the dogmatic assertions of *Dominus Iesus* to an
antecedent question of a determinate kind lies in the natural, spontaneous
"logic" of question and answer by which answers corresponding to one type of
question evoke other questions of a different type. A proposition, itself the answer to some question of the *whether*-kind, can lead in either of two directions
by giving rise to one or the other of two further questions, each asking something different from *whether* the proposition is so. The assertion that such-and-
such *is* so may, on the one hand, prompt one to wonder exactly what the proposition might mean, and thus to ask how it might be understood. Such a question
seeks to make sense of what is proposed; it is headed for intelligibility or coherence. It asks not *whether* but *how* a truth is true. On the other hand, however, the same assertion may instead prompt a different sort of question—not
whether, not *how,* but *for what reasons* such-and-such is proposed as true, on
what grounds its truth is asserted, what warrants there are for asserting it, assenting to it, believing it is so.

The distinctions I have just drawn pertain to any human intellectual investigation, theology included. Thus a doctrine or teaching or dogmatic statement is a
propositional utterance, corresponding at least implicitly to a *whether*-question.
As with other such utterances, one may ask how it is to be understood, what
sense it makes, how it can best be conceived, or how it coheres with other assertions, theological or otherwise. Such questions belong to a more or less def-
inite region of theological endeavor, which was once called speculative theology but might less misleadingly, following Bernard Lonergan, be called
"systematics." As I shall use the word from here on, "systematics" names one
of the functionally specialized tasks that Lonergan distinguishes within theology on the basis of distinctions between different kinds of questions such as I

have outlined above. So conceived, "systematics" has a different aim and procedure from dogmatic theology or, to continue with Lonergan's terminology, "doctrines." The functional specialty "doctrines" concentrates on *whether;* it is concerned with settling what is so. "Systematics" asks *how;* it is concerned with explanation in the sense of bringing to light the intrinsic intelligibility of the assertions that "doctrines" deals with. "Doctrines" annunciates truths; "systematics" aims at understanding them.

But a statement proposed as true, as an answer to "Is it so?", can initiate another, different line of questioning. One may ask what makes it so, why it is so, what reasons or warrants there are for holding that it *is* so. The theological counterpart of such questions is inquiry that investigates the external grounds of a doctrinal assertion—not at all the same thing as investigating its internal coherence or its similarity to other, non-theological assertions. To make the same point in terms of Lonergan's functional specialties, "foundations" is different from "systematics." These two sorts of theological inquiry stand, as it were, on either side of "doctrines." If the aim is to promote an understanding of some doctrinal statement, theological discussion will move along the lines of "systematics." If, on the other hand, the aim is to show what establishes or guarantees the doctrine's truth, the discourse will take another direction, toward "foundations."

Because these distinctions are grounded in the ubiquitous human performance of asking different kinds of questions, they are not limited to "Lonerganian" theology. I find them helpful in clarifying what *Dominus Iesus* is doing. Broadly speaking, the three methodological characteristics I listed earlier correspond respectively to "doctrines," "systematics," and "foundations." That is, *Dominus Iesus* is concerned mainly with the *whether*-questions proper to "doctrines." It does *not* go into questions that call for the kind of explanation that belongs to "systematics," and in fact eschews these explicitly in favor of what it calls an expository treatment. As for "foundations," the question about why the assertions in *Dominus Iesus* are asserted is given a straightforward answer, though the declaration gives it performatively rather than in as many words. These truths are being asserted as true because they have been truly asserted already. If the declaration does not explain, neither does it argue—or rather, the only argument it uses is the argument from authority. No warrant is given for the teachings it "reiterates," and none, it would seem, is required, except the authority of the other documents which this document quotes.

Before moving from analysis to comment and evaluation, it will be appropriate to take note of which documents *Dominus Iesus* does appeal to as authorities. They are various. The declaration opens with a biblical verse and goes on to transcribe the whole Nicene Creed. Several of the church fathers are cited, though not many medieval scholastics. But by far the greater part of the dogmatic statements reiterated in *Dominus Iesus* come from two twentieth-century sources. The substance of its teaching is drawn either from the Second Vatican Council or from the present Pope. For Roman Catholic theologians these are authoritative sources—how authoritative, I do not presume to say. Nor am I in a position to judge the degree of authority that quoting them confers on *Dominus Iesus,* or what additional authority accrues to the document from its having been issued by the Congregation for the Doctrine of the Faith (CDF) and ratified by the same Pope, or where the whole of it is therefore to be located on Roman Catholicism's finely graded scale of authoritative pronouncements.[6]

2. A POSSIBLY RELEVANT COMPARISON

However that may be, authoritative pronouncements of what is to be believed are not peculiar to Roman Catholic Christianity. Nor are the three methodological characteristics I find in *Dominus Iesus* peculiar to that pronouncement. It does nothing that has not been done in statements of Christian doctrine that claim catholic as well as Roman Catholic assent. One such dogmatic declaration is the "Definition of Faith" decreed by the ecumenical council of Chalcedon in 451, to which Anglicans are more or less formally committed,[7] and with which I think it will be instructive to compare *Dominus Iesus.* My comparison will endeavor to make two points. First, if *Dominus Iesus* expressly claims that what it teaches is not new—it "breaks no new ground," as Archbishop Carey said—it could also claim there is nothing unprecedented in its method. That in itself may open the declaration to objections, and I think it does. Thus my second point will be that there are enough differences between *Dominus Iesus* and the Chalcedonian definition to raise some doubt as to whether the means that suited Chalcedon's ends are suitable to the ends that *Dominus Iesus* pursues, in the situation in which it pursues them.

To resume, then: dogmatic declarations are not rare in Christian history. *Whether*-questions arise spontaneously, and from time to time they have given birth to disputes important enough to call forth yes-or-no judgments that come down on one side of the issue and rule out the other. Often enough, these disputes have been Christological. As Christ's person and work hold a pre-eminent place in Christian belief, so too many of the dogmas of the church were framed to define what it is (and is not) to say Jesus is Lord. Inasmuch as *Dominus Iesus* has this concern as well, it invites comparison with earlier doctrinal statements about the Lord Jesus; in particular, with *the* Christological dogma defined at Chalcedon. It might almost be thought that the declaration intentionally issues some such invitation. There are enough hints and echoes of Chalcedon in *Dominus Iesus* to suggest that it was meant to be seen, if not as a "new Chalcedon" in itself—the CDF is not, after all, an ecumenical council—at least as a latter-day sequel.

Be that as it may, what does seem clear is that *Dominus Iesus* and the Chalcedonian definition meet similar issues is a broadly similar way. Each of them was promulgated in order to stop "Christological drift." What *Dominus Iesus* in a nicely nuanced phrase calls "problematic and even erroneous propositions" were, in both cases, being put forward by Christian teachers, and in both cases the resulting controversy was grave enough to require official action. At Chalcedon, the question at issue came down to a single *whether*-question—whether the Lord Jesus is *one* or *two*. The answer the council arrived at begins, after a preamble, with a recitation of a text that the whole Christian community acknowledged as its doctrinal standard *par excellence,* the Nicene Creed. As I have mentioned, that is exactly how *Dominus Iesus* begins.[8] Chalcedon's definition claims to be expounding the creed, nothing more. Far from adding anything to what the bishops at Nicaea had already asserted, the definition professes itself to be "following the holy fathers." *Dominus Iesus* likewise claims to be asserting no more than has been definitively asserted before. Its teaching "takes up what has been taught...in order to reiterate certain truths" (§3). Not only, then, do both documents fall within the zone that Lonergan calls "doctrines," but both stand on the "foundations" of earlier doctrine. And to complete the methodological triad introduced in the previous section, there is no more "systematics" in the Chalcedonian decree than in *Dominus Iesus.*

This last point should perhaps be elaborated. Notoriously, the council of Chalcedon made use of certain technical terms without explaining what they should be understood to mean. More importantly, its dogmatic decree states over and over that there is one Christ; it states that one and the same Christ is perfect in divinity *and* perfect in humanity, truly God *and* truly man; it states, in words that will come up again below, that this divinity and this humanity are to be neither confused nor separated. But there it stops. There is no attempt at shedding light on *how* Christ can be one and the same, while divinity and humanity are not the same. *Dominus Iesus* is a much longer document, too long to summarize, but as I have noted already it does not undertake to show how its various assertions cohere, how they are to be understood, what their relation might be to other truths, theological or non-theological. Specific examples in the declaration will be mentioned presently; at the moment I want only to make the point that if *Dominus Iesus,* which certainly relies for its content on the authority of earlier pronouncements, does also stop short of providing insight into how its own "reiteration" of those pronouncements might be construed, there is on both counts a precedent that could scarcely be bettered.

The precedent might be employed in some such way as this. It has often been said that Chalcedon's Christological definition defines, not in the sense of stating an exact and fully articulated position, but only in the sense of setting boundaries and determining limits within which such a position must be worked out if it is to be an orthodox Christology. *Dominus Iesus,* it could be argued, restricts itself in much the same way. It acknowledges the importance of current questions about Christianity's relations to other religions, and acknowledges that many particular issues have yet to be resolved. However they are resolved, though, the resolution must keep within the perimeters stated (or reiterated) in the declaration. Some things are negotiable, some are not. *Dominus Iesus* states the ones that are not. Whether all the non-negotiable prescriptions and proscriptions that it states *can* be followed in a constructive way is a further question, which I think it is legitimate to ask and worthwhile to explore. It best can be sharpened, however, by taking into account four ways in which, despite their methodological similarities, *Dominus Iesus* and the Chalcedonian definition differ.

(1) The council of Chalcedon dealt with a single point of Christian belief. The "Christological drift" it sought to correct had to do with the distinction between the humanity and the divinity of the Lord Jesus. *Dominus Iesus* reconfirms this teaching—Chalcedon is one of the authorities it quotes—but reconfirms it as one among others. The *whether*-questions it deals with are many. They range over the theology of the sacraments, the Trinity, revelation, soteriology, pneumatology, and ecclesiology. If Chalcedon defined one dogma, *Dominus Iesus* is very nearly a conspectus of dogmatics.[9]

(2) Chalcedon's decree was an "in-house" decision. It addressed a dispute that had arisen entirely within the church, formulating what amounts to a rule of Christian grammar: if you are going to speak of Christ in and with the church—in homily, liturgy, devotion—*this* is how you should frame your speech.[10] Those who speak some other language, about someone else, are no concern of the council's. *Dominus Iesus* is not limited in the same way. True, it is formally addressed only to "the Catholic faithful." In fact, however, it addresses itself "to whom it may concern" and its implicit claim is that it concerns everyone. It is not methodologically irrelevant that, published as it was on a website in several languages, *Dominus Iesus* is as public a text as a text can be. For, like the Chalcedonian decree, it does in a sense prescribe what must be said about the Lord Jesus—among other things. The other things, however, begin with God—not some god, one of the gods, but the only God there is, the God whose will it is to save all human persons, and to do so, according to the declaration, through the Lord Jesus and not otherwise.

It is not, in other words, as though *Dominus Iesus* were saying: this is how to speak about Christ, *if* it happens to be Christ that you are interested in speaking about and not the Buddha or Joseph Smith or whomever. It is saying that if you are not interested in speaking about Christ, in confessing that Jesus is Lord, you should be. The notion of "salvific universality" as *Dominus Iesus* asserts it puts the document in quite another realm of discourse than the metaphysical pluralism that Mark Heim adumbrates in his essay. Salvation, for *Dominus Iesus,* is certainly Christocentric but not, for that reason, any less the one and only Deity's one and only intention for each and every mortal creature.

(3) A further difference between Chalcedon and *Dominus Iesus* is the converse, so to say, of the one I have just discussed. As the Chalcedonian decree does not speak *to* persons who are not Christians, so too it does not speak *about* them. *Dominus Iesus,* in covering so much more ground, does. At least implicitly, and at significant points explicitly, it instructs the Catholic faithful as to how they should regard those who are not of their number—Christians outside the Roman pale and, especially, non-Christians. In one sense this is the document's *raison d'être.* The "problematic and even erroneous propositions" it sets out to deal with were advanced, we may infer, in order to interpret non-Christian religions from a Christian standpoint in a positive way, instead of dismissing them *a priori* as false. Since it does regard these interpretations as problematic and even erroneous, *Dominus Iesus* has been interpreted in its turn, not

altogether without reason, as denigrating the religious value of traditions apart from the one it reconfirms. Hence the vexation, to say the least, that its judgments have aroused.

(4) Every text has a context, a cultural climate that affects its genesis and its reception alike. The culture of late antiquity to which the Chalcedonian definition belongs was "classicist." By culture I mean the set of meanings and values that inform a way of life, and by classicism I mean, borrowing again from Lonergan, culture that conceives itself normatively. For classicism there could be only one culture properly so called; what was outside it was simply uncultured.

The alternative to conceiving culture normatively is conceiving it empirically, by understanding in their concrete variety the ways in which men and women actually constitute the *Lebenswelt* of their individual and social existence, and how the meanings and values by which they live change, develop, go astray, or dissolve. Such an empirical approach to conceiving culture has been replacing classicism gradually for years and even centuries. The same communications media that allowed *Dominus Iesus* to be read throughout the world as soon as it was issued have made it impossible to suppose that there is only one culture with a capital C, that its achievements are permanent, or that it informs a way of life that has always been the same in every respect that really matters. And what is true of human living generally is true as well of religion. One aspect of the shift away from classicism toward an empirical understanding of a plurality of cultures has been the acknowledgment of religious pluralism in the sense in which that phrase is now customarily used.

In a word, culture has become historically minded. So too, a theology that "mediates between a cultural matrix and the significance and role of a religion in that matrix" will be, not a permanent achievement, but an ongoing process; and the methodology that guides the process will be historically minded.[11] Now, *Dominus Iesus* rightly observes that the momentous questions it treats call for theological reflection to proceed "in a way that is convincing and effective." But to be convincing is one thing in a classicist culture. It is something else in a historically minded one that conceives itself empirically. Consequently, it is at least a question whether the approach to "doctrines" taken in the fifth century can, at the turn of the twenty-first, address a context that has dropped the outlook and assumptions of classicism. To that question the next section will turn.

3. ASSESSING THE DECLARATION: TWO RESERVATIONS

In the first section I characterized *Dominus Iesus* as belonging roughly to "doctrines," as avoiding the kind of explication that "systematics" aims to provide, and as appealing to authoritative texts as "foundational" warrants. In the second section I suggested that these methodological characteristics are standard operating procedure for church pronouncements on Christian teaching, so that, other things being equal, there is no reason to fault *Dominus Iesus* for doing much the same as what the Chalcedonian decree does. I added, however, that other things are not equal. The disparity, I want now to propose, is such as to provoke reservations about the declaration.

My reservations are, basically, two. The "foundations" of *Dominus Iesus* are classicist, the "systematics" minimal. Given the breadth of the topics it treats and the situation that prompted the CDF to treat them, a treatment that is long on quotations and short on explanation is something less than satisfactory. This is by no means to say that the doctrine of the declaration, *qua* "doctrines," is wrong. Much of it is right. But as an Anglican I neither do nor can accord to *Dominus Iesus* the "implicit faith" or *de jure* assent which it can claim from Roman Catholics by virtue of being a formal teaching of their church's magisterium. I can only judge whether it is intrinsically convincing and internally coherent—methodological considerations for which the criteria do not depend on ecclesial allegiance.[12] If I find much in the declaration that is right, I also find that in certain respects it is right for the wrong reasons.

(1) As for my first reservation, there is little if anything historically minded about *Dominus Iesus*. Its very first quotation is a case in point, and sets the stage for all that follows. If the authors of the declaration wanted to begin it with a plain and pungent statement of the imperative of evangelizing, the necessity of belief, and the peril of unbelief, knowing that all these themes would figure prominently later in the document, they could not have found a better scriptural text than Mark 16:15-16—if Mark 16:15-16 were a scriptural text. It is, as Robert Imbelli insists, a text that appears in the Vulgate, and for that matter in the King James Version. What it is certainly not is a text that belonged to the gospel of Mark in its original form. The spuriousness of everything that follows verse 16:8 in the received version of Mark was not known, however, before the advent of historically-minded scholarship. It is true that the verses quoted at the beginning of *Dominus Iesus,* though not original, are ancient. They provide evidence for early and perhaps very early Christian belief and, as such, might well be useful for theology that takes history seriously.[13] But that is not the way the declaration uses textual sources—which is my point.

As Pheme Perkins discusses at length in her essay, *Dominus Iesus* marshals biblical passages without regard to their context, that is, to put it in methodological terms, without regard to the questions their authors were endeavoring to answer or the audiences the answers were meant to address. As with the Bible, so with other texts: *Dominus Iesus* tries to position itself above the flux of historical variation. It weaves together excerpts that come from widely different contexts to present a seemingly timeless tapestry. Similarly, its own terminology switches from a scholastic to a patristic to a contemporary idiom, as though language were atemporal and concepts had neither dates nor developments. Frederick Lawrence's essay makes the same point in a specific area: the ecclesiology of *Dominus Iesus* is normative and juridical, conceiving the church's identity in static terms independent of external influence or internal development.

In sum, *Dominus Iesus* is an excellent specimen of classicism. Whereas the Second Vatican Council, to judge from some of its documents, brought in at least a tincture of historical mindedness,[14] this document, though it quotes the council at every turn, cannot be said to have followed its methodological lead. It remains content with what Lonergan calls "foundations in the simple manner," which he sums up as follows:

> One must believe and accept whatever the bible or the true church or both believe and accept. But X is the bible or the true church or both. Therefore one must believe and accept whatever X believes and accepts. Moreover, X believes and accepts $a, b, c, d, \ldots$ Therefore, one must believe and accept $a, b, c, d, \ldots$ [15]

Why are "foundations in the simple manner" problematic, a cause for reservations about *Dominus Iesus?* Not, I would stress, because such classicist foundations are untrue. As Lonergan maintains, "they are as true as they ever were." [16] Nevertheless, they are inappropriate.

They are inappropriate for the reasons suggested at the end of the previous section here. "Catholic philosophy and Catholic theology are matters, not merely of revelation and faith, but also of culture. Both have been fully and deeply involved in classical culture," [17] a culture that is and has been passing away. One theologically significant result of its passing has been the emergence of new attitudes toward religious pluralism and, correspondingly, new questions about Christian uniqueness. Such questions have long been on the agenda for Protestant theologians, and lately, as Mark Heim observes in his essay, Roman Catholic scholars have been taking a prominent part in addressing them. The answers proposed have not all met with the approval of Roman Catholic authorities, and indeed the flagrant relativism involved in some of them is incompatible with Christian orthodoxy in any confessional form. *Dominus Iesus,* however, though it does recognize that out of the new dialogue between Christianity and other religions "new questions arise that need to be addressed through pursuing new paths of research" (§3), tries to put the new wine into old wineskins. The usual consequences can perhaps be expected.

(2) My first reservation about *Dominus Iesus* is largely a matter of principle: assembling a catena of quotations from respectable sources is not likely to meet the exigencies of a situation that could emerge only in a culture that is ceasing to be classicist. My second reservation needs careful statement. There is nothing wrong with pursuing one question at a time. "Systematic" theology deals with one kind of question, and to complain that *Dominus Iesus* is not "systematics" is to complain that it does not do something it evidently never meant to do. My reservation, nevertheless, is that the declaration's consistent avoidance of explanation in favor of "expository language" has resulted in an exposition which itself stands in serious need of being expounded. A kind of conceptual instability runs through the whole document, insofar as its statements bear on non-Christian religion and religions. Each of these statements is presented as true. How they can *all* be understood as true is, no doubt, a question more germane to "systematics" than to "doctrines." But to the extent that this question is left unaddressed, *Dominus Iesus* undermines its own credibility.

On the one hand, there are many passages that seem clearly to recognize and welcome the genuine holiness of religious traditions apart from Christianity. These passages are fairly general; the traditions are not named and, as Francis Clooney's essay points out, no distinctions are drawn between them. Not surprisingly, these positive evaluations are expressed using a Christian vocabulary—Christ, Spirit, grace, salvation, and so on—but *Dominus Iesus* does endeavor to use those terms in a respectful, inclusive way. God, it affirms, has not failed to make himself present in various ways (§8), so that various religious traditions have truly God-given elements (§21), which are truly salvific. Those persons who follow the promptings of the Spirit are on the way to salvation (§22), and through the Spirit the possibility of salvific participation extends to the whole human race (§12). Somewhat more specifically, the document says that this universally offered possibility is partnership in the paschal mystery (§12), that is, in the death and resurrection of the Lord Jesus Christ. And it says that this same Christ is the mediator of grace in all creation (§11), that such divine grace can be received by followers of other religions (§22), and that it is to be found in the sacred books of those religions (§8).

All this suggests an expansive conception of what Christian theologians call the divine "economy" by which salvation takes place and God draws all things to himself. That is on the one hand. On the other, *Dominus Iesus* qualifies its welcoming gestures by restricting in various ways the scope of salvation and the efficacy of any means of salvation that may be present outside Christianity. Thus, while Christ's mediation of saving grace is said to give rise to a manifold cooperation on the part of diverse persons and groups, any idea that there exist mediations independent of the Christian one is ruled out (§14). There is, for instance, no action of God's Spirit that is outside or parallel to the action of Christ (§12). Again, even though it is as the eternal Word that Christ mediates grace through creation itself (§11), still there is no economy of the Word outside the church (§9). Again, whatever beams of truth may shine through the pages of books other than the Christian Bible (§8), it remains that believing this truth amounts only to accepting human aspirations, humanly conceived and born of human religious experience (§7). Such believing is not faith, a term that *Dominus Iesus* reserves for assenting to revealed Christian truth. These are not the only examples of an ambivalence that can be found throughout the declaration. Others are discussed, from a different angle, in Clooney's essay. What then are we to make of the way *Dominus Iesus,* again and again, gives with one hand what it takes back with the other?

One possibility would be simply to admit that the problem of religious pluralism in general and, in particular, how the saving grace of God comes to non-Christians, has yet to be solved. To address it would be to take the step into "systematics" that *Dominus Iesus* declines to take, although it does, at one or two points, recognize the value of taking it. "Theologians," it observes, "are seeking to understand this question more fully. Their work is to be encouraged, since it is certainly useful for understanding better God's salvific plan and the ways in which it is accomplished" (§21). Yet if the declaration recommends encouraging theologians to do better than (it seems) they have done so far, it cannot be said to give them much encouragement itself. It acknowledges that in regard to other religions "theological research has a vast field of work under the guidance of the Church's Magisterium" (§14), but offers no guidance of its own as to how the work might be done. If, in sum, the problem that gave rise to *Dominus Iesus* was how God's salvation can be both inclusive and exclusive, universal and specifically Christian, the declaration has at best left it unresolved. Arguably it makes a solution more difficult to achieve. At least, there is no immediately obvious way to grasp in a single, intelligible view the positive judgments that *Dominus Iesus* unquestionably delivers, without falling afoul of its rather more evident strictures and negations.

4. ASSESSING THE DECLARATION: BEHIND METHODOLOGY

The two reservations set out in the previous section are both methodological, in the sense that each is concerned not so much with what *Dominus Iesus* says as with what it does or does not do and with how it does or does not do it. My argument has been that the contents of the declaration reflect methodological commitments that open it, as a whole, to objection. Because these commitments seem to have been made more or less deliberately, as I noted in the first section, a further question arises. Why? What lies behind them? If *Dominus Iesus* pieces quotations together with scant attention to historical scholarship— my first reservation—still the quotations had to be selected, presumably for some reason. And if there is a certain ambivalence in the way the document sets out its approval and disapproval of religion that is not Christian—my second reservation—still these judgments are presumably formulated by reference to some standard of what *is* Christian, presumably adopted for some reason. The reason, I think, is the same in both cases. There is a certain way of apprehending the "essence of Christianity" that informs and manifests itself both in the procedure that *Dominus Iesus* follows and in the contents it includes. I do not mean that the declaration is, after all, "systematic" theology. It is not. It does, however, take its bearings from what David Kelsey names a *discrimen,* a single vision that gathers up the complexities of the "Christian thing" and so guides decisions about "manner" and "matter" alike.[18]

The key to this *discrimen* is to be found, I believe, in one word—the word *one,* together with its English and Latinate cousins *only, alone, unique, union, unity, unicity.* Oneness is an emphasis from beginning to end of *Dominus Iesus.* A great number of things are said to be united, or unique, or one in some other sense. And I would say that the grand theme of the whole document is that all these various *ones,* these *onenesses,* are themselves *one.*

It is a theme that unfolds gradually, following a sequence announced at the outset. The introduction to *Dominus Iesus* tells us that in what follows it will deal with "the personal *unity* between the Eternal Word and Jesus of Nazareth" and with "the *unity* of the economy of the Incarnate Word and the Holy Spirit"; and this is what we find in section II. Then the declaration will deal with "the *unicity* and salvific *universality* of the mystery of Jesus Christ," as it does in section III; it will deal with "the *universal* salvific mediation of the Church," as it does in section IV; and it will deal with the oneness of the kingdom, the one church, and the Roman Catholic Church, as it does in section V (emphases mine).

In keeping with this prolepsis, *Dominus Iesus* sets out from the unity of humanity and divinity in the one person of Christ—with the "hypostatic union," that is, just as the council of Chalcedon defined it. Into that oneness, however, the declaration gathers, one by one, the other onenesses I have mentioned, beginning with the mission of the one Spirit of God. First, and most decisively, it states—without explanation—that the incarnation of the Word was a "trinitarian event" such that the work of the Spirit is coextensive with the "salvific action" of Christ (§12). Next, in section III, the declaration insists that this salvific action is unique, *one* gift offered by the Father through Jesus Christ in the Spirit, accomplished *once* for all in the incarnation, death, and resurrection of the only Son of God (§14). In the sections that follow in section IV, the uniqueness of this saving mediation is specified more exactly: "The fullness of Christ's salvific mystery belongs also to the Church, inseparably united to her Lord" (§16). It is true that Christ and the church are not identical, but their oneness is such that there is a single "salvific mystery." As the mission of the Spirit is included within the one economy of salvation, so too is the church's existence and mission. Finally, in section V we find that while certain distinctions can be drawn between the kingdom of God and the church "in her visible and social reality," still the unity of Christ with God, the unity of the kingdom of God with the kingdom of Christ, and the unity of Christ with the church mean—somehow; again no explanation—that the church and the kingdom are just as inseparably united.

Let us pause here. Stated in the most general terms, the *oneness* that has so far unfolded in *Dominus Iesus* is a oneness of finite and infinite—God's presence to the world. More, it is a divine-human unity that *saves* the world, that was initiated in God the Word's incarnation within space and time, and that extends, without lessening or ceasing to be one, through other space and later time, as the church. This presence of the divine with the human embraces in its oneness both God's Spirit and his kingdom, in such a way that they are neither apart from nor parallel to nor independent of the church.

Nor are we presented with a conception of this church that is at all indistinct or idealistic. That the church is *one* is affirmed in the Nicene Creed; but in *Dominus Iesus* its oneness is more than an article of faith or a "goal which all Churches and ecclesial communities must strive to reach." Here and now, the unity of the church is a fact, constituted by "elements" that are "already given" (§17) and exist in its "visible and social reality." Pre-eminent among those elements is baptism, the oneness of which is likewise asserted in the Creed, and which frames the whole of *Dominus Iesus*. With baptism its first paragraph begins, quoting the (doubtfully authentic) verse from the gospel of Mark that portrays the risen Christ as saying, "He who believes and is baptized will be saved"; and with baptism the declaration finishes in the last paragraph before its concluding section, which echoes the first paragraph by insisting on "the necessity of conversion to Jesus Christ and of adherence to the Church through Baptism...in order to participate fully in communion with God, the Father, Son and Holy Spirit" (§22).

In this last quotation, however, where I have put ellipsis dots, *Dominus Iesus* adds a further requirement, beyond conversion to Christ and baptismal adhesion. Also necessary are "the other sacraments." Which sacraments, we are not at this point told; but identifying them by inference is not difficult. Christian sacraments are said to have "a divine origin" and "an *ex opere operato* salvific efficacy," and together with other indications the Latin phrase suggests that two other sacraments in particular are intended. One of the two is clearly the Eucharist. But this sacrament depends on another one, the sacrament of orders, for its "genuine and integral substance." Ordination, in turn, cannot take place without a "valid Episcopate" (§17), which guarantees a "valid Eucharist" by maintaining "an historical continuity—rooted in the apostolic succession— between the Church founded by Christ" and the church of the present day (§16). At this point, then, the oneness of Christ, the Spirit, the economy of salvation, the kingdom, and the church, has been made to include not only "one Lord, one faith, one baptism, one God and Father of us all" (Eph 4:5) but also one continuous succession through space and time of validly ordained bishops.

Bishops, however, are not the final step in the declaration's unifying of unities, though Anglicans might wish they were. For bishops are not one but many, and more than one ecclesiastical community claims, as Anglicans do, to have preserved the unity of "apostolic succession." *Dominus Iesus* acknowledges the claim to the extent of allowing that the Eastern Orthodox churches are churches in the true sense. Other Christian groups, which baptize but lack (according to the declaration) the valid episcopate that would validate their other sacraments, are "ecclesial communities" merely. Even the Orthodox, moreover, are only on the margin of the oneness of Christ-Spirit-salvation-kingdom-church. For their bishops, however validly ordained, are not at one with the final "element" of the "visible and social reality" of the church's unity. They are not "governed by the Successor of Peter" (§16, §17).

The point I have been drawing out is that *Dominus Iesus* elides the unicity of the hypostatic union in the incarnate Word, the unicity of God's salvation of the world, the unicity of the Christian church, and the unicity of a juridical office, the papacy. The document's descriptive subtitle is perfectly accurate. *Dominus Iesus* does pronounce "on the unicity and salvific universality of Jesus Christ and the church." The conjunction *and,* however, does not mean that the church has a unicity and a saving universality, and so does its Lord. It means that Christ's unicity and universality, and the church's unicity and universality, are one. And what makes the church one, in the last resort, is its chief officer. So, while it may be partly due to an Anglican hermeneutic of suspicion, I cannot help thinking that the role of the "successor of Peter" has been somewhat downplayed in commentaries on *Dominus Iesus*. To be sure, the papacy is not emphasized, nor even mentioned very often. But when the declaration speaks of universality—that is, catholicity—it very plainly has Roman catholicity in view. Absent the Roman pontiff, there are certainly baptized Christians, but just as certainly they are disunited and remote from the complete divine-human oneness that for *Dominus Iesus* is Christianity's essence. Together with whatever concessions and friendly gestures the document may make to "particular Churches" and "ecclesial communities," to say nothing of world religions, the teachings that it reiterates and reconfirms include the doctrine plainly stated in one of the authoritative sources that *Dominus Iesus* itself refers to—the doctrine that "it is absolutely necessary for the salvation of every human creature that he be subject to the Roman Pontiff."[19] That doctrine does not stand alone; it has been qualified in various ways, not least by Vatican II; but it has never been retracted, and it is by no means an incidental component of "salvific universality" as *Dominus Iesus* envisions it.

In this regard, it may be recalled that a good part of the declaration transcribes writings of the present pontiff, who also approved it "in a special way." For, as William Abraham argues perceptively, the Pope has acquired a role that is not only uniquely sacramental or uniquely juridical but also uniquely methodological:

> The articulation and deployment of a doctrine of papal infallibility …transformed what was originally a tacit claim about divine guidance in the Church as a whole into an explicitly formulated canon of divine revelation which gave precedence to the Pope in resolving crucial disputes about the very content and meaning of divine revelation itself.[20]

Whereas orthodoxy was once guaranteed, as Chalcedon puts it, by "following the holy fathers," the guarantee came to consist in following the Holy Father.

Abraham is careful to emphasize that it is equally possible to construe papal infallibility either as a precious gift of divine grace or as a lapse into "foundationalism." But, either way, it is "a kind of epistemic mechanism… a norm of knowledge, a criterion of truth."[21] And this is all of a piece with the importance that *Dominus Iesus* assigns to the notion of revelation. Just what *is* "salvific" about Jesus Christ and the church? The answer that *Dominus Iesus* presents is not framed in terms of justification or *theiosis* or atonement or redemption, none of which is mentioned by name. Salvation lies in "the full revelation of divine truth" (§5), which has its source and fulfillment in the Word made flesh, which his Spirit has taught "to the Apostles and, through them, to the whole Church" (§6), and which is properly responded to by the obedience of faith in the sense of assent (§7). Hence the (pseudo-)Marcan verse that opens the declaration. "He who believes and is baptized will be saved; he who does not believe will be condemned." *Dominus Iesus* is thus not only a statement of doctrine. It is a doctrine *about* doctrine, to the effect that doctrine is at the heart of the Christian gospel, and that assenting to it is *de esse* for salvation. That is why the declaration can marshal its propositions from authoritative sources regardless of their context: revealed truth is "objectively" certain no matter how or by whom it was uttered. Perhaps too it is why the declaration offers so few explanations: *understanding* revealed truth is unimportant compared with the "obedience of faith."

Such is the *discrimen* that informs *Dominus Iesus,* substantively and methodologically—an image of unity at once human and divine that pertains at once to one Lord Jesus, one saving revelation, one church, one episcopate, one Pope. In some obscure way all these unique units are part and parcel, each of the others. In *what* way, *how* they are all one, we are not told. No doubt this unity is mysterious in the theological sense; but the declaration itself says that mystery can in faith be penetrated "in a way that allows us to understand it co-herently" (§7). Articulating the coherence, understanding the mystery, however imperfectly, would be the "systematic" theology that *Dominus Iesus* omits. Over and over again it *asserts* union, unity, uniqueness; over and over again it forbids separation. But when it says, for example, that "the connection is clear between the salvific mystery of the Incarnate Word and that of the Spirit" (§12), it can only mean that it is clear there must *be* a connection, because what the connection consists in is not made clear at all. And it is the same everywhere in the declaration: things are "closely linked," "single and indivisible," they exist "inseparably," "in intimate connection," "united in a mysterious way." These and similar terms are the ligatures that *Dominus Iesus* uses to hold together its essential vision of Christianity. Verbally, they unite its many unities. Yet it may be doubted whether the unification is anything more than verbal.

It may be doubted because the word *one* has not one meaning but several. In scholastic parlance, it is a "transcendental": not only is it used in senses that are analogous rather than univocal, but only by analogy can it be understood. Now things that are analogous are partly similar and partly different. The greater the similarity, the stronger the analogy. But the onenesses that *Dominus Iesus* insists upon are unquestionably different. The oneness of the one Lord Jesus is the oneness of a person, and that one a divine person. The person of the Son or Word is not the same as the person of the Spirit or the person of the Fa-ther. The oneness of the Trinity, therefore, is not the same as the oneness of the Incarnation, for in the Incarnation two natures are united whereas in the Trinity three persons are one God. Nor is the oneness of the economy of salvation the same as the oneness of God, for the Word's role and mission in that economy begins with his taking on a human nature; the role and mission of the Spirit does not. Nor is the oneness of the incarnate Word the same as the oneness of the extension of the Incarnation in revelation, church, and sacrament. For in the Incarnation there is one man and one historical life, whereas revelation, church, and sacrament involve many men and women, who are one inasmuch as they share a common life constituted by common understanding, common beliefs and practices, common ends and purposes. And so on.

My point is not that *Dominus Iesus* ignores these distinctions. Some of them it draws itself. My point is only that the unities they distinguish are not the same. What it is to understand any one of them, *as* one, is to understand dif-ferently from what it is to understand any of the others. The fact that *Dominus Iesus* offers no explanation of *how* the unities it asserts might be understood makes it easier to use ligature-words to amalgamate them into one overall scheme. The declaration begins from a perfectly orthodox Chalcedonian doctrine of the Incarnation: the eternal Word existing and operating through a human nature. But it goes on to transfer Chalcedon's conception of a unity of human and divine out of its original, specifically Christological context into others. By asserting intimate connections and denying separations it falls little if at all short of taking theological positions which, in its own phrase, are "problematic or even erroneous"—positing that the whole Trinity was incarnate, that the Word is eternally incarnate, that the Word's human nature in space and time is the church, and that the kingdom of God is ruled by the successor of Peter.

8

A JEWISH RESPONSE

Ruth Langer

Christians in general and the Catholic church in particular have, in the past half-century, made immense strides toward forging new and positive relationships with other religious groups, especially with Jews. These changes have put us on a path toward what Judaism terms *tiqqun 'olam,* an eschatological repair of our flawed world. However, this task is never easy. Almost two millennia of polemic, supersessionism, and hatred have formed many of the fundamental structures of Christian theology and practice. As a result, the process of reform, officially set in motion in the Catholic world by the Second Vatican Council, has not been simple. This process has regularly encountered major bumps, unexpected turnings, and forks in the road, including times when seeming progress has been reversed. To many in the Jewish world, *Dominus Iesus* appears to be a major crisis point, for it apparently undercuts many of the fundamental principles which allow Jews to enter into dialogue with Catholics. Much of this perception, however, arises from the fact that *Dominus Iesus* communicates through internal Catholic theological language and categories, easily misunderstood by most Jewish readers. Most critically, *Dominus Iesus* never mentions "Jews"; it discusses the church's relationship with "non-Christian religions," a category that some suggest means everyone except for Christians and Jews, but that Jewish readers automatically and reflexively understand as referring to themselves.

In this paper, I explore some of the Jewish responses to *Dominus Iesus,* seeking to clarify what led to their vehemence, and then exploring how and whether these responses were generated by misunderstandings of the declaration. I also suggest that some of the issues raised in this process themselves suggest important topics for theological dialogue between Jews and Catholics, presuming, of course, that the fundamental misunderstandings raised by the document can be clarified.

While the Christian world undertakes the difficult theological task of ridding itself of anti-Judaism, the Jewish world has a matching task, of learning to trust the sincerity of its Christian neighbors. Jewish anti-Christianity certainly exists, but it is driven more by lived experience than by theology. If Jews can feel that Christianity honors them and their religion, that it seeks co-existence and mutual glorification of God rather than baptism, then Jewish anti-

Christianity can disappear. But when Jews read the printed words of *Dominus Iesus:*

> Indeed, the Church, guided by charity and respect for freedom, must be primarily committed to proclaiming to all people the truth definitively revealed by the Lord, and to announcing *the necessity of conversion to Jesus Christ and of adherence to the Church through Baptism and the other sacraments,* in order to participate fully in communion with God, the Father, Son and Holy Spirit (§22, emphasis mine).

this echoes not with the processes set in motion by the Second Vatican Council's *Nostra aetate,* but with the Christian world's history of forced baptisms and persecutions. Mistrust rises to the surface very easily, given the Jewish community's consciousness of its own history on the margins of Christian Europe. Language like this re-irritates still raw nerves.

For Jews, contemporaneous events in the Catholic world only reinforced the impact of this statement. On September 3, only two days before the publication of the English translation of *Dominus Iesus,* Pope John Paul II beatified Pope Pius IX. There are certainly good internal Catholic reasons for celebrating the life's work of this man who led his church through the political and social upheavals of the mid-nineteenth century. But Jews remember Pius IX as an evil man and cannot comprehend how he can be celebrated by the church as holy. They remember that Pius called Jews "dogs," declaring that there were too many of them in Rome.[1] In a time when Jews were gradually gaining civil rights and free residence throughout the Western world, he refused Roman Jews residence outside of the ghetto or relief from other measures designed to keep Jews in a political and economic state demonstrably inferior to that of their Catholic neighbors.[2] Most famously, he publicly supported the removal of Edgardo Mortara from his parents' home. This child was a six-year-old Jewish boy whose Catholic nursemaid had secretly baptized him during an illness in his infancy. The claim was that the child, now a Christian, could no longer be raised by his Jewish parents. The Pope's support extended to his personal adoption of the child as his own son.[3]

Nor was the Mortara affair unique, except in the depth of furor it caused.[4] Kidnapping of Jewish children to raise them in Christian religious communities happened at least up to the Second World War.[5] Even in the current context of the furor over Pius IX's beatification, Daniel Ols, of the Holy See's Congregation for the Promotion of Saints, announced on Italian television that he would "find it beautiful" for a child such as Mortara to be baptized without his parents' consent. Ols was quoted as saying that the "good of the eternal life" supersedes any "natural good," including the rights of a parent over a child. Obviously, this further inflamed the sensitivities of Jewish participants in dialogue who understand the contemporary church to have disavowed just such sentiments.[6] From a Jewish perspective, the Mortara affair and all similar incidents before and after constitute kidnapping and forced conversion, expressing a pro-

found disrespect for Judaism as a valid religion and creating a situation of in-
credible vulnerability for Jewish parents and for the community in general.

By itself, though, the beatification of Pius IX might have been a minor
bump in Jewish-Catholic relations, packaged in the Jewish mind with other incomprehensible beatifications and canonizations.[7] But *Dominus Iesus* appeared
in this context, complete with its assertions that either puzzle or infuriate Jews
committed to Jewish-Catholic dialogue and that make those Jews who have
been lukewarm or uninvolved shrug, respond "What did you expect?" and turn
away entirely. The Jubilee Day of Jewish-Christian Dialogue was postponed indefinitely because, under the leadership of the Chief Rabbi of Rome, the same
man who had welcomed John Paul II to his synagogue in 1986, the Jewish delegation called off its participation.[8] Weeks later, long-time and highly respected
Jewish participants in high-level dialogue are wondering whether they need to
reconsider their public positions on Jewish-Catholic relations.

Not only has *Dominus Iesus* itself set back the process of Jewish-Catholic
reconciliation, but it almost totally eclipsed a simultaneous and very important
step forward within the Jewish world. The following Sunday, September 10, a
group of just under two hundred Jewish scholars and rabbis published in the
New York Times and the *Baltimore Sun* a full-page advertisement entitled
"*Dabru Emet:* A Jewish Statement on Christians and Christianity." This statement, years in the making, is an articulation of a contemporary Jewish positive
theology of Christianity. It is accompanied by a book, *Christianity in Jewish
Terms,*[9] that addresses many of the same categories in significant depth. This
statement had a two-fold aim: to express to the Christian world how the process
of dialogue is affecting Jews and Judaism; and to deepen the Jewish world's
awareness of the progress made in Jewish-Christian relations—that is, to make
a major stride in fighting Jewish anti-Christianity. That the publication of this
document occurred in the shadow of *Dominus Iesus* significantly affected its
immediate impact. While the leading national Jewish papers gave these two
documents a joint article buried in the middle of the paper,[10] the Boston *Jewish
Advocate* completely ignored *Dabru Emet.*

The *Jewish Advocate*'s reaction was extreme but illustrative. It devoted
three columns of its front page to *Dominus Iesus,* including a two-column edi-
torial with the banner headline "Jewish-Catholic Relations: Dangerous or
Wasted Effort?" In this, the editor called for the cessation of all dialogue, and
accompanied his remarks with reprints of the most inflammatory sentences of
Dominus Iesus.[11] The paper only eventually printed a clarificatory op-ed submitted by a coalition of leading local Jewish groups suggesting that, while concern was valid, cessation of dialogue was not the way to move forward. After
reviewing the problematic assertions of *Dominus Iesus* and then the positive
strides made in Jewish-Christian relations since Vatican II, this group wrote:

> It is precisely because we have come so far that the Vatican's recent
> declaration is so unsettling. And, for this very same reason it is of great
> importance that we not abandon the process of dialogue, but use it to
> better understand what lies behind this document. It is possible that in

the end we may not agree with what the Vatican has to say and may discover new and perhaps significant hurdles to Catholic-Jewish reconciliation. On the other hand, we may learn, as some experts in the Jewish community have speculated, that this statement was never intended for a Jewish audience and that the authors may be prepared to offer a clarification at a later date.[12]

Should *Dominus Iesus* be "unsettling" to the Jewish community? According to various Catholic spokesmen, the answer is absolutely "no." They remind us that this document needs to be read within the context of both the cumulative formal statements of the church beginning with *Nostra aetate* and also the formal and informal statements and actions of John Paul II. In interpreting *Dominus Iesus* for their own communities, one American bishop after another has deliberately emphasized the positive value of dialogue. Cardinal Roger M. Mahoney of Los Angeles, in responding to the negative coverage of the declaration in the *Los Angeles Times,* said:

> I would like to take this opportunity to reassure our partners in dialogue that our mutually beneficial conversations and joint pursuit of the truth will continue. I pledge my unyielding support for these efforts... Nowhere in the declaration is there criticism of the fruits of bilateral agreements or of new initiatives taken in inter-religious dialogue ...The actions of Pope John Paul II himself have demonstrated his own profound respect for peoples and traditions other than Roman Catholic... The tone of *Dominus Iesus* may not fully reflect the deeper understanding that has been achieved through ecumenical and inter-religious dialogues over these last 30 years or more... It is my sincere hope that our ongoing dialogue and partnership will proceed unabated... Only in this way can we continue to move beyond the tragic estrangement which has characterized so much of our past.[13]

Cardinal Bernard Law of Boston, in beginning the process of teaching this declaration to his archdiocese, wrote:

> Catholics recognize that other religious traditions search for God and have found God, though without knowing Christ Jesus. Inter-religious dialogue, as part of the Church's missionary life, represents a sincere desire to seek *understanding* with the adherents of other religions so that all human beings may come to the knowledge of the truth...*Dominus Iesus* does not signal a lessening of the Church's commitment to ecumenical and inter-religious dialogue. Rather it is a statement of truth so that the dialogue may proceed on a firm foundation and not be open to misunderstandings and misinterpretations. *Dominus Iesus* is not a proclamation of some human superiority in contrast to any other person or institution. It is a re-affirmation of what the Church believes.[14]

Pope John Paul II himself recently wrote:

> [*Nostra aetate*] states that the Church, "in her tasks of promoting unity
> and love among human beings and among nations, considers, above
> all, what they have in common and leads them to share their common
> destiny" (n. 1). Dialogue among religions has to take account of this
> requirement and proceed along these lines. Today, with the Grace of
> God, this dialogue is no longer only a hope; it has become a reality,
> even if the path ahead of us is still long. How could we not be grate-
> ful to the Lord for the gift of this mutual opening, which is at the base
> of a deeper understanding between the Catholic Church and Judaism?
> The memories of the unforgettable pilgrimage in the Holy Land are
> still alive in me.[15]

The almost total absence of such sentiments and attitudes in the text of
Dominus Iesus itself made it necessary that these men and others remind the
world of the text's larger context.[16] When read alone—which is the way that
most non-Catholics will hear this declaration—one finds such comments as:

> The Church's proclamation of Jesus Christ . . . today also makes use of
> the practice of inter-religious dialogue. Such dialogue certainly does
> not replace, but rather accompanies the *missio ad gentes,* directed to-
> ward that "mystery of unity," from which "it follows that all men and
> women who are saved share, though differently, in the same mystery
> of salvation in Jesus Christ through his Spirit." Inter-religious dia-
> logue, which is part of the Church's evangelizing mission, requires an
> attitude of understanding and a relationship of mutual knowledge and
> reciprocal enrichment, in obedience to truth and respect for freedom
> (§2).

> *Equality,* which is a presupposition of inter-religious dialogue, refers
> to the equal personal dignity of the parties in dialogue, not to doctri-
> nal content (§22).

While the final sentence quoted from article 2 here might indicate a relationship in which true dialogue can take place, the rest of this declaration makes
clear that "obedience to truth" refers to the content of official Catholic doctrine.
Within this document, dialogue exists only as an opening for proclamation, that
is, for teaching the world about Christianity with the ultimate goal of baptism.
As Archbishop Alexander J. Brunett of Seattle, consultant to the U.S. bishops'
Committee for Ecumenical and Interreligious Affairs, has written:

> Dialogue partners usually understand that there is much give and take
> and that one should come to the table with a clear understanding of
> their own religious convictions and ecclesial identity. From that per-
> spective, this declaration does not add much to the process nor does it

further the cause of mutual understanding and respect... In general, those who know well the Vatican documents and the thinking of Pope John Paul II and his leadership role in the quest for Christian unity and religious understanding will recognize that this declaration does not add to the dialogical process. Some perhaps will wonder why it does not reflect the ecumenical sensitivity achieved through 30 years of dialogue and cooperation.[17]

Hence, while the text of *Dominus Iesus* itself legitimately raises concerns in the Jewish community, there are serious indications that these concerns may be obviated in the process of its interpretation and application by those Catholic leaders personally engaged in and committed to dialogue. Particularly heartening are the calls to read this declaration in the light of—and not in contrast to—the fruits of the past decades of dialogue.

Certain points require clarification to begin to answer Jewish concerns about this declaration. Most fundamentally, does *Dominus Iesus* apply to Catholic-Jewish dialogue at all? The declaration itself is ambiguous. It explicitly mentions two categories of dialogue partners: non-Christians and Christian non-Catholics. The only reference to something explicitly Jewish is embedded in its statement that only the Christian Bible, both Old and New Testaments, can be understood as wholly *inspired,* with God as their author, as opposed to the sacred books of other religions (§8). While this does place Jewish Scriptures into a special category, it is solely a consequence of Christianity's historical development out of Judaism and makes no explicit or implicit statement about the theological status of today's Jews.

In their interpretations of *Dominus Iesus,* American bishops, the Catholic community most intimately involved in Catholic-Jewish dialogue, rarely clarify this issue. For example, Cardinal Law in his restatement of the declaration for the Boston community explicitly devotes a paragraph to Orthodox and Protestant churches and another, broadly, to "our brothers and sisters of other religions." He perhaps makes oblique reference to Judaism in his closing sentence: "The Catholic Church is sustained in this task by the revelation made to Abraham, Moses, and the prophets that God's promises are eternal."[18] However, this does no more than vaguely hint at *Nostra aetate*'s recognition that "Jews remain very dear to God, for the sake of the patriarchs, since God does not take back the gifts he bestowed or the choice he made."[19]

Clearer are the statements that seem to place Judaism in a somewhat separate category. Bishop Robert Lynch at one point lists the participants in interreligious dialogue with Catholics as "Buddhist, Muslims, Taoists, Hindus, etc.," but later, in his discussion of ecumenical Christian dialogue, he refers to the "local Episcopalian bishop, Lutheran bishop and Jewish rabbis with whom I have contact."[20] He apparently places Judaism within the ecumenical Christian categories addressed by the declaration, and not as a "non-Christian" religion. This itself is curious from a Jewish perspective and will be discussed below. In like manner, Bishop Joseph Fiorenza of Houston, president of the National Conference of Catholic Bishops, devotes separate attention to the Jewish community "to which Christians are closely related through Christ himself and the revealed word of God in the Old Testament," followed by a general reference to "other great religions."[21] Similarly, in his letter to the Lisbon conference, the Pope made specific reference, first to issues of Christian ecumenism, then to Judaism (in the section quoted above), and then, in a single sentence, to the church's "encounter with Islam, with the Eastern religions, and with the great cultures of the contemporary world."[22] All of these statements imply that Jews are indeed among the communities of faith with which Catholics dialogue and that *Dominus Iesus* addresses. However, there remains an ambiguity as to whether or not Jews are "non-Christians."

The Pope and Bishop Fiorenza's formulations are consistent with the documents of the Second Vatican Council, where *Nostra aetate,* titled in English "Declaration on the Relation of the Church to *Non-Christian* Religions," treats first Hinduism and Buddhism,[23] then Islam,[24] and then Judaism.[25] This suggests that Judaism is indeed "non-Christian." Such an understanding appears explicitly in the 1968 document *Humanae personae dignitatem* (On Dialog [*sic*] with Unbelievers), which speaks of three circles of dialogue: with all humanity, with non-Christians, and with non-Catholic Christians.[26] This formulation persists in the "Rules for Promoting Dialogue" where separate subsections address dialogue with each category. It explicitly looks for "cooperation . . . between Christians and members of non-Christian religions, especially Jews and Muslims."[27] The ranking of these non-Christian religions, implied in *Nostra aetate,* receives a more explicit formulation in *Lumen gentium,* which details the relationship of "those who have not yet received the Gospel…to the people of God."[28] This text deliberately begins with Jews as "a people most dear for the sake of the fathers, for the gifts of God are without repentance"—followed then by Muslims because of their faith in God, and then all those who seek God. Given this understanding, then, in addressing the church's relationship with non-Christian religions, *Dominus Iesus* must include Jews. How can a document, so comprehensive in its address to both non-Christians and non-Catholic Christians, that is, everyone outside Catholicism, simply omit Jews?

However, there are suggestions that *Dominus Iesus* does not address Jews and Judaism at all because in contemporary Catholic theology, Judaism constitutes a *sui generis* category, falling under the rubric of neither Christian nor non-Christian. Although the documents of the Second Vatican Council consistently considered Jews to be "non-Christian," in 1974, the Vatican established its Commission for Religious Relations with the Jews within its Pontifical Council for the Promotion of *Christian* Unity. As the religion that gave birth to Christianity, as the community to which God made unbreakable covenantal promises, Judaism has, in John Paul II's language, a special status *within* the church as a beloved (elder) brother.[29] As a consequence, the concerns for the salvation of non-Christians that drive much of *Dominus Iesus* and its discussions of evangelization and mission are not relevant to the church's relationship with Jews. Because God promised salvation to the Jews before the advent of Christianity, the Catholic Church consequently has no mission to the Jews (and does not mention Jews in its 1990 encyclical *Redemptoris missio*). *Dominus*

Iesus's discussions of the intra-Christian issues of valid sacrament and apostolic succession also cannot apply to Jews.

Given this ambiguity, and given the public outcry over *Dominus Iesus* within the Jewish world, we can justifiably wonder why, to my knowledge and as of this writing, no spokesperson for the church has publicly and formally stated that *Dominus Iesus* simply does not apply to the church's relationship with Jews. Certainly the withdrawal of the Italian rabbis from the Jubilee Day of Dialogue communicated the urgency and created the opportunity for such a statement. Eugene J. Fisher, associate director of the Secretariat of Ecumenical and Inter-religious Affairs of the National Council of Catholic Bishops, has openly taken this position,[30] but such a statement needs to come publicly and officially from a level in the church hierarchy comparable to that of the Congregation for the Doctrine of the Faith that issued the declaration.[31] Cardinal William H. Keeler of Baltimore, the United States episcopal moderator for Catholic-Jewish relations, in an address to a Jewish synagogue in Virginia Beach, stressed the continuity of *Dominus Iesus* with the teachings of the Second Vatican Council, especially the irrevocable nature of God's covenant with the Jews, and suggested that media reports have deliberately distorted the intent of the document. According to the report of his talk, he emphasized that *Dominus Iesus* "is a technical document, intended for Catholic theologians in Asia and in some teaching centers." He thus implied that it is irrelevant to Catholic-Jewish relations—but he did not state so in an explicit, official manner.[32]

Obviously, the Catholic theological placement of Jews within the human community, as discussed here, remains ambiguous.[33] Jewish self-perception does place Judaism outside the Christian world, although it also acknowledges a closer relationship with Christianity and Islam because of their historical derivations from Judaism. Judaism also distinguishes Christianity for its reverence of the Hebrew Bible (Old Testament) and Islam for its uncompromising monotheism. In many ways, the church's grouping of Judaism with "non-Christian" religions fits better with Judaism's own categories than the "elder brother" label that brings Judaism within the Christian sphere. The *sui generis* category for Judaism suggested by contemporary church leaders is a comfortable compromise; by preserving Jewish distinctiveness, it conforms better with Judaism's self-image. This understanding also has the real advantage of allowing the church explicitly to disavow mission to the Jews and to deny the calls for baptism that are so disturbing in *Dominus Iesus*.

Dominus Iesus does bring to the fore several other elements deserving of further reflection and clarification by the Catholic Church, by the Jewish community, and by those engaged in dialogue. As mentioned briefly above, the declaration (§8) restricts the category of "inspired text" to the Old and New Testaments and defines these as the foundation of "faith" as opposed to mere, humanly developed "belief" which grounds itself on texts containing "gaps, insufficiencies, and errors." This understanding obviously places Judaism's holiest text into a privileged category. However, it would seem to relegate Judaism to its biblical formulation, that which I prefer to consider the "elder sibling" of Judaism itself as well as of Christianity. This relegation does not readily encourage a Catholic affirmation of the Judaism even of Jesus' time (which, for Jews, is already post-biblical), let alone the Judaism reformulated by the rabbis after the destruction of the Temple, or the Judaism of today. Traditional forms of Judaism consider the Oral Torah, the rabbinic heritage, to be *inspired* by God; in contrast, we discuss the Written Torah and even the prophetic texts in the language of *revelation*. In its formulation, then, *Dominus Iesus,* while it reflects the perspective of *Nostra aetate,* ignores the teachings of the 1974 "Guidelines and Suggestions for Implementing the Conciliar Declaration, *Nostra Aetate,* No. 4"[34] and the 1985 "Notes on the Correct Way to Present Jews and Judaism in Preaching and Catechesis in the Roman Catholic Church"[35] which call for engagement with contemporary Judaism. This necessarily must include Judaism's self-understanding and its understanding of its own texts. Note that these church documents represent only the first rather tentative steps toward a new positive understanding of Judaism.

Dominus Iesus employs triumphalist language that seemingly denigrates the validity of all non-Catholic Christian and non-Christian religious traditions, particularly with regard to their claims to truth and salvific abilities.[36] This, in itself, is not a major stumbling block to continued dialogue, but it certainly should be a subject of dialogue. Judaism also makes absolutist claims, although they are framed differently. It teaches that its community, the people Israel, is distinctive, chosen by God for a holy task, a task that does have redemptive implications (even if it is not always framed in these categories). Once one places *Dominus Iesus* in the context of post-Vatican II Catholic understandings that God's covenant with the Jews is eternally valid and a source of salvation, then our particularistic understandings of our own communities and their relationship to God should be a fruitful topic for dialogue.

Finally, *Dominus Iesus* presents only one facet of the church's current understanding of evangelization. Jewish readers notice immediately that the declaration begins and ends with only the most familiar and threatening mode of evangelization, that of seeking to baptize the nations of the world. Jews, and probably all non-Christians, need to be educated about the other aspects of the church's evangelizing mission, set forth in detail in *Redemptoris missio,* that do not threaten Jewish identity but rather present openings to mutual understanding and growth *within* our distinct religious traditions. Where Jews can trust Christian mission to operate at the levels of seeking justice and peace, of social service, of looking to discern God's will in the world and to realize it, then Jews can join in this mission because it is our mission too. Then we have a place to dialogue over our understandings of this mission, its motivations, its means, and its eschatological goals. Without feeling threatened, Jews can learn why the church must frame this work in the language of mission and evangelism—and Christians can similarly learn why Jews today frame this task as *tiqqun 'olam* (repair of the world). Many Jews are comfortable with accepting this common task of reaching for the eschaton, as long as we can wait for God to clarify then whether He has or has not already sent His messiah.[37]

Hence, if *Dominus Iesus* does not apply to Jews at all, its primary problematic from the perspective of Jewish-Catholic dialogue is one of communication. Cardinal Keeler suggests that a hostile press gathered for the release of the declaration, at which he was present, "did not want to understand what was being presented but seemed determined to misconstrue its content."[38] Perhaps. But why release a document intended for a limited elite audience at a press conference and on the Internet? Conversely, if one wants to place a document in the hands of as many people as possible, it needs to be written in language that will prevent misinterpretation as much as possible. *Dominus Iesus* is composed in internal Catholic language for an audience with sophisticated theological training. It presumes a sophisticated knowledge of thirty-five years of church teachings at all levels on relationships with non-Catholics, not even referencing many of their important points. Many of its details and much of its tone were miscommunicated when heard by the wider audience who, in our day, had easy access to the text, creating an unnecessary public relations problem for the church and its agenda of dialogue.[39]

As Francis Cardinal Arinze, president of the Holy See's Secretariat for Inter-religious Dialogue, acknowledged in his conversations with Boston College's Theology Department on October 31, 2000, such a dialogue cannot exist if Catholics enter it with the explicit goal of converting and baptizing their dialogue partners, for they will have no partners. Similarly, he continued, dialogue is dishonest if Catholics hold this goal secretly in their hearts. *Dominus Iesus*'s explicit call for baptism as a stated goal of dialogue ignores this reality and threatens to end dialogue. If, as Catholic leaders suggest, the substance of this declaration is really a restatement of established church teachings, then this substance (which I deliberately have not addressed here because it is an internal concern of the church) needs to be restated with deep sensitivity to the way that this voice will be heard by non-Catholics. This sensitivity itself grows from personal participation in dialogue, from learning to know and appreciate the religious other, and from struggling to understand one's own religion's role in relationship to the other in the other's presence.

9

IMPLICATIONS FOR CATHOLIC MAGISTERIAL TEACHING ON JEWS AND JUDAISM

Philip A. Cunningham

There can be little doubt that *Dominus Iesus* lends itself to being read in ways that damage Catholic-Jewish relations. However, clarifications offered by Catholic leaders in the months since the document's release on September 5, 2000 have the potential to advance the Catholic-Jewish relationship. This essay will explore these developments, summarize Catholic magisterial teaching about Jews and Judaism, and offer some ideas for further theological reflection that are suggested by the declaration.

A. PROBLEMATIC ASPECTS OF *DOMINUS IESUS* FOR CATHOLIC-JEWISH RELATIONS

There are five main reasons why *Dominus Iesus* has created tensions for the Catholic-Jewish relationship. *First,* it was issued only two days after Pope John Paul II beatified two of his papal predecessors, Pius IX and John XXIII. Elsewhere in this volume Ruth Langer has described the troublesome inter-religious aspects of so honoring Pius IX. Here it suffices to note the sensitized situation produced by the unfortunate timing of issuing *Dominus Iesus* so soon after the beatification. Renewed Jewish apprehension and doubt about the Catholic Church's intentions made it almost inevitable that Jewish readers would interpret pessimistically any imprecise or ambiguous statements in the declaration.

Second, the writing style of *Dominus Iesus* has also proved unhelpful for Catholic-Jewish relations. As the text itself notes:

> The expository language of the Declaration corresponds to its purpose, which is not to treat in a systematic manner the question of the unicity and salvific universality of the mystery of Jesus Christ and the Church, nor to propose solutions to questions that are matters of free theological debate, but rather to set forth again the doctrine of the Catholic faith in these areas, pointing out some fundamental questions that remain open to further development, and refuting specific positions that are erroneous or ambiguous (§3).

This "expository" setting forth of doctrine produces a declaratory mode, filled with nuanced technical language, which does not attempt to provide systematic explanations of its assertions. Readers unfamiliar with Catholic theological terms or their usage elsewhere would unavoidably misread important aspects of the text. Furthermore, the expository approach seems to have precluded any of the penitential and congenial sentiments seen in other recent ecumenical and inter-religious documents, giving rise to a tone that readers from other religious communities have found haughty and offensive.

It might be argued that *Dominus Iesus* was intended only for the narrow readership of Catholic theological specialists in ecumenical and inter-religious research and so should not be faulted for its technicality or expository tone. If this were true, however, one would have expected it to be disseminated through bishops' conferences and theological societies instead of to the religiously diverse global audience evoked by the press conference at which it was promulgated.

Whatever rationale lay behind this press conference, in the present mass media age even materials circulated internally eventually become publicly known. For instance, a letter from Cardinal Joseph Ratzinger to the presidents of Catholic bishops' conferences regarding the expression "sister churches" received massive electronic and printed media attention only a week before the release of *Dominus Iesus*.[1] This worsened the impact of the declaration on other-than-Roman Christian readers, just as the beatification of Pius IX had exacerbated the reactions of Jewish readers.

Since instantaneous global communication is a growing reality, it would seem reasonable to conclude that a new responsibility is incumbent upon the Roman Catholic magisterium. Its instructions must henceforth be written with an awareness of the varied populations who will read and be affected by them. Precise and unambiguous phrasing must be used. Technical language must be explained. This would seem to have been especially needed in a text issued during a Jubilee Year that John Paul II hoped would "provide a great opportunity, especially in view of the events of recent decades, for inter-religious dialogue."[2]

Third, as an instance of the declaration's lack of consideration for its worldwide readership, Jewish readers in particular would naturally assume that the phrases "non-Christian religions" or "the religious traditions of the world" in *Dominus Iesus* would include themselves. With this presupposition, Jews would tend to read the declaration's effort to distinguish between "faith" and "belief" with considerable alarm:

> The proper response to God's revelation is *"the obedience of faith"*
> ... The obedience of faith implies acceptance of the truth of Christ's revelation, guaranteed by God, who is Truth itself: "Faith is first of all a personal adherence of man to God. At the same time, and inseparably, it is a *free assent to the whole truth that God has revealed."*
> ... For this reason, the distinction between theological faith and belief in the other religions, must be firmly held. If faith is the acceptance in grace of revealed truth, which "makes it possible to penetrate

the mystery in a way that allows us to understand it coherently," then belief, in the other religions, is that sum of experience and thought that constitutes the human treasury of wisdom and religious aspiration, which man in his search for truth has conceived and acted upon in his relationship to God and the Absolute.

This distinction is not always borne in mind in current theological reflection. Thus, theological faith (the acceptance of the truth revealed by the One and Triune God) is often identified with belief in other religions, which is religious experience still in search of the absolute truth and still lacking assent to God who reveals himself. This is one of the reasons why the differences between Christianity and the other religions tend to be reduced at times to the point of disappearance (§7).

To Jews, who by definition understand themselves as belonging to "another religion" than Christianity, this section reads as saying that Jews have no faith and no divine revelation, but possess only humanly derived beliefs about God. This construal would delegitimate the Jewish tradition in its entirety, since it denies God's election of Israel and the establishment of the Sinaitic covenant. The identification of "obedience of faith" with "the acceptance of the truth of Christ's revelation" adds to the impression that Jews are without authentic faith when they seek to be obedient to God. Those Jews who are aware of the numerous recent Catholic statements that affirm Israel's abiding covenant with God would have to wonder whether this *Dominus Iesus* section represented a retrenchment in official Catholic teaching.

Over the past several months, however, Catholic officials have insisted that the writers of *Dominus Iesus* did not intend such a construal. They have indicated that the Catholic Church does not, in fact, consider Judaism to be a "non-Christian religion" in the sense of not possessing inspired scriptures or not being in covenant with God. Cardinal Edward Idris Cassidy, outgoing president of the Pontifical Commission for Religious Relations with the Jews, explained:

> In fact, the Declaration *Dominus Iesus* did not deal at all with relations between the Christian revelation and the faith of Israel, but with the other religions of the world. The Catholic Church does not consider the faith of Israel one among the other religions of the world. Rather it has an absolutely special relationship to Christianity, and the document itself makes clear that the Hebrew Testament is considered by the Catholic Church, together with the New Testament, as inspired by God in the strict sense of the term.[3]

Cardinal Cassidy's successor as president of the Commission, Cardinal Walter Kasper, made a similar point in an address on *Dominus Iesus* delivered at the 17th meeting of the International Catholic-Jewish Liaison Committee in May 2001:

The document *Dominus Iesus* does not affect Catholic-Jewish relations in a negative way. Because of its purpose, it does not deal with the question of the theology of Catholic-Jewish relations, proclaimed by *Nostra aetate,* and of subsequent Church teaching. What the document tries to "correct" is another category, namely the attempts by some Christian theologians to find a kind of "universal theology" of interreligious relations, which, in some cases, has led to indifferentism, relativism and syncretism. Against such theories we, as Jews and Christians, are on the same side, sitting in the same boat; we have to fight, to argue and to bear witness together. Our common self-understanding is at stake.[4]

In the first section of *Dominus Iesus* itself there is a clear (if subtle) indication that its authors understood Judaism to be in a special (if not described) category of religious tradition. In comparing the "sacred writings of other religions" with the church's scriptures, the declaration states: "The Church's tradition, however, reserves the designation of *inspired texts* to the canonical books of the Old and New Testaments, since these are inspired by the Holy Spirit" (§8, emphasis in the original). This acknowledgment of the inspired status of the *Tanakh* means that the Hebrew and Jewish traditions cannot be understood as falling on the "human belief" side of the distinction between faith and belief that *Dominus Iesus* attempted to draw. Cardinal Joseph Ratzinger, who as president of the Congregation for the Doctrine of the Faith was presumably the principal author of the document, seemed to refer precisely to this distinction in December 2000:

> It is evident that, as Christians, our dialogue with the Jews is situated on a different level than that in which we engage with other religions. The faith witnessed to by the Jewish Bible (the Old Testament for Christians) is not merely another religion to us, but is the foundation of our own faith. Therefore, Christians—and today increasingly in collaboration with their Jewish sisters and brothers—read and attentively study these books of Sacred Scripture, as a part of their common heritage.[5]

Given this unanimous claim by major Vatican hierarchical leaders, it would seem that Jews and Judaism were indeed not subjects under consideration in *Dominus Iesus*. This does not mean that the declaration has no implications for Jews, as will be noted below. Nonetheless, *Dominus Iesus* can be faulted for failing to specify and reaffirm the unique place that Judaism holds in Catholic understanding. Much consternation could have been avoided had the covenantal status of Judaism been forthrightly reiterated.

Fourth, a similar lack of clarity concerning the purposes of inter-religious dialogue has also raised questions in Jewish minds about Catholic motives in seeking dialogue. Words such as "'Because she believes in God's universal plan of salvation, the Church must be missionary.' Inter-religious dialogue, therefore, as part of her evangelizing mission, is just one of the actions of the Church in her mission *ad gentes* [to the nations]" (§22) are readily misunderstood if the meaning of "evangelizing mission" is not known from other Catholic documents. Given their long history of interaction with Christians, Jewish readers are wary of language smacking of proselytization or assimilation, particularly with the appearance of the word "missionary" just before the phrase "evangelizing mission." Without knowledge of the technical meaning of certain terms, the sentence seems to be saying that the Roman Catholic Church enters into inter-religious dialogue with a desire to convert Jews. This impression is strengthened by the declaration's emphasis on the fullness of divine revelation that the church possesses. What need is there for inter-religious dialogue with traditions not based on divine revelation? What could be learned about God from people who do not share the church's fullness of revelation? Although the declaration also notes that "inter-religious dialogue, which is part of the Church's evangelizing mission, requires an attitude of understanding and a relationship of mutual knowledge and reciprocal enrichment" (§2), the mere mention of "reciprocal enrichment" does little to correct any mistaken ideas about "evangelizing mission" that a reader might have.

Nonetheless, reciprocal enrichment has for several years been the stated Roman Catholic purpose for inter-religious dialogue, especially with Jews. Such dialogue was understood to demand a deep respect for the religious identity of the other. The 1974 "Guidelines and Suggestions for Implementing the Conciliar Declaration *Nostra aetate,* No. 4," issued by the Pontifical Commission for Religious Relations with the Jews, discussed the subject of dialogue in some detail:

> To tell the truth, such relations as there have been between Jew and Christian have scarcely ever risen above the level of monologue. From now on, real dialogue must be established. Dialogue presupposes that each side wishes to know the other, and wishes to increase and deepen its knowledge of the other. It constitutes a particularly suitable means of favoring a better mutual knowledge and, especially in the case of dialogue between Jews and Christians, of probing the riches of one's own tradition. Dialogue demands respect for the other as he is; above all, respect for his faith and his religious convictions.[6]

While witnessing to their faith in Jesus Christ, the text explained, Catholics have a responsibility to maintain "the strictest respect for religious liberty in line with the teaching of the Second Vatican Council...In order not to hurt (even involuntarily) those taking part, it will be vital to guarantee, not only tact, but a great openness of spirit and diffidence with respect to one's own prejudices."[7] This sensitivity to the integrity of the Jewish religious life, intense enough to warn Catholics to be critical of their own motives for dialogue, is unthinkable if the dialogue is only a pretext for conversionary campaigns.

In a recent book, *Many Religions, One Covenant,* Cardinal Ratzinger cautioned against a misguided conception of inter-religious dialogue. "Let me speak

plainly: Anyone who expects the dialogue between religions to result in their unification is bound for disappointment. This is hardly possible within our historical
time, *and perhaps it is not even desirable.*"[8] He goes on to observe that Catholics
"may find it relatively easy to criticize the religion of others, but we must be
ready to accept criticism of ourselves and of our own religion."[9] Such openness
to criticism and the expression of the desirability of religious diversity is inconsistent with a view of inter-religious dialogue as a strategy for proselytization.

Indeed, inter-religious dialogue with Jews is now understood as an essential goal of Catholic religious education, at least in principle. "Religious teaching, catechesis and preaching should be a preparation not only for objectivity,
justice, and tolerance but also for understanding and dialogue. Our two traditions are so related that they cannot ignore each other. Mutual knowledge must
be encouraged at every level."[10]

Sadly, without a background in this teaching readers of *Dominus Iesus* can
all too readily draw different conclusions. Even with such knowledge, readers
have been troubled by the declaration because it failed to reiterate the urgent
need for and reciprocal benefits of inter-religious dialogue. It also did not distinguish between the different senses of evangelization as *witnessing* to faith in
Christ through the words and actions of one's life (which is appropriate in the
setting of inter-religious dialogue) and *instructing* or *proclaiming* the Christian
faith in order to prepare someone for conversion (which has no place in inter-
religious dialogue).

Fifth, the overarching theological emphasis of *Dominus Iesus* points to unresolved questions in the Catholic-Jewish relationship. This is evident in the
declaration's one specific reference to Jews. "It was in the awareness of the one
universal gift of salvation offered by the Father through Jesus Christ in the
Spirit (cf. Eph 1:3-14), that the first Christians encountered the Jewish people,
showing them the fulfillment of salvation that went beyond the Law" (§13).
This appears in a section upholding that "the truth of Jesus Christ, Son of God,
Lord and only Savior, who through the event of his incarnation, death and resurrection has brought the history of salvation to fulfillment, and which has in
him its fullness and center, must be *firmly believed* as a constant element of the
Church's faith" (§13). Prescinding from the anachronistically neat distinction
between "the first Christians" and "the Jewish people" and the questionable
presumption that the earliest, Jewish apostles understood "salvation" in the
same way as *Dominus Iesus* does, this passage leaves little room for any religious value for Judaism beyond its fulfillment in Christianity.

One Jewish commentator, David Berger, deems this perspective to be thoroughly supersessionist, an opinion he finds confirmed in Cardinal Ratzinger's
book, *Many Religions, One Covenant.*[11] However, Berger does not judge his
type of supersessionism to be morally objectionable because in his other writings the Cardinal does not disparage Judaism as his Christian ancestors did.
"As long as Christians do not vilify Judaism and Jews . . . they have every right
to assert that Judaism errs about religious questions of the most central importance, that equality in dialogue does not mean the equal standing of the parties'
religious doctrines, that at the end of days Jews will recognize the divinity of

Jesus, even that salvation is much more difficult for one who stands outside the Catholic Church."[12] Reciprocally, Berger adds, Jews also have every right to "believe that the worship of Jesus as God is a serious religious error displeasing to God even if the worshiper is a non-Jew, and that at the end of days Christians will come to recognize this."[13]

The problem with all of this is that *Dominus Iesus* confirms for Berger the dangers in engaging in theological or doctrinal dialogue with Catholics. In his reading of the declaration, Catholics must constantly try to bring their conversation partners to an awareness of the fullness of the truth of salvation. Therefore, the conversion of Jews is always on the Christian agenda. This remains true by virtue of the document's emphasis on the unicity and universality of Christ, irrespective of clarifications about the varying technical senses of evangelization as witness and mission.

Given the statements presented above from other Catholic documents about inter-religious dialogue, I do not agree with the inevitability of Dr. Berger's reading, but it is a perfectly reasonable construal. In my view, he has accurately detected that the Catholic community has not yet integrated its recent recognition of God's perpetual covenant with Israel into its theologies of Christ, church, and salvation. As Cardinal Kasper has noted:

> Besides the already mentioned main problem raised by *Dominus Iesus,* there are other questions that I cannot deal with in this paper, since they would need a much more thorough discussion. These questions have already been object of our dialogue and should be on the agenda also in the future. In this context, I can only mention them, without claiming to solve them. Neither has *Dominus Iesus* the intention to enter these issues: they are beyond its intra-theological and intra-catholic intention.
>
> One of these questions is how to relate the covenant with the Jewish people, which according to St. Paul is unbroken and not revoked but still in vigor, with what we Christians call the New Covenant. As you know, the old theory of substitution is gone since the Second Vatican Council. For us Christians today the covenant with the Jewish people is a living heritage, a living reality. There cannot be a mere coexistence between the two covenants. Jews and Christians, by their respective specific identities, are intimately related to each other. It is impossible now to enter the complex problem of how this intimate relatedness should or could be defined. Such a question touches the mystery of Jewish and Christian existence as well, and should be discussed in our further dialogue.[14]

To some extent, *Dominus Iesus* itself recognizes such unresolved questions: "In the practice of dialogue between the Christian faith and other religious traditions...new questions arise that need to be addressed through pursuing new paths of research, advancing proposals, and suggesting ways of acting that call for attentive discernment" (§3). One wonders how it is possible for the declaration simply to expound traditional formulas in the face of such unresolved and unprecedented questions as the relationship between the church and Israel, whose enduring covenant the church has only recently acknowledged. In any case, it is counterproductive to the church's desire to encourage non-conversionary inter-religious dialogue when it issues documents that can defensibly be read as promoting conversion through dialogue.

B. CATHOLIC MAGISTERIAL TEACHING ABOUT JEWS AND JUDAISM

In his remarks to the May meeting of the International Catholic-Jewish Liaison Committee, Cardinal Kasper stated that "the Declaration [should be] read and interpreted—as any magisterial document should—in the larger context of all other official documents and declarations [on Jews and Judaism], which are by no means cancelled, revoked or nullified by this document."[15] To see the fuller implications of *Dominus Iesus* for the future, it must be situated within official Roman Catholic post-*Nostra aetate* documents about Jews and Judaism. The second part of this essay, therefore, will summarize the relevant aspects of this teaching, which is to be found primarily in documents issued by the Pontifical Commission for Religious Relations with the Jews, in instructions by local bishops' conferences, and in numerous addresses by Pope John Paul II.[16]

1. The Roman Catholic Church recognizes that Jews are in an eternal covenant with God

Although only implied by *Nostra aetate*, Pope John Paul II has explicitly declared this in many speeches. He has described Jews as "the people of God of the Old Covenant, never revoked by God,"[17] "the present-day people of the covenant concluded with Moses,"[18] and "partners in a covenant of eternal love which was never revoked."[19] No doubt the full theological ramifications of this affirmation will be worked out only over time, but already its impact can be seen in a Vatican description of Jews and Christians as "the people of God of the Old and New Testaments."[20] The use of the singular "people of God" instead of the plural "peoples of God" reflects the Catholic conviction about the intimate bonds between Judaism and the church. Even though Jews do not share the church's faith in Christ, they are participants in a faith-covenant with God and, together with Christians, somehow constitute the "people of God."

2. Catholics need to understand Jews in the light of their own religious experience

This important idea was first articulated in the Prologue of the Pontifical Commission's 1974 "Guidelines." "On the practical level in particular, Christians must therefore strive to acquire a better knowledge of the basic components of the religious tradition of Judaism; they must strive to learn by what essential traits Jews define themselves in the light of their own religious experience."[21] To put this another way, Jews need to be able to recognize themselves and their heritage in Roman Catholic references to them. Catholics need to incorporate accurate understandings of Judaism into their understanding of their own faith. Ideas that do not accord with the Jewish religious experience (for instance: Judaism is legalistic; the Pharisees didn't care about people) do not belong in Catholic thought. *Dominus Iesus* has raised objections from some Jewish readers precisely because they mistakenly, if understandably, find Judaism being ignored or caricatured in its sweeping assessments of non-Christian religions.

3. Catholics repent of the teaching of contempt and are committed to genuine fellowship with Jews

The "teaching of contempt" is a now-common phrase coined by Jules Isaac to refer to the incessant Christian anti-Jewish theological claim that God cursed Jews because they allegedly killed Christ. Cardinal Cassidy has summarized this teaching of contempt very well:

> There can be no denial of the fact that from the time of the Emperor Constantine on, Jews were isolated and discriminated against in the Christian world. There were expulsions and forced conversions. Literature propagated stereotypes, preaching accused the Jews of every age of deicide; the ghetto which came into being in 1555 with a papal bull became in Nazi Germany the antechamber of the extermination.[22]

On March 12, 2000, as part of the Catholic Church's celebration of the Great Jubilee 2000, Pope John Paul II presided over a Mass of Pardon at St. Peter's Basilica. During this unprecedented liturgy, the leaders of the Catholic community engaged in an ecclesial examination of conscience and prayed for God's forgiveness for the sins of Christians during the preceding millennium. Cardinal Cassidy implored, "Let us pray that, in recalling the sufferings endured by the people of Israel throughout history, Christians will acknowledge the sins committed by not a few of their number against the people of the Covenant and the blessings, and in this way will purify their hearts."[23] This "purification of memory," as the Pope put it during his homily,[24] was seen as essential for the church at the beginning of the third Christian millennium. It is an important aspect of the church's ongoing rapprochement with the Jewish people.

This connection between penitence and reconciliation in Catholic-Jewish relations was reiterated in an equally solemn moment during the Pope's visit to Israel two weeks later. While visiting the holiest site of the Jewish people, the Western Wall in Jerusalem, the Pope inserted into the wall a profound pledge before God:

> God of our fathers, you chose Abraham and his descendants to bring Your name to the nations: we are deeply saddened by the behavior of those who in the course of history have caused these children of Yours to suffer and asking Your forgiveness we wish to commit ourselves to genuine brotherhood with the people of the Covenant.[25]

The sense of Jubilee penitence and conversion embodied by these two prayerful events will hopefully outlive the temporary furor generated by *Dominus Iesus*. The declaration would surely not have been so negatively construed had it conveyed some of the humility prominent in these other Roman Catholic statements issued during the year 2000. Be that as it may, it is true that *Dominus Iesus* said nothing to contradict the papal pledge made in Jerusalem.

4. Catholics seek dialogue with Jews for mutual enrichment

Some quotations offered in discussing the fourth item in the first section of this essay have already demonstrated this present point. However, two additional aspects of this teaching can be further developed here.

John Paul II has noted that the Christian and Jewish "common spiritual heritage is considerable. Help in better understanding certain aspects of the church's life can be gained by taking an inventory of that heritage, but also by taking into account the faith and religious life of the Jewish people as professed and lived now as well."[26] This statement was significant because it encouraged Christian engagement with the Jewish tradition not only in terms of Christian origins through biblical and historical studies but also through contemporary encounters with the living faith of the Jewish people today. The Commission for Religious Relations with the Jews cited and developed this idea when it instructed:

> The history of Israel did not end in 70 A.D. It continued, especially in a numerous Diaspora which allowed Israel to carry to the whole world a witness—often heroic—of its fidelity to the one God and to "exalt Him in the presence of all the living" (Tobit 13:4)... The permanence of Israel (while so many ancient peoples have disappeared without trace) is a historic fact and a sign to be interpreted within God's design... We must remind ourselves how the permanence of Israel is accompanied by a continuous spiritual fecundity, in the rabbinical period, in the Middle Ages and in modern times, taking its start from a patrimony which we long shared, so much so that "the faith and religious life of the Jewish people as they are professed and practiced still today, can greatly help us to understand better certain aspects of the life of the Church [citing John Paul II, 6 March 1982]."[27]

This recognition of the perpetual life of faith of the Jewish people, a people covenanting with the same God whom the church knows through Christ, is the basis for understanding that, to put it simply, Roman Catholics can learn from Jews. Indeed, taken in tandem with the frequently quoted papal declaration that Jews are the dearly beloved elder brothers of Christians,[28] it is clear that Catholics can learn *about God* from Jews.

This appreciation of the Jewish spiritual heritage also applies to the Roman Catholic approach to the first part of the Christian Bible, traditionally called the "Old Testament." The church's post-*Nostra aetate* appreciation of the spiritual wealth of the Jewish tradition also applies to Jewish traditions of interpretation of the scriptures:

> It is true, then, and should be stressed, that the Church and Christians read the Old Testament in the light of the event of the dead and risen Christ and that on these grounds there is a Christian reading of the Old Testament which does not necessarily coincide with the Jewish reading. Thus Christian identity and Jewish identity should be carefully distinguished in their respective reading of the Bible. But this detracts nothing from the value of the Old Testament in the Church and *does nothing to hinder Christians from profiting discerningly from the traditions of Jewish reading*...
>
> Typological reading only manifests the unfathomable riches of the Old Testament, its inexhaustible content and the mystery of which it is full, and should not lead us to forget that *it retains its own value as revelation that the New Testament often does no more than resume.*[29]

In this context, typology is the practice of reading persons or events in the Old Testament as foreshadowings of persons or events in the New. It has been the predominant Christian approach to those scriptures. The remarkable development seen in this quotation is the acknowledgment of legitimate, non-christological readings of the Old Testament from which Christians can benefit, and the recognition of a vast spiritual treasury in the Old Testament that the New Testament by itself does not fully convey.

Applying these concepts, the U.S. Bishops' Committee on the Liturgy has advised Catholic preachers to "show that the meaning of the Hebrew Scriptures for their original audience is not limited to nor diminished by New Testament applications," to "avoid approaches that reduce them to a propaedeutic or background for the New Testament," and to "draw on Jewish sources (rabbinic, medieval, and modern) in expounding the meaning of the Hebrew Scriptures and the apostolic writings."[30]

Thus, as is reflected in the relevant magisterial documents and despite the impressions that *Dominus Iesus* has produced, Roman Catholic interest in dialoguing with Jews is faith-centered and devoid of proselytizing intent. Catholics are encouraged to dialogue with Jews in order to grasp Jewish self-definition more accurately, to understand their own faith tradition better, to increase their understanding of what it means to covenant with God, and, as shall be seen below, to collaborate with Jews in preparing the world for God's Reign.

5. The Catholic Church believes that Jews have an ongoing, divinely ordained vocation in the world

This still-emerging understanding is based on the previous convictions. It represents the church coming to grips with the ongoing covenantal dynamism of Judaism so as to conceive of the Jewish mission in the world beyond *prepara-*

tio Christi, preparing for the coming of Christ. John Paul II has reflected on Jewish mission in connection with the Shoah:

> I think that in this sense you continue your particular vocation, show-
> ing yourselves to be still the heirs of that election to which God is
> faithful. This is your mission in the contemporary world before the
> peoples, the nations, all of humanity, the church. And in this church all
> peoples and nations feel united to you in this mission ... [Our meeting]
> helps me and all the church to become even more aware of what unites
> us in the disposition of the divine covenant.[31]

Also noteworthy are two more recent statements in Cardinal Ratzinger's *Many Religions, One Covenant.* In a discussion about Christ in the context of the divine promise that Abraham would be a source of blessing for all the nations, Ratzinger observes:

> The history of Israel should become the history of all, Abraham's son-
> ship is to be extended to the "many". This course of events has two as-
> pects to it: the nations can enter into the community of the promises of
> Israel in entering into the community of the one God, who now be-
> comes and must become the way of all because there is only one God
> and because his will is therefore truth for all. Conversely, this means
> that all nations, *without the abolishment of the special mission of Is-
> rael,* become brothers and receivers of the promises of the Chosen
> People; they become People of God *with* Israel through adherence to
> the will of God and through acceptance of the Davidic kingdom.[32]

This idea of a "special mission of Israel" is repeated later in the volume:

> Israel may find it impossible to see Jesus as the Son of God as Chris-
> tians do; but it is not impossible for them to see him as the Servant of
> God who carries the light of his God to the nations. Conversely, even
> if Christians look for a day when Israel will recognize Christ as the
> Son of God and the rift that separates them will be healed, they should
> also acknowledge God's providence, which has obviously given Israel
> a particular mission in this "time of the Gentiles."[33]

Several points should be made about this quotation. Cardinal Ratzinger here expresses the expectation that Jews would someday acknowledge Jesus as God's Son. This is not new in the tradition of Christian thought. What is significant is the linkage of a postponement of this anticipated Jewish acknowledgment into the eschatological future with the cardinal's perception that God has "obviously given Israel a particular mission" during the intervening eras. His call for Christians to acknowledge in the present reality that Jews have a (presumably positive) divinely ordained mission has not, in fact, been very obvious to Christians for the past two millennia. Quite properly, the cardinal does not seek to delineate what this Jewish vocation in the world might be. That is because Christians must learn how "Jews define themselves in the light of their own religious experience."[34]

A text issued early in 2001 by the U.S. Bishops' Committee on Ecumenical and Inter-religious Affairs, "Catholic Teaching on the Shoah: Implementing the Holy See's *We Remember,*" is also relevant here. It indicates that education about the Holocaust in Catholic schools should

> encourage a positive appreciation of Jews and Judaism and the ongoing role of the Jewish People in God's plan of salvation. This role, the Church teaches, was not exhausted in preparing the way for and giving birth to Jesus. It will continue until the End of Time. Thus, Pope John Paul II has spoken of the Church and the Jewish People being "joint trustees and witnesses of an ethic... drawn from our common heritage in the Law and the Prophets... and marked by the Ten Commandments, in the observance of which [humanity] finds its truth and freedom [citing John Paul II, 1986]."[35]

Here again is evident the emerging Catholic understanding that Jews have a mission in the world until the eschaton because of their perpetual covenantal bonding with God.

6. Catholics and Jews share a mission to prepare the world for the Messiah

As suggested by the previous quotation, among the tasks of Jews in the world is one in which the church also participates:

> Attentive to the same God who has spoken, hanging on the same word, we have to witness to one same memory and one common hope in Him who is the master of history. We must also accept our responsibility to prepare the world for the coming of the Messiah by working together for social justice, respect for the rights of persons and nations and for social and international reconciliation. To this we are driven, Jews and Christians, by the command to love our neighbor, by a common hope for the kingdom of God, and by the great heritage of the prophets. Transmitted soon enough by catechesis, such a conception would teach young Christians in a practical way to cooperate with Jews, going beyond simple dialogue.[36]

It should be noted that this vision of Jews and Christians sharing a responsibility to promote justice and peace in the world was introduced by an eschatological comment:

> Furthermore, in underlining the eschatological dimension of Christianity we shall reach a greater awareness that the people of God of the

Old and New Testaments are tending toward a like end in the future: the coming or the return of the Messiah—even if they start from two different points of view. It is more clearly understood that the person of the Messiah is not only a point of division for the people of God but also a point of convergence.[37]

Here we see additional evidence from Roman Catholic magisterial documents that a new recognition of the "not yet" or unfinished dimension of Christian expectations accompanies the affirmation of the eternal covenant between God and the people of Israel. This enables: (1) a stress on the joint witness of Jews and Christians in the world; (2) an acknowledgment of an authentic Jewish mission in the world that is not *preparatio Christi;* and (3) a deferral of the formerly thorny issue of Jewish recognition of Jesus' divine Sonship out of the present temporal frame and into the eschatological future. Again, *Dominus Iesus* addressed none of this developing magisterial teaching. In my view this was a regrettable omission.

C. FUTURE THEOLOGICAL DEVELOPMENTS
SUGGESTED BY *DOMINUS IESUS*

In considering the ramifications of *Dominus Iesus* for future Catholic-Jewish relations, these implications come to mind:

First, concerns about whether the declaration disclosed a latent or inevitable missionizing agenda when dialoguing with Jews suggests that the time may have come for the Roman Catholic Church to declare formally that it has no interest in undertaking conversionary campaigns that target Jews. I would submit that the magisterial statements of the Catholic hierarchy to date justify and unavoidably lead to such a statement. Three essential Catholic teachings are involved:

(1) The Catholic Church has officially declared that God's covenantal love for the Jewish people is eternal. Covenanting with a saving God must by definition be saving, as Cardinal Kasper recently professed: "The Church believes that Judaism, i.e., the faithful response of the Jewish people to God's irrevocable covenant, is salvific for them, because God is faithful to his promises."[38] If the Jewish people are in a saving covenant with God, then there is no need to convert them for the sake of their salvation.

(2) Moreover, if seeking conversions or missionizing is understood as bringing people who previously were idolaters or did not know God into relationship with the One God, then obviously Jews are excluded from such a campaign. Once again, Cardinal Kasper has made this point: "The term mission, in its proper sense, [refers] to conversion from false gods and idols to the true and one God, who revealed himself in the salvation history with his elected people. Thus mission, in this strict sense, cannot be used with regard to Jews, who be-

lieve in the true and one God. Therefore—and this is characteristic—[there] does not exist any Catholic missionary organization for Jews. There is dialogue with Jews; no mission in this proper sense of the word towards them."[39]

Thus, the command of the risen Christ in Matthew 28:19, "Go therefore and make disciples of all the nations," should be understood as referring not to Israel, but to the "nations" (Hebrew = *goyim,* Greek = *ethnoi*), the Gentiles. Cardinal Kasper verbally made this point twice during the May 2001 International Catholic-Jewish Liaison Committee meeting.

(3) Finally, as discussed under point 5 above, the Catholic Church acknowledges that the Jewish people have an ongoing divinely ordained mission in the world that goes beyond *preparatio Christi* and that only Jews themselves can articulate (see endnotes 31-35). If this is so, then, to be blunt, and using the words of Michael McGarry, God does not want a world without Jews.[40] To seek to convert Jews to Christianity would be to oppose the will of God who has covenanted with the Jewish people to bear witness before the nations (*ad gentes*) to the sacred Name in a distinctive way throughout historic time. Christians seeking to convert Jews could be found to be "fighting against God" (Acts 5:39)!

Thus, it can now be theologically argued that the church's mission *ad gentes* is related to the ongoing mission of the Jewish people *ad gentes.* Both Jews (as Jews) and Christians are each essential to God's plan for preparing the world for the coming or return of the Messiah.

Although the Roman Catholic Church indeed has no office dedicated to the conversion of Jews, it should officially make *de jure* its current *de facto* renunciation of any conversionary campaigns that target Jews, and do so with clearly expressed theological explanations. This is *not* to say that the church should cease announcing the good news of Christ universally. Indeed, Jews (and everyone else!) should see and hear the gospel manifested in the lives of Christians. Some individual Jewish men and women may decide to receive baptism as a result of this Christian witness. However, the developing Catholic magisterial theological teaching about Jews and Judaism rules out a focused ecclesial campaign aimed at Jews *qua* Jews to promote their conversion to Christianity.

This would go an enormous way to assuaging the legitimate Jewish concerns so well articulated by David Berger in the wake of *Dominus Iesus.* Furthermore, as John Pawlikowski noted at the International Catholic-Jewish Liaison Committee meeting, such a Catholic declaration would offer a public theological rebuttal to Christian communities such as the Southern Baptist Convention which fund proselytizing efforts aimed at Jews. No definitive Christian statements have offered a systematic theological rationale against such initiatives.[41] The casual observer is left with little alternative than to conclude that Christians naturally should be about the business of converting Jews. Public Catholic witness on this matter would be a form of evangelization to our fellow Christians.

Second, Dominus Iesus has major implications for soteriology. *Dominus Iesus,* of course, maintains the centrality of Christ for salvation, but, as noted earlier, drew attention to a particular question that needs further theological research:

> With respect to the *way* in which the salvific grace of God—which is always given by means of Christ in the Spirit and has a mysterious relationship to the Church—comes to individual non-Christians, the Second Vatican Council limited itself to the statement that God bestows it "in ways known to himself." Theologians are seeking to understand this question more fully. Their work is to be encouraged, since it is certainly useful for understanding better God's salvific plan and the ways in which it is accomplished (§21; see also §14).

Although the declaration was presumably not referring to Jews in this regard, Cardinal Kasper later *did* discuss Jews in relation to this question immediately before the sentence on the salvific value of Israel's covenant noted above. "[*Dominus Iesus*] declares that God's grace, which is the grace of Jesus Christ according to our faith, is available to all. Therefore, the Church believes that Judaism, i.e., the faithful response of the Jewish people to God's irrevocable covenant, is salvific for them, because God is faithful to his promises."[42]

The saving grace of God that covenantally "saves" Jews is somehow also the saving grace of Jesus Christ. How that might be explained or conceptualized is an unresolved issue in Catholic theology. Given the relevant magisterial teaching, however, this soteriological question would need to be predicated upon Israel's perpetual covenant with God. I am convinced that one fruitful path to explore involves conceiving of Jesus Christ as incarnating Israel's covenanting life with God, but the limits of a paper concerned with *Dominus Iesus* prevent any expansion upon this prospect.[43]

Third, in conclusion I note the declaration's claim that, "with the incarnation, all the salvific actions of the Word of God are always done in unity with the human nature that he has assumed for the salvation of all people" (§10). This statement raises profound theological possibilities, since the human nature in question, unless understood in some bloodless generic way, was that of a *Jewish* human being. It suggests that Christians could understand that the covenantal bonding between God and Israel took on a new intimacy with the incarnation of the divine *Logos* in Jesus the Nazorean. Since the Son of God was incarnated as a son of Israel, all of God's saving actions are intensely linked to the covenantal love between God and Israel.

10
CHALLENGES
TO MUSLIM-CHRISTIAN RELATIONS

Qamar-ul Huda

The recent Congregation for the Doctrine of the Faith (CDF) document *Dominus Iesus* forces members outside the Catholic tradition to reassess their understanding of the church and the faith they profess to their believers. *Dominus Iesus* as a document is affirming publicly the Catholic faith, and is probably one of the most important Vatican documents on other religious traditions since the Second Vatican Council. While it does not specifically refer to the Islamic tradition or to contemporary Muslim-Christian relations, it speaks about other traditions in relation to the Catholic faith. The document is not meant to be an instructive guide for Christian believers attempting to deal with other religious traditions, but rather to "clarify certain truths of the faith" (§23).

A quotation from the Second Vatican Council's dogmatic constitution *Lumen gentium,* which says that the mission of the church is to "proclaim and establish among all peoples the kingdom of Christ and of God, and she is on earth, the seed and the beginning of that kingdom," indicates that the authors of *Dominus Iesus* are primarily interested in this aspect of the Second Vatican Council (§18). *Dominus Iesus* is selective in what it presents as the doctrine of faith. Its repetitive reference to missionary activity and evangelizing is discouraging to modern Muslim-Christian relations and disheartening to Muslims. It disappoints expectations following the Second Vatican Council that the two faiths would grow in inter-religious dialogue.

In its opening section, *Dominus Iesus* states: "Inter-religious dialogue, which is part of the Church's evangelizing mission, requires an attitude of understanding and a relationship of mutual knowledge and reciprocal enrichment, in obedience to the truth and with respect for freedom" (§2). But all forms of understanding the "other" are designed to convert them to the church. This essay is a response to some of the problems *Dominus Iesus* poses to Muslims in general, and specifically to Muslim-Christian relations.

MY SALVATION *VERSUS* YOUR SALVATION

One of the more pertinent areas of concern for Muslims in *Dominus Iesus* is section VI, entitled "The Church and the other religions in relation to salvation." As a document of faith intended to reflect the church's role in salvation for its believers, it affirms the church's temporal and spiritual function. It states that "it must be *firmly believed* that 'the Church, a pilgrim now on earth, is necessary for salvation: the one Christ is the mediator and the way of salvation; he is present to us in his body which is the Church. He himself explicitly asserted the necessity of faith and baptism . . . and thereby affirmed at the same time the necessity of the Church which men enter through baptism as through a door'" (§20). In *Dominus Iesus,* the importance of faith and baptism is paralleled with the church's role in bringing salvation to its believers, with support from the gospels of Mark (16:16) and John (3:5). One problem with this assertion, at least for Islamic theology, is the interference of an institution between God and believers. Any claims about the necessity of an intermediary, human or organizational, between God and his servants contradicts the Islamic affirmation of the doctrine of *tawhîd* or the oneness of God. For Muslims, every moment and every level of existence requires the believer to assert *tawhîd.*[1] Through daily prayers, fasting, charity, social work, pilgrimage, and other faith-related activities, believers must struggle to submit themselves to God's supremacy at every conceivable level—mind, heart, and soul. The Qur'ân, the revelations received by the Prophet Muhammad, commands its believers to work toward establishing a life of *tawhîd.* It describes this task as a human struggle or a human effort, "*jihâd.*"[2] Commonly mistaken in contemporary language as a "holy war against non-Muslims," the word *jihâd* is used over and over in the Qur'ân to mean striving toward a life of God-consciousness, which often means resisting the attractions of things that are ungodly.[3]

HOLY CHURCH AND HOLY MOSQUE

The insistence in Islam on maintaining a non-central institution to govern its theological, eschatological, spiritual, and temporal affairs was intended to prevent any single authority over believers. The *shahadah* or basic testimony in Islam that "There is no God but one God, and the Prophet Muhammad is the Messenger" affirms that God is supreme in all affairs. Human beings were created to worship God and follow the guidance of divine revelations. The Qur'ân recognized the important theological notion of *ecclesia,* or a church, for the followers of Jesus, but it also noted problems that come with an authoritative body in religious matters. The Qur'ân was not interested in recreating the religious and social structures of Christianity but in returning to an absolute, non-intermediary identity. Since the growth and development of Christianity and Islam differ in numerous ways, it appears that the historical experiences of Enlightenment, reformation, and modern secularism have pressed the church to be marginalized, particularly as constituting the means of salvation. Then, from a historical point of view, it is natural for *Dominus Iesus* to reassert the church's role in salvation. For Muslims, all ideas of faith, spirituality, law, and life are contained in the Qur'ânic revelations and there cannot be another statement to supersede the final revelations.

Dominus Iesus is mainly intended for Christian believers; however, there are statements that refer to "others"—presumably meaning Protestant Christians and non-Christians—who still benefit from a mysterious relationship to the church and Holy Spirit. For example, it states:

> For those who are not formally and visibly members of the Church, "salvation in Christ is accessible by virtue of a grace which, while having a mysterious relationship to the Church, does not make them formally part of the Church, but enlightens them in a way which is accommodated to their spiritual and material situation. This grace comes from Christ; it is the result of his sacrifice and is communicated by the Holy Spirit"; it has a relationship with the Church, which "according to the plan of the Father, has her origin in the mission of the Son and the Holy Spirit" (§20).

This statement does not recognize the fact that other religious traditions do not adhere to belief in a Holy Spirit communicating to believers. For Muslims, all work and communication is performed by the one and only God.

Once *Dominus Iesus* establishes the church's function in salvation, it tries to invalidate other religious traditions and their respective ways of understanding salvation. It speaks about their prayers, rituals, sacred scriptures, and general beliefs as not completely salvific. It concedes that other traditions may have some spiritual elements, but then regards them as preparation for the truth of the Christian gospel. For example, *Dominus Iesus* states that "it is clear that it would be contrary to the faith to consider the Church as *one way* of salvation alongside those constituted by the other religions, seen as complementary to the Church or substantially equivalent to her, even if these are said to be converging with the Church toward the eschatological kingdom of God" (§21). While the intention of *Dominus Iesus* is to reaffirm the "true" distinctions of the Catholic doctrine of faith, it is problematic when it makes exclusive claims about salvation and claims a single ownership of truth. The paragraph does not stop at sole custody of salvation; instead, it continues to undervalue other religious traditions as having inherent obstacles to obtaining salvation. For instance: "Indeed, some prayers and rituals of the other religions may assume a role of preparation for the Gospel, in that they are occasions or pedagogical helps in which the human heart is prompted to be open to the action of God. One cannot attribute to these, however, a divine origin or an *ex opere operato* salvific efficacy, which is proper to the Christian sacraments. Furthermore, it cannot be overlooked that other rituals, insofar as they depend on superstitions or other errors...constitute an obstacle to salvation" (§21).

According to Qur'ânic theology, God made human beings as his vicegerents or representatives (*khalîfâh*) on earth (Q 2:30). The Qur'ân calls this representation a type of trust that no other creature can carry out (Q 33:72). The corruption or disobedience of this trust between God and human beings is what brings about evil consequences. This type of conflict and violation leads to further violation of the earth. For medieval Muslim scholars like Imâm al-Ghazalî (d. 1111) and Ibn 'Arabî (d. 1240), the closer human beings are connected to divine mercy (*rahma*), the tighter the bond is built on harmony with divine peace. However, if believers stray away from this bond, they inevitably fail to be trustworthy custodians on earth. This corruption or *fasâd,* mentioned in the Qur'ân over fifty times, is produced by human error and free will. Islamically, God is actively involved with human affairs and desires his creatures to accept their submission to him. As the Qur'ân notes: "Corruption has spread over land and sea from what men have done themselves that they may taste a little of what they have done: They may happily come back to the right path" (Q 30:41). The Creator desires his creatures to witness the result of their capriciousness. Human corruption, or the ongoing drama of *fasâd,* is meant to help human beings to find ways to rectify the corruption they have created. The Qur'ân speaks on this subject of violence on earth (*fasâd*) that can have a positive return to God through repentance. Human disobedience not only violates the responsibility of custodianship of the earth, but, more importantly, it also fails to affirm God's unity.

RELIGIOUS PLURALISM AND THE OTHER

One of the more distressing aspects of *Dominus Iesus* is the way it demarcates Catholic faith and identity at the expense of other religious traditions. On the one hand, it reveals the power behind the Christian faith and affirms that the church is continuing the tradition of teaching all nations, baptizing them in the name of the Father, and of the Son, and of the Holy Spirit, teaching them to observe all that has been commanded.[4] On the other hand, in attempting to reassert the Christian faith, *Dominus Iesus* simultaneously undermines the validity of other faiths by calling into question their legitimacy. The declaration states: "This truth of faith does not lessen the sincere respect which the Church has for the religions of the world, but at the same time, it rules out, in a radical way, that mentality of indifferentism 'characterized by a religious relativism which leads to the belief that one religion is as good as another'" (§22). Here the difficulty is not so much the zealous language used to affirm the Christian faith, as it is the way the document claims that faith's supremacy over other religious traditions. For Islamic theology this is not a new claim. The Qur'ân addresses it, referring to the claims made by Jews and Christians who felt that they were not like any other people whom God created, that their special covenant gave them an elevated status with God, and that they were "friends of Allâh to the exclusion of other people."[5] Along with this unique status came inherent purity and the belief that the afterlife was exclusively saved for them. As the Qur'ân states, "They claim to be children of Allâh and His beloved" (Q 5:18) and "considered themselves pure" (Q 4:48). The Qur'ân consistently teaches that any exclusive claim remains with Allâh alone; that is, no religious group has the authority or the power to judge any other people because God alone decides the fate of all created things.

> And they say: None shall enter paradise unless he [or she] be a Jew or
> a Christian. Those are their vain desires. Say to them: Produce your
> proof if you are truthful. Remember, whoever submits his [or her]
> whole self to Allâh and is a doer of good, will get reward with his [or
> her] Lord. For God's is the kingdom of the heavens and the earth and
> all that lies between them (Q 5:18).[6]

This not only serves as a reminder to Muslims of how other religious groups
have made exclusive truth claims, but more importantly, it shows that Muslims
themselves need to be careful never to proclaim divine exclusivity, because
everything is dependent on God's will and it is he who has power over all
things.[7]

Another example of *Dominus Iesus*'s exclusive theological and salvific
claims, which raise grave issues having to do with real respect for other religious traditions, is the way it speaks of "others" who only by chance can receive divine grace because they stand outside of the church's borders. Even if
the authors of *Dominus Iesus* wanted to emphasize the unique status of members of the church, it is unfortunate that they felt compelled to denigrate other
religious traditions and other Christian groups as "gravely deficient." They
write, for instance: "If it is true that the followers of other religions can receive
divine grace, it is also certain that *objectively speaking* they are in a gravely deficient situation in comparison with those who, in the Church, have the fullness
of the means of salvation" (§22). This approach undermines their own legitimacy in professing the kingdom of God and the kingdom of Christ in the
church, because it is antithetical to the peaceful proclamation of Jesus Christ as
"the way, the truth, and the life" (Jn 14:6). *Dominus Iesus* is meant to oppose
defenders of religious relativism, a new secular ideology that appears to be a
threat to the church's authority. For example, it states, "The Church's constant
missionary proclamation is endangered today by relativistic theories which
seek to justify religious pluralism, not only *de facto* but also *de iure* (or 'in principle')" (§4). The authors are interested in displaying an uncompromising faith
in the church as the inheritance from Jesus Christ and in declaring that they
cannot in any way risk allowing anything less.

The heart of this issue is respect for other religious traditions and whether
the church views other traditions as equally important with respect to divine
revelation. *Dominus Iesus* states that in order to reiterate certain truths of the
faith and "faced with certain problematic and even erroneous propositions, theological reflection is called to reconfirm the Church's faith and to give reasons
for her hope in a way that is convincing and effective" (§23). Yet it is not consistent theologically for the church to reaffirm truths of its own tradition by
weakening the validity of other religious traditions. In Islamic theology the
Qur'ân acknowledges Jews and Christians as "people of the Book" (*ahl al-
kitâb*) with a common shared scriptural history. Both Jews and Christians have
a special status in Islam where they are considered to be communities that have
had divine revelations from messengers of God. While there is in all three traditions a history of apologetics and polemics, the Qur'ân does recognize in two

ways the legitimacy of all revealed religious tradition: it recalls the coexistence of other religious communities with separate rituals, beliefs, laws, and social practices, and it recalls that these communities' believers are believers in one God. The Qur'ân acknowledges the distinct qualities of other traditions, and Muslims are commanded to accept religious pluralism. This is evident and explicit in Islamic law in areas of food and marriage. Muslims are allowed to eat food prepared by the people of the Book (Q 5:5) and Muslim men are legally permitted to marry chaste women who are people of the Book (Q 5:5). This is to say that in such intimate relationships as marriage and in social interactions, the Qur'ân acknowledges, and hence Muslims sincerely believe, that there is no alternative to the recognition of multiple religious traditions. It is religious pluralism that allows us completely to submit as servants to God, and any attempt to invalidate the other is, at least for Muslims, a rejection of faith and of God's will.[8] In Islam, religious pluralism means not just tolerating the existence of other religious traditions as separate communities but acknowledging that the other traditions are integrally tied to the divine message, that the essence of the message in Torah, Bible, and Qur'ân brings us back humbly to submit ourselves in front of the one God.

THE QUESTION OF MUSLIM-CHRISTIAN INTER-RELIGIOUS DIALOGUE

The single most damaging passage in *Dominus Iesus* for contemporary Muslim-Christian relations is article 22: "In inter-religious dialogue as well, the mission *ad gentes* 'today as always retains its full force and necessity.'" It is significant to recall that Muslim-Christian relations have historically been characterized by violence, polemical literature, and straightforward agendas to destroy the other. When an official document like *Dominus Iesus* refers to inter-religious dialogue and mission *ad gentes* in the same sentence, it brings back memories of evangelical missionary work to convert the "infidel" Muslims. Preaching the gospel to those who are "deficient" and "not equal" is hardly a productive way to learn from others or teach oneself about another religious tradition. If *Dominus Iesus* is significantly tied to the assertion that "the Church proclaims and is in duty bound to proclaim without fail," then there will be little inter-religious dialogue between the two faiths. The conversions forced by the Crusaders, the Inquisition, and the colonial experience are all still in the collective imaginations of Muslims. Clearly the two communities will not learn from each other if inter-religious dialogue is another opportunity to convert Muslims to Christianity.

    Dominus Iesus's reference to inter-religious dialogue as a way of conversion is alarming because Muslims had hoped that after Vatican II there could be serious theological progress in Muslim-Christian relations. This idea of conversion also undermines the goal stated recently by the president of the Pontifical Council on Inter-Religious Affairs, Francis Cardinal Arinze, who declared that dialogue is about real collaboration and cooperation between the religious traditions.[9] *Dominus Iesus* undermines this work when it states that "the

Church, to whom this truth has been entrusted, must go out to meet their desire, so as to bring them the truth. Because she believes in God's universal plan of salvation, the Church must be missionary. Inter-religious dialogue, therefore, as part of her evangelizing mission, is just one of the actions of the Church in her mission *ad gentes*" (§22).

The same section of *Dominus Iesus* refers to other religious traditions as having equal personal dignity but not equal worth with respect to doctrinal content. Clearly, the authors of *Dominus Iesus* know very little of other religious traditions, doctrinally or historically. They are interested in affirming the superiority of the Catholic faith and the church. When the document states that "the Church, guided by charity and respect for freedom, must be primarily committed to proclaiming to all people the truth definitively revealed by the Lord, and to announcing the *necessity of conversion* to Jesus Christ and of adherence to the Church through Baptism and the other sacraments, in order to participate fully in communion with God, the Father, Son and Holy Spirit" (§22, emphasis added), it reflects pre-modern attitudes characterized by exclusive claims of truth and supreme authority on all matters on faith. This type of thinking creates a step back in Muslim-Christian relations and it will unfortunately build barriers between the two communities.

It must be admitted that it is admirable for the Roman Catholic Church to remain committed to missionary work in a world of religious indifference and growing secularization. Similarly, Muslims are undergoing a process of re-assessing their faith and reflecting on how to express it in acceptable terms. Some of these parallel questions point me to one of Islam's distinguished philosophers and sûfîs, 'Alî ibn 'Uthmân al-Jullâbî al-Hujwîrî (d. 1070), who wrote an influential sûfî treatise that is still used in some parts of the Islamic world, entitled *Kashf al-Mahjûb,* "Unveiling the Veils." In this instructional manual for Muslim mystics, al-Hujwîrî wrote about specific techniques involved in the growth of reunion with God; with the success of each inner practice, the sûfî unveils another veil that divides the believer from the Creator. He stated, "Bowing oneself in prostration forces humility and the prostration of the head brings about self-knowledge, and the profession of faith is an intimate statement. Real salutation takes the place of detachment from the world and escape from the problems of stations."[10] I think that the problems posed by *Dominus Iesus* for Muslim-Christian relations are tied to these stations of worldly positioning and of claiming truths for one's own tradition while dismissing the other as just another misguided religion. For any sincere dialogue to occur between the faiths, both Muslims and Christians will need to move beyond stagnant pronouncements and toward the mutual and humble process of unveiling of the veils that divide us from each other and from God.

11

IMPLICATIONS FOR THE PRACTICE OF INTER-RELIGIOUS LEARNING

Francis X. Clooney, S.J.

A GOOD BEGINNING

By its own admission *Dominus Iesus*[1] does not intend "to treat in a systematic manner the question of the unicity and salvific universality of the mystery of Jesus Christ and the Church, nor to propose solutions to questions that are matters of free theological debate" (§3). Rather, it is an instruction about the identity of Christ, the integral interconnection of Christ, revelation, and the church, and consequently[2] the correct nature of the Christian encounter with people who belong to the "non-Christian religions." Much in the declaration is clear and helpful in enunciating important rules which should fruitfully guide the thinking of Catholic Christians who accept the creed as central to their faith: believe in Christ in accord with the creed as a whole, and as it is understood in the Catholic tradition; acknowledge the unique and universal salvific importance of Christ with reference to all theological issues; safeguard the unity of the Word and Son of God with Jesus of Nazareth, whose Spirit it is working in the world, and understand this unity as it has been remembered and passed down in the church; avoid responses to pluralism which posit the leveling of religious differences; engage conscientiously in an inter-religious dialogue characterized by "an attitude of understanding and a relationship of mutual knowledge and reciprocal enrichment, in obedience to the truth and with respect for freedom" (§2); but do not enter that dialogue with the presupposition that all paths are equal; instead, begin—and end—with the firm conviction that Christ is the Way.[3] Some conservatives will be bothered by some parts of the declaration and some progressives by other parts, but it ably brings to the fore some key elements of Christian faith in a plausible fashion that will ring true for most Catholics. For this we can be grateful to the authors.

But an affirmation of the creed as understood in the Roman Catholic Church and a rejection of relativism as the foundation for dialogue establish a beginning to useful instruction, not an end. When we look for guidance in the declaration regarding more difficult issues, we can still learn, but less fully. Some points are well taken, yet remain incomplete; some points are unclear as stated in the declaration, and need clarification.

LANGUAGE IS AN UNRULY AFFAIR

We are correctly reminded, for instance, to avoid positing a radical opposition between "the logical mentality of the West and the symbolic mentality of the East" (§4). This is a sensible point, since there is much in Western thought that is not logical and much in Eastern thought that is not symbolic. In any case, sweeping generalities that persist in referring to "East" and "West" (east of what? west of what?) do not bear scrutiny, whether they are positive or negative, since it is not clear what is being asserted or ruled out.

We are rightly advised to use words carefully (§7), and in particular to avoid stretching terms to a "one size fits all" accommodation of the Christian reality and the reality of other religious traditions. Certainly, it never helps to use terms indiscriminately as if they were easily applicable across religious boundaries. For instance, we are told it is important to distinguish "faith" (what we Christians have) and "belief" (what others have). "Faith" is "a personal adherence of man to God," "the acceptance in grace of revealed truth," "the acceptance of the truth revealed by the One and Triune God," "a dual adherence: to God who reveals and to the truth which he reveals, out of the trust which one has in him who speaks" (§7), and it must be reserved exclusively for Christians' act of adherence to God and acceptance of God's truth. By contrast, "belief" is "that sum of experience and thought that constitutes the human treasury of wisdom and religious aspiration, which man in his search for truth has conceived and acted upon in his relationship to God and the Absolute." This term may be used to name what people in other religious traditions have and do.

This is a serious distinction which gets at important aspects of what we believe about ourselves as Christians; yet even in the declaration itself "faith" and "belief" do not seem to function entirely in separation from one another. We notice, for instance, that "belief" and "believe" are used at least twenty-five times to refer to what Christians have and do. One might conclude that Christians have faith and also believe, while other people only believe, although it may be that the authors simply found it convenient to use both words in order to express themselves.

More seriously, the "faith-belief" distinction does not seem to do justice to the richer affirmation, cited above, that faith is a *dual* adherence, "to God who reveals" *and* "to the truth which he reveals." Were faith only "the acceptance in grace of revealed truth" and "the acceptance of the truth revealed by the One and Triune God," and assuming too that God reveals the truth in a single all-or-nothing gift, then it might fairly be stipulated that only Christians have this faith. But given the declaration's explanation of faith as a "personal adherence of man to God" too, the denial of "faith" to the people of other religious traditions must be interpreted as also indicating that in other religious traditions there can be no relationship with God of the sort that counts as that personal adherence which is also faith. This is sad enough in itself, but it would also be contrary to what the declaration asserts later on, that God "does not fail to make himself present in many ways, not only to individuals, but also to entire peoples through their spiritual riches" (§8). If God is present to people in their own religions, God surely is present in such a way that those people can respond to God and adhere to God even before assenting fully to revelation as understood in the teachings of the Roman Catholic Church. But if God does not fail in the divine intention to communicate with all human beings, and if knowing God invites humans to adhere to God, then it does not seem entirely reprehensible to say that the devout Muslim or Hindu who adheres to God does in some real way have not only "a life of belief" but also "a life of faith" as defined in the declaration.

Later we are instructed that the scriptures of other religious traditions are not inspired by God's Spirit (§8). Here too, it is possible to respect the declaration's double stipulation that while Christian scriptures and those of other religious traditions can both be called "sacred,"[4] "inspiration" is uniquely descriptive of biblical texts "since these are inspired by the Holy Spirit" (§8). But it gets confusing because we are also told that "in actual fact" those other sacred texts "direct and nourish the existence of their followers, [and] receive from the mystery of Christ the elements of goodness and grace which they contain"; that "there are some elements in these texts which may be *de facto* instruments by which countless people throughout the centuries have been and still are able today to nourish and maintain their life-relationship with God"; and (as above) that God "does not fail to make himself present in many ways, not only to individuals, but also to entire peoples through their spiritual riches" (§8). By the Congregation's own description, then, it might reasonably be conceded that God is working among people of other religious traditions and guiding them through the action of Christ. We also know that the Spirit cannot be separated from Christ, who works in and through the Spirit; so one might dare to presume that the sacred scriptures of other traditions are already enlivened by the Holy Spirit. Even if they are not "inspired" according to the declaration's stipulation, nonetheless one might innocently conclude from the declaration that these other sacred scriptures are in some way really "inspired" by God, since the Spirit is at work in them.

All of this may appear confusing to those of us not well versed in the subtleties of this topic, and there is always the chance that I have not fully understood the intent of the authors. But in any case my point is not to suggest that the authors of the declaration ought not stipulate specific meanings for terms such as "faith" or "inspiration," but only that they themselves have not yet succeeded in making an exceptionless case for the stipulations they propose. They do not seem to have entirely resolved the problems that have led some theologians to speak of the "faith" of people in other religious traditions and of the "inspiration" at work in their sacred texts. Until things are made clearer by the Congregation, it seems right that we show sympathy toward those theologians who keep trying to find human words expressive of what God does in meeting us, becoming present even in the diverse sacred texts of the human race, and inviting each human being to a personal relationship, even now.

ASSERTING THE UNIQUE TRUTH

The declaration asserts, firmly and rightly, that what we believe is actually true; and rightly so, because it is true. Even in a comparative context, this is not a problem. It is not a peculiarly Roman Catholic insight to hold that the content of faith is true or that the truth about reality can be normatively apprehended. I have known many Hindus over the years who are quite willing to assert the truth of what they believe. In my years of study of Indian Hindu theologies, too, I have encountered numerous claims by theologians as to the truth of a community's faith. For example, numerous Hindu theologians devoted to the deity Narayana (Vishnu, Krishna) as the supreme Lord hold strict views about Narayana's supremacy: God is truly and fully known in this tradition and its scriptures; Narayana alone is the one true God and the sole Lord of the universe; he is eternally accompanied by the Goddess Shri; he saves the world by graciously and unexpectedly entering it in forms such as Krishna and Rama; other beliefs and other forms of worship are deficient in light of scripture, and they are faulty in logic too; other gods are inferior and dependent beings, and not other names for the same Reality.[5]

The great theologian Ramanuja, writing in the eleventh century CE, makes such claims about Narayana as the one supreme God. In his early treatise *The Vedartha Samgraha* he argues this position largely on scriptural grounds, and to some extent largely in regard to scriptures widely shared among leading Hindu intellectuals of his time and class. At the heart of his teaching is his faith that God, as he knows God from revelation (in the Sanskrit Veda and the Tamil hymns of devotion), is the supreme God. Ramanuja also elaborates a consequent theory of human and divine nature, language, and religion in order to explain how traditions are to be ranked in relation to one another. He develops a fruitful analogy between the divine-human relationship—God is as it were the inner self of each human self, enlivening selves as selves enliven bodies—and the force of linguistic reference; because of the way the world is, all nouns, in their full signification, refer to God, Narayana.

When we claim that "my faith is true, unique, and even superior," we may be correct, but the claim itself is not unique or even particularly unusual. Catholics who make this claim are in important ways like Ramanuja and his community who make a comparable claim. It is not surprising that Catholics and south Indian Vaishnavas hold similarly strong views, defend them with similarly strong judgments, and undergird them with similarly complicated theories. Such is the way in which believers often assert their beliefs as true. External error too is explained according to the tradition's internal norms. In Ramanuja's tradition, it is assumed that those who understand how to read scripture properly, as it has been read in the tradition, will recognize the truth of these claims, while those who fail to understand nature and language will also fail to understand the truth, that Narayana alone is the one Lord of the universe. In the declaration, similarly, it is assumed that only Roman Catholics will have the ability to grasp as fully as humans ever can the truth that God has given in some way or another to people everywhere.

My intent in making these points is not to relativize the claims made in *Dominus Iesus,* but rather to put them in context. Similarity does not rule out truth; truth does not fear similarity. Rather, comparative study helps us to assess better the nature of our claims to certitude, winnowing them so as to remove extraneous arguments and needless presuppositions about our distinctiveness. Positively, we do well to differentiate our relationships with people of other religious traditions, since we often have much in common with them regarding important religious truths: the world is intelligible, material realities must be understood in the context of larger spiritual realities, there is an ultimate personal source and goal, there is a divine person who is compassionate as well as just, God and not humans takes the initiative in the divine-human encounter, God decides to become involved in the world even to the point of speaking in human words which are in fact recorded in sacred texts, and God ventures to become embodied in the world in human form. Similar truth claims exist, as well as interesting differences. It does not seem necessary to claim that every truth we discover in biblical revelation can be found only there. Nor is there great value in seeming anxious to show that all important Catholic beliefs are different from Jewish or Muslim or Buddhist or Hindu teachings on the same issues. The trick is to be able to recognize which reasonable and sacred truths we share with which traditions, to rejoice in this similarity and even to suppose that there is more to it than we have thus far suspected. In this way we can avoid making unnecessary or distracting claims about the truths we are obliged to hold.

One important difference must be noted. The declaration is also correct in reminding us that the Christian claim about Jesus Christ is distinguished by the fact that we couple it with the intent of bringing Christ to all people, and all people to Christ. While most religious traditions, I venture to guess, actually believe that their truths are universally true, most do not announce an active agenda of the ideals of evangelization and conversion. Since we do, we are all the more obliged to understand that world to which we are sent. Neither evangelization nor dialogue is strengthened by separating one from the other. Whether evangelical intent is manifest in a strictly missionary agenda or in the allied practices of arranging dialogues or writing treatises evaluating other people's religions, there are special obligations which the Christian must honor if this evangelical dynamism is to be honestly cherished in a way that is genuinely global and not parochial. We must be able to present the gospel in a way that makes at least some sense to people not already inclined to be well-disposed toward Vatican teachings; to communicate sensibly, we must be able to speak knowledgeably about those other traditions; to do this, we must listen to persons in those traditions and even learn from them.

A DISTURBING INDIFFERENTISM

Oddly enough, it is not the theologians who observe similarities and differences and take them seriously who encourage indifferentism, but rather the authors of the declaration. The declaration treats different religious beliefs, acts, and communities generically, as if such differences do not matter enough to be noted. Religions are described simply as "other religions," the "religious traditions," the "other religious experiences," and the adherents of those religions as the "non-Christians." Perhaps we should assume that Judaism stands in a separate category distinct from that comprised of non-Christians, although the declaration gives no hint of this. But if we are being asked to group all other religions together, the effect is quite unusual. Religions devoted to a personal, loving God would be treated the same as religions in which the idea of God is not central; religions deeply interconnected with our own religious roots, such as Islam, would be treated the same as religions with no such common roots, such as Shintoism. Just as relativism is improperly vague, it is also improper to imply, as do the authors of the declaration by their silences, that there are no important distinctions among the various religious traditions that need to be noticed. To treat everyone else as "the non-Christians" is also counterproductive and contrary to the declaration's own goal of reaffirming religious truth, since some of our strongest allies on issues of religious and moral significance are members of those other religious traditions. But to differentiate our attitudes toward different religions in an intelligent manner is a complicated task that requires learning and intelligent, informed judgments which can be received and critiqued by members of those religions themselves.

NAMING THE ERRORS

A similar indifference seems to underlie the still sharper assertion that all people in all other traditions are objectively speaking "in a gravely deficient situation" (§22), which I take to mean that the religious traditions to which Hindus and Muslims and Buddhists and others adhere are, in all their communal forms and all their local expressions throughout all of history and in every culture, gravely deficient. But a sweeping claim that "all religions err" is not much more helpful than its twin, the sweeping claim that "all religions are nice." If I wish to point out someone else's errors, I am obliged to name those errors in some particular and verifiable form.

The declaration gives us no illustrative examples, but only calls our attention to other religions' "gaps, insufficiencies and errors" (§8, echoing a phrase apparently first used by Paul VI in 1963). Since we are not fideists and rightly expect faith and unfaith to have observable effects on how people think and live, it is reasonable to expect that if religious traditions err, they will do so in ways that become manifest in erroneous thoughts, words, and deeds that can be named specifically. It would have been helpful had the declaration given some examples of the kinds of gaps, insufficiencies, and errors which make traditions demonstrably deficient, lest the faithful fear error where there is none, or warmly admire as spiritual wisdom what the authors of the declaration know to be merely erroneous.

The declaration states that while "some prayers and rituals of the other religions may assume a role of preparation for the Gospel, in that they are occasions or pedagogical helps in which the human heart is prompted to be open to the action of God," "other rituals, insofar as they depend on superstitions or other errors (cf. 1 Cor 10:20-21), constitute an obstacle to salvation" (§21). It is not clear whether these "other rituals" are superstitious and erroneous simply because they are Hindu or Jewish or Buddhist, or rather, more narrowly, only when they are erroneous according to criteria internal to the traditions themselves.

It seems extreme to claim that every act of worship in a synagogue or mosque is intrinsically erroneous; if this is not the declaration's intent, then some more sophisticated criteria for superstition and freedom from superstition are required, lest we be less or more generous in our judgments than is fitting. If the authors do wish to assert that the various traditions are erroneous simply because their beliefs diverge from Roman Catholic faith and practice, this merely reaffirms in other words the necessity of adhering to the Christian creed, and seems to make scholarly inquiry unnecessary. For example, are some Confucian rites (in China) and Brahmanical rites (in India) superstitious and others not? Or are they all superstitious insofar as "Confucian" and "Brahmanical" refer to "non-Christian religious realities"? This is an old question which vexed missionary theologians such as Mateo Ricci and Roberto de Nobili in the seventeenth century and prompted papal pronouncements in the eighteenth century and more recently as well. Surely by now we should be able to understand more clearly the nature of the superstition and error at stake. Perhaps the point really is that it is inherently superstitious for Vaishnavas in Ramanuja's tradition to worship Narayana as Lord, and not merely that superstition can be present if fears and misconceptions taint temple worship. If the point is simply that some rituals are in fact performed with mistaken intent or driven by misguided fears and desires, I doubt that scholars in other religious traditions will disagree, although they might also observe that Roman Catholics too may suffer from superstitious beliefs and on occasion worship improperly.

A NEW SCRIPTURAL NORM

It is remarkable that in this crucial paragraph (§21) the authors of the declaration choose to gloss "superstitions" and "other errors" by citing, without further explanation, 1 Corinthians 10, a text which seems not to have been used before in recent Vatican statements regarding religious pluralism. Consider the actual text:

> Therefore, my dear friends, flee from the worship of idols. I speak as to sensible people; judge for yourselves what I say. The cup of blessing that we bless, is it not a sharing in the blood of Christ? The bread that we break, is it not a sharing in the body of Christ? Because there is one bread, we who are many are one body, for we all partake of the

one bread. Consider the people of Israel; are not those who eat the sacrifices partners in the altar? What do I imply then? That food sacrificed
to idols is anything, or that an idol is anything? No, I imply that what
pagans sacrifice, they sacrifice to demons and not to God. I do not
want you to be partners with demons. You cannot drink the cup of the
Lord and the cup of demons. You cannot partake of the table of the
Lord and the table of demons (1 Cor 10:14-21).[6]

There seems to be no room here for a differentiation of the good and the
bad in pagan practices. According to Paul's passionate rhetoric, the participation in Christian worship and Christian community is diametrically opposed to
other participations, since all other rituals can be traced to demonic origins.
Since 1 Corinthians 10 has not customarily been cited in papal or Vatican documents, it is striking that it is the sole biblical text cited at this crucial point in
the declaration. It is not entirely clear what the authors of the declaration intend, but we may most easily conclude that this text is to be taken as normative
in the Catholic judgment on the rituals of other religious traditions. By this
standard, all the ritual practices of all religious traditions are to be collected
under the title of idolatry; Hindu, Buddhist, Muslim, Native American rites are
all rooted in the work of demons and signify nothing of value. If this is the
point, it is a difficult but important one, and it is imperative that the authors
write something more, soon, to explain what they intend readers to learn from
this key citation.[7]

But even here a comparative perspective is helpful; the vehemence of
Paul's resentment of idolatry reminds me again of similar sentiments in Ramanuja's tradition. A traditional anecdote recorded by the fourteenth-century
commentator Attanjiyar tells us of Ramanuja's intense dislike of other religions, particularly their sacred places:

One day Lord Narayana was being carried in procession, when it
began to rain. For shelter, the Lord was carried into the premises of another temple, a temple of Shiva. Ramanuja and the other elders who
had accompanied the procession remained outside the premises in the
rain. Someone asked Ramanuja, "Sir, if the Lord has taken shelter inside, why do you not do the same?" Ramanuja answered, "Fool, if the
emperor elects to make love to a courtesan, does this mean that his
queen should imitate her Lord and make love to a courtier?"[8]

Attanjiyar cites this anecdote approvingly in the course of glossing a verse by
the ninth-century poet saint Tirumalisai Piran. In the verse Death instructs his
roaming ministers, who seize those due to die, to observe the purity of devotion
among those who follow Narayana.

Death summons his servants and whispers in their ears,
"Don't fail to notice how

even if they forget the name of the One whose feet are holy,
his devotees still don't worship in alien ways;
go then and be virtuous yourselves, worship in that way too."[9]

Even when devotees stop chanting the names of the "one whose feet are holy" (possibly due to the approach of death) they still know enough to reject all contact with other gods and their "alien ways." The anecdote about Ramanuja is introduced in support of this exclusive attitude. In this Hindu context too the passion is intense, and Ramanuja, Attanjiyar, and Tirumalisai Piran would surely be able to recognize what Paul meant. Unlike the authors of the declaration, though, their heirs today do not seem interested in making claims about other religions or in converting those who worship in those alien ways. But for us who are Catholic and intend to bring the good news to all people, a pious horror in the presence of the other is no excuse for not paying attention and learning something of what those people do and believe.

TOWARD A UNIVERSAL SYLLABUS OF ERRORS

Given the logic of the declaration's critique, it would have been more forceful had its authors gotten more particular about the errors they have in mind. They should easily have been able to do this. Given the certitude that underlies the declaration and the nearly universal publication of its claims in the world media, there really can be no reason to postpone a global syllabus of errors on the grounds that more research must be done. At the present time we know an enormous amount about each religious tradition. Catholic theologians have known about Islam, for example, for over a thousand years, and Catholic scholars have been studying Hinduism and the religions of China and the Americas for five hundred years. Learned treatises have been written about Native American religions since the seventeenth century. There is already a very adequate body of learning available as a resource for specific and presumably verifiable claims about the truth and error of what other people believe.

It is not satisfactory that the Congregation should simply restate settled truths and affirm that the traditions are gravely deficient, while leaving the discovery of actual errors to others. After all, the latter task is harder than the former, and more dangerous, since it involves theologians in the task of studying traditions carefully and learning about and from them and then devising a workable language to express their findings. Inevitably, positive claims and genuine respect creep in, as theologians discover acutely intelligent, highly moral, deeply theological, and profoundly spiritual dimensions in the traditions being dissected in order to uncover their errors and deficiencies. Some positive or negative conclusions drawn by these scholars may invite specific criticisms from learned scholars and from theologians within those other traditions themselves. Other conclusions, nuanced or even positive, will annoy those who have never studied the traditions and have no sympathy for scholars who would understand them in reasonable detail before judging them. Better to have the Congregation involve itself in this more difficult and subtle work of studying other religious traditions instead of leaving it to experts.

It would be interesting, for instance, to invite the authors of the declaration to read Ramanuja's treatise on the meaning of sacred scripture, the *Vedarthasamgraha,* or his commentary on the *Bhagavad Gita,* both of which are readily available today in English and other global languages. It would be very instructive to hear what they have to say about particular texts such as these, how they identify erroneous concepts and statements within them, and how they respond to reactions from scholars and theologians within Ramanuja's tradition. If they cannot do this, they may end up in the odd position of being like those relativists who are similarly unwilling to argue the truth of their positions with informed representatives of opposing viewpoints.

A MOST UNUSUAL DIALOGUE

It is legitimate to wonder about the practicality of the dialogue that is to be carried on according to the declaration, and here too we must hope for more guidance from the authors of the declaration. As I have already mentioned, the declaration certainly does reaffirm the value of a dialogue carried forward with understanding and respect. Near its end, though, the declaration adds another dimension: "*Equality,* which is a presupposition of inter-religious dialogue, refers to the equal personal dignity of the parties in dialogue, not to doctrinal content, nor even less to the position of Jesus Christ—who is God himself made man—in relation to the founders of the other religions" (§22). Here too the key underlying point is appropriate. Uncritical dialogue is not helpful and one must not dishonor one's own beliefs in order to honor those of another. There is no reason for Catholics to become diffident or halting in their confession of the Lordship of Jesus. In my own experience of dialogue, a strong and deep devotion to the truth of one's own faith is not an obstacle to encounter or to sharing with people possessed of similarly deep and intense faith commitments. It is only when faith is obscured by the belief that nothing of importance can be learned from anyone other than people just like oneself that dialogue becomes impossible and the integrity of faith diminished.

According to the declaration, dialogue should proceed according to a distinctive pattern. Proper dialogue will be urgent, equipped with features such as mutuality, reciprocity, a recognition of the dignity of all the individual participants. At the same time, the mentality of the Catholic participants in the dialogue—usually the hosts—must also be reinforced with a determination to respect neither the doctrinal content nor the founders of the other religions; Catholic participants in dialogue will also move forward with an assured and incontestable foreknowledge that every other religion represented in the dialogue is deeply and irremediably defective.

It is not entirely clear how this kind of dialogue can be fruitful, and the Congregation itself needs to give us some good examples of successful dialogue along these lines. Potential dialogue partners will probably have already read *Dominus Iesus* when they come for dialogue; I certainly will make sure that anyone I invite to a dialogue has had a chance to read it beforehand, lest they confuse my own attitude with the official position of the Roman Catholic Church. Attentive members of other religious traditions will be a tough audience to please or intimidate. Centuries of missionary work have not convinced them that their souls are in peril; innumerable Bible translations and Christian publications have not persuaded them to abandon the sacred texts of their traditions. They may be amused or upset by the declaration's characterization of their traditions as gravely deficient, but they will probably not be swayed by its claim to authority, since they have no reason to revere the Congregation as an unquestionable authority on religious matters. Even well-disposed members of other traditions will want to know whether there are still good reasons—for them, regardless of the reasons Catholics might have—why they should agree to participate in dialogues pursued according to the declaration.

It is imperative that the Congregation itself—not theologians who did not write the document, nor officials in other Vatican offices who might well have written it quite differently—speak directly to the people of other religious traditions, explain things to them in a convincing fashion, and engage them in an honest back-and-forth conversation where authors of the declaration show themselves willing to listen. Otherwise, the declaration might appear persuasive and beyond criticism only when buttressed by the disciplinary authority of the Congregation.

Those of us who are Catholic are in the meantime justified in holding back, until the Congregation shows us how this new dialogue is to work in practice. Since the declaration reminds us too that dialogue is "part of the Church's evangelizing mission" (§2), our understanding of the practice of evangelization in relation to dialogue will also be incomplete until we can observe the authors of the declaration engaged in dialogue, at least with people of other religious traditions. Were theologians to venture where the authors of the declaration themselves have not yet trod, they might well be rebuked for going too far in attempting to explain in a satisfactory fashion the positions proposed in the declaration.

A MATTER OF WILL, AND OF HEART AND MIND

In the preceding pages I have stressed the possibilities and challenges that arise when other traditions are studied in their particularity instead of being grouped together as "the religions." I have referred to the Hindu tradition of devotion to Lord Narayana, in the theology of Ramanuja, but innumerable other examples might have been brought to the fore as well. When the discussion remains abstract, one either remains uselessly vague or gets caught in intellectual relativism or arrogance, both of which render religious learning almost impossible. Once we get particular and learn people's beliefs and practices and theologies, progress can be made and Christian beliefs and practices and theologies put forward even more strongly.

A person who is, or by God's grace seeks to be, entirely committed to Christ, is also a person willing to take other religious traditions seriously, listening with a critical but deeply open mind to what people in that tradition have said. Then the dynamic of encounter with other religious traditions and the people in those traditions comes to life in a deeply creative and deeply religious way, as the firmest of faith convictions is toughened by the most resolute determination to listen and learn.

ON THE EDGE

I have been carefully but honestly ambivalent in the preceding paragraphs. Much in the declaration makes immediate sense to me. Its intense focus on Jesus of Nazareth as the Son of God and Savior seems very important, very beautiful, very true. I appreciate the document, respect its authority, take to heart its admonitions. But I also know that it is not enough. I have also been visiting India and studying the Hindu religious traditions for over twenty-five years; it is my form of obedience to Christ, one might say. I am disappointed that the declaration remains incomplete while yet giving little indication of how anything learned in study and dialogue might be permitted to contribute to the completion of what it does say.

More will indeed be said, since we are only at the beginning of the millennium of dialogue. Pope John Paul II was a prophet when he said, in India in 1986, "By dialogue, we let God be present in our midst, for as we open ourselves in dialogue to one another, we also open ourselves to God."[10] It may take us much of the new millennium to understand how it is that in dialogue we are opening ourselves to God. Surely, we must continue to see other religious traditions in the light of Jesus of Nazareth, but when we do, we will also be learning to see him newly radiant in the light of those other traditions. Learning from other religions does not change the timeless truths of our faith, but it certainly does transform, enrich, and deepen our way of following Jesus. It drives out not only relativism and indifferentism but also arrogance and ignorance. As far as I can see, it is God who desires dialogue among people of faith; it is God who is not offended by our stumbling, imperfect efforts to include every particular religious idea and image and practice within the love of Christ; and it is God who will leave us restless and unsatisfied until we succeed in finding the Lord Jesus present, everywhere.

12

A TIMELY REAFFIRMATION
AND CLARIFICATION OF VATICAN II[1]

Anthony A. Akinwale, O.P.

The publication on August 6, 2000 of the declaration *Dominus Iesus* by the Vatican Congregation for the Doctrine of the Faith generated a lot of heat. Two highly contested statements of the declaration are discernible. According to the first, "ecclesial communities which have not preserved the valid Episcopate and the genuine and integral substance of the Eucharistic mystery, are not Churches in the proper sense" (§17). And, according to the second, "If it is true that the followers of other religions can receive divine grace, it is also certain that *objectively speaking* they are in a gravely deficient situation in comparison with those who, in the Church, have the fullness of the means of salvation" (§22). While the first statement is interpreted as putting down other churches and ecclesial communities, the second is interpreted as denigrating non-Christian religious traditions. To judge by most comments made in some sections of the print and electronic media, the impression is registered that the fundamental thrust of the declaration represents what has often been referred to as a "restorationist agenda" and an antithesis of the openness demonstrated by the church at the Second Vatican Council. Using this as premise, the inference is drawn by some critics that the declaration is an untimely setback for ecumenical initiative and inter-religious dialogue.

My aim in this short essay is to attempt to demonstrate that both the premise and the conclusion drawn from it misrepresent the purpose, the functional specialty, and the contents of the declaration. Rather than seeing the declaration as a contradiction of Vatican II and an obstacle to ecumenical and inter-religious dialogue, it is my contention that a careful reading of *Dominus Iesus* reveals that it is consistent with the Vatican II understanding of the church's nature, identity, and mission. Such careful reading requires at least a liberal formation in theology and in the history of Catholic doctrines. Such formation and such reading can hardly be found among the most respected journalists in the secular and even in the Catholic media. Consequently, whoever substitutes personal reading of the declaration with journalistic commentary does so at his or her own risk.

But of greater importance than my aim is the aim of the declaration itself. This purpose can be better apprehended and appreciated when one apprehends and appreciates Bernard Lonergan's distinction between the aim of the functional specialty of "doctrines," which is the statement of doctrine; and that of the functional specialty of systematics, which is the explication of doctrine. In this respect, the purpose of *Dominus Iesus,* and this must not be overlooked, is more doctrinal than systematic. The words of the declaration are instructive here. The purpose of *Dominus Iesus*

> is not to treat in a systematic manner the question of the unicity and
> salvific universality of the mystery of Jesus Christ and the Church, nor
> to propose solutions to questions that are matters of free theological
> debate, but rather to set forth again the doctrine of the Catholic faith
> in these areas, pointing out some fundamental questions that remain
> open to further development, and refuting specific positions that are
> erroneous or ambiguous (§3).

These words clearly point out that the purpose of *Dominus Iesus* is more doctrinal than systematic. As such, the declaration does not propose any new doctrine. The doctrines it sets forth have been taught in previous documents of the church's magisterium, and these are being proposed to reiterate certain truths that are part of the church's faith.

It is my contention that when the declaration is subjected to careful scrutiny, the teachings of the Second Vatican Council will be seen to be largely represented in the sources cited by the writers of the declaration. Consequently, whether or not it will aid or hinder ecumenical and inter-religious dialogue is not an issue that will be determined by the positions taken in the declaration as such. Rather, it is an issue that will be determined by two factors: first, whether *Dominus Iesus* represents or misrepresents the doctrinal propositions of Vatican II, and, second, whether Vatican II itself represents an aid or an obstacle to ecumenical and inter-religious dialogue. If it can be shown that the document is a reaffirmation and not a repudiation of Vatican II, and if it is accepted that Vatican II opens up the path of ecumenical and inter-religious dialogue—a position which, to the best of my knowledge, remains largely accepted more than three decades after the conclusion of the Council—then the prognostic can be reasonably made that the future of and the desire for Christian unity, as well as the future of and the desire for harmony among adherents of the different religions of the world, will be determined not by the doctrinal positions of *Dominus Iesus* but by its interpretation and or misinterpretation.

The English title of the declaration, "On the Unicity and Salvific Universality of Jesus Christ and the Church," is indicative of the two fundamental preoccupations of the document. The issues here are what the church says of herself in relation to other churches and ecclesial communities, and what the church says of her Lord. The hermeneutical principle which is *conditio sine qua non* for a fair and accurate reading of the document is such that what is said of the church is derived from what is said of Christ. Ecclesiology is presented as a derivative of Christology, and a further examination of this Christological presupposition of the document shows its inseparable link with an underlying theology of revelation. This presents anyone who desires a careful commentary on the declaration with three layers of reading: a theology of revelation, a Christology, and an ecclesiology. While Vatican II proposes a theology of revelation and an ecclesiology, the council does not devote any document to Christology. Instead, the Christology of the ecumenical councils of Nicaea, Constantinople, Ephesus, and Chalcedon are taken for granted. However, in the course of setting forth its doctrine on divine revelation, the Second Vatican Council makes its Christological positions known. I shall first examine the Christological presuppositions of the document, that is, in its relationship with the underlying theology of revelation; then I shall present the position of the declaration on the church's self-understanding as a reaffirmation of the major ecclesiological insights of Vatican II.

REVELATION AND CORRESPONDING
CHRISTOLOGICAL PRESUPPOSITIONS

The underlying theology of revelation of *Dominus Iesus* is a reaffirmation of the theology of revelation of Vatican II's *Dei verbum.* According to *Dei verbum,* "By this revelation then, the deepest truth about God and the salvation of man shines forth in Christ, who is at the same time the mediator and the fullness of all revelation."[2] The same *Dei verbum* goes on to assert, in a statement reaffirmed in *Dominus Iesus,* that, given the fullness of revelation in Christ,

> The Christian dispensation, therefore, as the new and definitive covenant, will never pass away, and we now await no further new public revelation before the glorious manifestation of our Lord Jesus Christ (cf. 1 Tim 6:14 and Tit 2:13).[3]

Through the instrumentality of his humanity—that is through his words, deeds, and entire history—Jesus fully and definitively reveals God's salvific ways because his person is the divine Person of the Incarnate Word who is "true God and true man."[4]

This has a consequence for the life of faith of the Christian, a consequence of which *Dominus Iesus* reminds its readers by taking its inspiration from the Second Vatican Council. According to the theology of revelation of Vatican II, the fullness of revelation in Jesus Christ demands an obedience of faith in which the human creature is to fully submit his intellect and will to God.[5]

The declaration goes on to distinguish between theological faith and belief in the other religions. According to this distinction, theological faith, which is the acceptance in grace of the truth revealed by the One and Triune God, is not identical with belief in other religions, which is religious experience in the form of the human quest for the Absolute.[6] Disregard for this distinction leads to the reduction and even disappearance of the differences between Christianity and other religions.

In discussing the theology of revelation of Vatican II, or any theology of Christian revelation for that matter, one has to contend with the sacred writings of other religions. In this connection, *Dominus Iesus* does not propose any new doctrine. While it recognizes that "there are some elements in these texts which may be *de facto* instruments by which countless people throughout the centuries have been and still are able today to nourish and maintain their life-relationship with God," the declaration also recognizes that church tradition "reserves the designation of *inspired texts* to the canonical books of the Old and New Testaments, since these are inspired by the Holy Spirit."[7] In a nutshell, while the ongoing tradition of the church does not deny that they are *sacred* texts, it explicitly denies that they are *inspired* texts. *Dominus Iesus* sees the spiritual riches of these sacred texts of other religions as ways by which God makes himself present in many ways to individuals and to entire peoples, "even when they contain gaps, insufficiencies and errors," and as receiving their elements of goodness and grace from the mystery of Christ.[8]

The doctrine of the fullness of revelation in Christ and the doctrine of the unicity and universality of the salvific mystery of Jesus Christ provide mutual support for each other. To affirm the fullness of revelation in Jesus is to affirm his unicity and uniqueness, and to affirm his unicity and uniqueness is to affirm that there is fullness of revelation in him. He is unique because "no one knows the Father except the Son and whosoever the Son chooses to reveal him" (Mt 11:27). And he is unique because "no one has seen God ... and he alone has revealed him" (Jn 1:18). Since he reveals the Father in a way no one ever did, and since this revelation is for salvation, he is the Savior of the world. There is salvation in no one else.

The doctrine of the fullness and definitive character of the revelation of God in the person of Jesus can be seen as preparing the ground for the declaration's restatement of the Christological doctrines of Nicaea and Chalcedon. Jesus is able to reveal the Father in such fullness because he is one with the Father. To use the creedal definition of Nicaea, he is

> the Son of God, the only begotten generated from the Father, that is, from the being of the Father, God from God, Light from Light, true God from true God, begotten, not made, one in being with the Father...

And using the creedal statement of Chalcedon he is

> the one and the same Son, our Lord Jesus Christ, the same perfect in divinity and perfect in humanity, the same truly God and truly man ... one in being with the Father according to the divinity and one in being with us according to the humanity..., begotten of the Father before the ages according to the divinity and, in these last days, for us and our salvation, of Mary, the Virgin Mother of God, according to the humanity.

It is important to see what is at stake here. *Dominus Iesus,* following Vatican II's *Dei verbum,* affirms that the fullness of revelation is in Jesus. The affirmation of this theology of revelation goes together with the Christology of Nicaea's affirmation of the divinity of Christ, and this affirmation is reappropriated by *Dominus Iesus.* Subsequent to this Christological doctrine of Nicaea is the Chalcedonian Christological doctrine of one Person in two natures. The teaching of Vatican II on the fullness of revelation in Jesus is contradicted by the consideration of Jesus as a particular, "finite, historical figure, who reveals the divine not in an exclusive way, but in a way complementary with other revelatory and salvific figures," in which case Jesus would be one medium of divine revelation among many other media. Such a position, which is common in much of contemporary theology, is considered by *Dominus Iesus* to be "in profound conflict with the Christian faith." The corollary of this contradiction of Christian faith is the neo-Arian position which contradicts the doctrine of Nicaea by denying the divinity of Christ. Again, this is not uncommon in contemporary theology. The separation of the Word from Jesus Christ, another common feature of contemporary Christology, would introduce or reintroduce the Nestorian two-person Christology repudiated by Chalcedon. Against this, *Dominus Iesus* quotes John Paul II's *Redemptoris missio:*

> To introduce any sort of separation between the Word and Jesus Christ is contrary to the Christian faith...Jesus is the Incarnate Word—a single and indivisible person...Christ is none other than Jesus of Nazareth; he is the Word of God made man for the salvation of all ...In the process of discovering and appreciating the manifold gifts—especially the spiritual treasures—that God has bestowed on every people, we cannot separate those gifts from Jesus Christ, who is at the center of God's plan of salvation.[9]

By virtue of the Incarnation, the action of the Word as such cannot be separated from the action of the Word made man without compromising the Christian faith. The operations of the two natures are the operations of one subject, the single person of the Word, in communion with his Spirit. The unicity and salvific universality of the mystery of Christ in one salvific economy of the One and Triune God is expressed in the words of Paul to the Corinthians: "Indeed, even though there may be so-called gods in heaven or on earth—as in fact there are many gods and many lords—yet for us there is one God, the Father, from whom are all things and for whom we exist, and one Lord, Jesus Christ, through whom are all things and through whom we exist" (1 Cor 8:5-6). In the first letter to Timothy, the sole mediation of Christ is taught: "God desires all men to be saved and to come to the knowledge of truth. For there is one God; there is also one mediator between God and men, the man Jesus Christ, who gave himself as a ransom for all" (1 Tim 2:4-6).

In all this, it is clearly evident that the theology of revelation of Vatican II is the starting point and guiding principle of the Christological positions of

Dominus Iesus, Christological positions which are not new, insofar as they simply repeat Nicaea and Chalcedon. The church recognizes her faith in the creedal statements of the Councils and therefore considers any contradiction of these creedal statements to be "in profound conflict" with her faith.

FROM CHRISTOLOGY TO ECCLESIOLOGY

Let us return to the two statements to which I referred at the beginning of this essay: that "ecclesial communities which have not preserved the valid Episcopate and the genuine and integral substance of the Eucharistic mystery, are not Churches in the proper sense" (§17); and "If it is true that the followers of other religions can receive divine grace, it is also certain that *objectively speaking* they are in a gravely deficient situation in comparison with those who, in the Church, have the fullness of the means of salvation"(§22). The first statement is in the realm of the church's self-understanding, while the second is in the realm of inter-religious dialogue. If I have devoted so much attention to Christology in the previous part of the essay it is because these statements are to be seen in the light of this theology of revelation and its corresponding Christology. I shall first examine the ecclesiological statement.

"Not Churches in the proper sense"

The first statement is a consequence of adherence to the Christology of Chalcedon. What the authors of *Dominus Iesus* have done in making this statement is to move from the Christological doctrine of the unicity of Christ, as put forward by Chalcedon, to the doctrine of the unicity and unity of the church. In concrete terms, given the teaching that Christ himself is one person and not two—a teaching which the Council of Chalcedon laid down against the two-person Christology of Nestorius—the church, which is his body, can only be one, not two, and subsists in the Catholic Church. This foundation of the assertion of the unicity and uniqueness of the church of Christ in the unicity and uniqueness of Christ has a patristic inspiration which should not escape our attention.

Cyprian of Carthage, in reaction to the Aquarii who taught that water alone sufficed for the eucharistic sacrifice, explained the symbolism of the mingling of wine and water in the eucharistic cup in a way that emphasizes the mystical union of the church of Christ with Christ himself:

> By water is meant God's people, whereas Scripture reveals that by wine is signified the blood of Christ. When, therefore, water is mixed with wine in the cup, the people are made one with Christ and the multitude of believers are bonded and united with Him in whom they have come to believe. And this bonding and union between water and wine in the Lord's cup is achieved in such a way that nothing can thereafter separate their intermingling. Thus there is nothing that can separate the

union between Christ and the Church, that is, the people who are established within the Church and who steadfastly and faithfully perse-
vere in their beliefs: Christ and his Church must remain ever attached
and joined to each other by indissoluble love.

Hence, when we consecrate the cup of the Lord, water alone cannot
be offered, no more than can wine alone. For should anyone offer up
only wine, then the blood of Christ will be there, but without us, whereas
if there is only water, the people will be there, but without Christ. So it
is only when both are mingled, bonded, united, and fused one with the
other that this spiritual and divine mystery is accomplished.[10]

As Tillard pointed out, from Cyprian, Augustine, John Chrysostom, Cyril of
Alexandria, to name but these, we learn that the personal body of Christ is
joined to the ecclesial body of Christ by the eucharistic body.[11] *Dominus Iesus,*
drawing inspiration from this patristic symbolism, affirms that the oneness of
the personal body implies the oneness of the ecclesial body. But this was not
original to *Dominus Iesus,* since the declaration was not the first magisterial
pronouncement on this issue. This teaching is contained in the ecclesiology of
the Second Vatican Council which is largely a patristic ecclesiology. The words
of the Council deserve to be quoted here:

This is the sole Church of Christ which in the Creed we profess to be
one, holy, catholic and apostolic, which our Savior, after his resurrection, entrusted to Peter's pastoral care (Jn 21:17), commissioning him
and the other apostles to extend and rule it, and which he raised up for
all ages as "the pillar and mainstay of the truth" (1 Tim 3:15). This
Church, constituted and organized as a society in the present world,
subsists in the Catholic Church, which is governed by the successor of
Peter and by the bishops in communion with him. Nevertheless, many
elements of sanctification and of truth are found outside its visible
confines. Since these are gifts belonging to the Church of Christ, they
are forces impelling towards Catholic unity.[12]

Concerning these words of Vatican II, *Dominus Iesus* is not just reaffirming but
also clarifying the Council. According to this clarifying statement:

With the expression *subsistit in,* the Second Vatican Council sought to
harmonize two doctrinal statements: on the one hand, that the Church
of Christ, despite the divisions which exist among Christians, continues
to exist fully only in the Catholic Church, and on the other hand, that
"outside of her structure, many elements can be found of sanctification
and truth," that is, in those Churches and ecclesial communities which
are not yet in full communion with the Catholic Church. But with respect to these, it needs to be stated that "they derive their efficacy from
the very fullness of grace and truth entrusted to the Catholic Church.[13]

But the position that the church of Christ, like Christ, is one and not two, and that this one church subsists in the Catholic Church necessitates a statement on the status of other Christian communities. Here, again like the Second Vatican Council, *Dominus Iesus* makes a distinction between a church and what Vatican II calls an "ecclesial community." A simple but not simplistic way of understanding this distinction is to bear in mind that while every church is a community of Christians, not every community of Christians is a church. There is a theological distinction to be made between a church and a Christian community. And what distinguishes a church from a mere community or assembly of Christians can be traced to the description of *the authentic Pentecostal church* in Acts 2:42: "they [the earliest Christians] remained steadfast in the teaching of the apostles and in communion, and in the breaking of bread and in prayer."

Three elements are discernible in the common life described here: apostolic teaching, the breaking of bread, and prayer. While the third, prayer, can be taken for granted, it is not always the case that the first two can be found in every assembly of Christians today. For today, especially in our Nigerian society, noted for the proliferation of places of worship, there are fissiparous Christian communities where a valid episcopate and the Eucharist are lacking. That a church, in a proper sense, must have these three characteristics is attested to in patristic ecclesiology for which where the bishop is there the church is, and for which the Eucharist makes the church and the church makes the Eucharist. Fathers like Ignatius of Antioch, Cyprian of Carthage, and Augustine of Hippo have a lot to teach us in this regard. It is my contention that *Dominus Iesus* was following them and Vatican II when it declared that: "ecclesial communities which have not preserved the valid Episcopate and the genuine and integral substance of the Eucharistic mystery, are not Churches in the proper sense."

With that, we have thus come from the one-Person Christology of Chalcedon to the unicity and uniqueness of the church of Christ, from the unicity and uniqueness of the church of Christ to the affirmation that this one church of Christ subsists in the Catholic Church, and from the subsistence of the one church of Christ in the Catholic Church to the use of the criteria set out in Acts 2:42 and in patristic ecclesiology in declaring the deficiency of ecclesial communities which preserve neither a valid episcopate nor the genuine and integral substance of the eucharistic mystery. To say that they are not churches "in the proper sense" is not to deny that there is a sense in which they can be called churches. The document does not say they cannot be called churches, but that they cannot be called churches "in the proper sense," and the proper sense here must include the ecclesial characteristics described in Acts 2:42. When, out of ecumenical sensitivity, they are called churches, the proper sense of "church" should be borne in mind. There is no church without a valid episcopate. Nor is there a church where there is no Eucharist. Nonetheless, consistent with the awareness and recognition of many elements of sanctification in such ecclesial communities, *Dominus Iesus* states, following the inspiration of Vatican II, that those who are baptized in these communities are, by Baptism, incorporated in Christ and thus are in a certain communion, albeit imperfect, with the Church. Baptism in fact tends per se toward the full development of life in Christ, through the integral profession of faith, the Eucharist, and full communion in the Church.[14]

"A gravely deficient situation"

The position of *Dominus Iesus,* according to which even though followers of other religions can receive grace they are *objectively speaking* in a gravely deficient situation, is to be seen against the background of the words of the Nicaean-Constantinopolitan Creed. In those words, the church professes faith in Jesus Christ, "God from God, Light from Light, true God from true God, begotten not made, one in substance with the Father." Again, the movement of the discourse is from Christology to other religions in relation to salvation as *Dominus Iesus* finds support in the teaching of the Second Vatican Council. Before the declaration, Vatican II had already affirmed that

> the Church, a pilgrim now on earth, is necessary for salvation: the one Christ is the mediator and the way of salvation; he is present to us in his body which is the Church. He himself explicitly asserted the necessity of faith and baptism (cf. Mk 16:16; Jn 3:5), and thereby affirmed at the same time the necessity of the Church which men enter through baptism as through a door.[15]

Since Christ is the one Mediator who is indispensable for salvation, the church that is mysteriously united to him has, in God's plan, an indispensable relationship with the salvation of every human being.[16] In this regard, the declaration, echoing Pope John Paul II, introduces a distinction between a mysterious relationship and a formal relationship. Going by this distinction, a human being may be related to Christ and the church in a way that we cannot objectively grasp. Such a human being does not have a formal relationship with Christ and the church but has a mysterious relationship. This is possible by virtue of a salvific grace which God bestows on such persons "in ways known to himself."[17] The grace that makes this possible comes from Christ's sacrifice on the cross and is communicated by the Holy Spirit.

The statement that followers of other religions are, objectively speaking, in a gravely deficient situation is made in comparison to those who are in a formal relationship with Christ by way of a formal relationship with the church. The absence of this formal relationship is not necessarily the absence of any relationship. Since what is being asserted is not the total absence of any relationship but the absence of a formal relationship, the followers of other religions are possible recipients of grace. But in the absence of a formal relationship with Christ, who alone is the Mediator because he is true God and true man, as we learn from the New Testament and from the ongoing magisterium of the church, *Dominus Iesus* affirms that adherents of other religions are in a gravely deficient situation.

CONCLUSION

In this essay, I set out to refute the claim that *Dominus Iesus* is doctrinally antithetical to the Second Vatican Council. This premise of doctrinal antithesis is used to draw the conclusion that *Dominus Iesus* is equally a contradiction of ecumenical initiative and inter-religious dialogue. It is my contention that *Dominus Iesus* reaffirms and clarifies the teachings of Vatican II and of other magisterial pronouncements of the church. The theology of revelation of the Second Vatican Council is used together with the Christological doctrines of Nicaea and Chalcedon as the basis of the position taken on the relationship between the Catholic Church and other churches and ecclesial communities, and between that church and non-Christian religions.

The issue here is not whether non-Catholics and non-Christians can attain salvation. That they can be saved is taken for granted. How or how not to say it in a way that is consistent with the faith of the church is the bone of contention. The purpose of the declaration is not to denigrate other ecclesial communities or religious traditions. Rather, this declaration is directed primarily at theologians whose task of searching for a better understanding of faith, of God's salvific plan and the way it is accomplished, needs to be encouraged (see §21). This task cannot be accomplished by espousing the self-refuting thesis of religious relativism according to which all religions are relative since there are no more absolutes.

REFERENCES

1. INTRODUCTION AND ECCLESIOLOGICAL ISSUES

1. See, for instance, the decree for the Jacobites of the Council of Florence (1452) which states: "[The holy Roman Church]...firmly believes, professes and preaches that no one outside the Catholic Church, neither pagans nor Jews nor heretics nor schismatics, can become partakers of eternal life, but they will go to the eternal fire prepared for the devil and his angels, unless before the end of their life they are joined to it" (DS 1351).

2. Pius XII, *Mystici Corporis:* DS 3821; Letter of the Holy Office to Archbishop Cushing, DS 3866-3873.

3. LG 14-16. Translations of Vatican II documents are from *The Documents of Vatican II,* ed. Walter M. Abbott, S.J. (New York: America Press, 1966).

4. LG 16.

5. LG 48; GS 45; AG 1.

6. LG 9.

7. RM 10.

8. Jacques Dupuis, S.J., insists that the mediation of the church in the strict, theological sense, has to be understood as instrumental efficient causality. See his work, *Toward a Christian Theology of Religious Pluralism* (Maryknoll, N.Y.: Orbis Books, 1997) 350. For this reason he denies the church's mediation in the salvation of those whom it does not reach with its ministry of word and sacrament.

9. See my book *Salvation Outside the Church?* (New York/Mahwah: Paulist Press, 1992) 158-160.

10. LG 8.

11. London: SCM Press, 1985.

12. This is quoted in footnote no. 56 of *Dominus Iesus.*

13. *One in Christ* 22 (1986) 115-123.

14. UR 22.

15. *Acta Synodalia Concilii Vaticani Secundi* III/2, 335.

16. LG 23.

17. Apostolic Letter *Orientale lumen,* 20: *Origins* 15/1 (May 18, 1995) 10.

18. *Acta Synodalia Concilii Vaticani Secundi* III/2, 335.

19. UUS 11: *Origins* 25/4 (June 8, 1995) 53.

2. A RAHNERIAN RESPONSE

1. Leonardo Boff's and Robert Kaiser's infelicitous responses to the declaration (to give but two examples) prompted me to remark that it used to be said that there is no salvation outside the Catholic Church; now there is no salvation in the church.

2. The negative way demands the abandonment of all concepts, thoughts, images, and symbols—even and especially those of God. God is thereby experienced and known only through unknowing, darkness, and negation. God is not this, not that. The person

of Jesus Christ in such mysticisms is usually absent and his role ambiguous. See my "Negative Way," *The New Dictionary of Catholic Spirituality,* ed. Michael Downey (Collegeville, Minn.: The Liturgical Press, 1993) 700-704.

3. Trans. George E. Ganss, S.J. (St. Louis: The Institute of Jesuit Sources, 1992) §22.

4. Trans. William V. Dych (New York: The Crossroad Publishing Co., 1978).

5. For examples of Rahner's uncompromising Christocentrism, see the two sections in *Foundations* on "The History of Salvation and Revelation" and "The One Christ and the Universality of Salvation," 128-321; "One Mediator and Many Mediations," *Theological Investigations IX,* trans. Graham Harrison (New York: Herder and Herder, 1972) 169-184; "The One Christ and the Universality of Salvation," *Theological Investigations XVI,* trans. David Moreland, O.S.B. (New York: The Seabury Press, 1979) 199-224.

6. *Faith in a Wintry Season* (New York: The Crossroad Publishing Co., 1990) 177.

7. Only a few months before his death, Rahner said in an interview: "That idle chatter 'why do I still stay in the Church?' turns my stomach." See his *Bekenntnisse: Rückblick auf 80 Jahre,* ed. Georg Sporschill, S.J. (Munich: Herold Druck, 1984) 44, my translation.

8. Co-authored with Heinrich Fries, trans. Ruth C. L. Gritsch and Eric W. Gritsch (Philadelphia: Fortress Press, 1985).

9. *Prayers for a Lifetime* (New York: The Crossroad Publishing Co., 1984) 163-165.

10. *Theological Investigations XVIII,* trans. Edward Quinn (New York: The Crossroad Publishing Company, 1983) 288-295.

11. Co-authored with Herbert Vorgrimler, *Dictionary of Theology,* 2nd edition (New York: The Crossroad Publishing Co., 1981) 163-164.

12. My colleague Francis A. Sullivan alerted me to the problem of translating the Italian word *deficitaria* as deficient. "Disadvantage" is, perhaps, a better rendering.

13. See Gavin D'Costa *The Meeting of Religions and the Trinity* (Maryknoll, N.Y.: Orbis Books, 2000) for an excellent debunking of the pluralist proposal, which he refers to as "veiled exclusivism." Also see, Gavin D'Costa, ed., *Christian Uniqueness Reconsidered: The Myth of a Pluralistic Theology of Religions* (New York: Orbis Books, 1990). The subtitle says it all.

14. *Foundations of Christian Faith,* 321.

15. DV 16. Translation from *The Documents of Vatican II,* ed. Walter M. Abbott, S.J. (New York: America Press, 1966).

16. Rahner would not deny that these rites and rituals might also be expressions of metaphysical aberrations, superstition, error, and depravity.

17. "Aspects of European Theology," *Theological Investigations XXI,* trans. Hugh M. Riley (New York: The Crossroad Publishing Co., 1988) 97-98. Translation emended.

18. *Karl Rahner in Dialogue,* ed. Hubert Biallowons, Harvey Egan, and Paul Imhof (New York: The Crossroad Publishing Co., 1986) 196.

19. "Thomas Aquinas: Patron of Theological Studies," *The Great Church Year: The Best of Karl Rahner's Homilies, Sermons, and Meditations,* ed. Albert Raffelt and Harvey D. Egan, S.J. (New York: The Crossroad Publishing Co., 1993) 313.

3. A PROTESTANT REFLECTION ON ECUMENISM
AND INTERFAITH ISSUES

1. Lutheran and Reformed Churches in the U.S. (the Evangelical Lutheran Church in America, the Presbyterian Church [U.S.A.], the Reformed Church in America, and the United Church of Christ) have entered full communion on the basis of "A Formula of

Agreement." The Evangelical Lutheran Church in America has also entered a full communion relationship with the Episcopal Church through a "Concordat of Agreement." These can be accessed at the Evangelical Lutheran Church in America's home page (www.elca.org).

2. Michael Kinnamon and Brian E. Cope, eds., *The Ecumenical Movement: An Anthology of Key Texts and Voices* (Geneva: World Council of Churches, 1997) 467.

3. *Baptism, Eucharist and Ministry* (Geneva: World Council of Churches, 1982) was the fruit of a study process over some thirty years. A formal study process on common confession of the apostolic faith, focused on the Nicene-Constantinopolitan creed, started later and has produced a preliminary text, *Confessing the One Faith* (Geneva: World Council of Churches, 1991).

4. See, for instance, *The Nature and Purpose of the Church* (Geneva: World Council of Churches, 1998) and Alan Falconer, ed., *Faith and Order in Moshi* (Geneva: World Council of Churches, 1998).

5. Quoted in "Negative Reaction to *Dominus Iesus* Continues," *America*, October 7, 2000, p. 5.

6. Gavin D'Costa, *The Meeting of Religions and the Trinity* (Maryknoll, N.Y.: Orbis Books, 2000).

7. D'Costa, *Meeting,* 83.

8. Philip Kennedy, "Rome & Relativism," *Commonweal*, October 20, 2000, 14-15.

4. NEW TESTAMENT ESCHATOLOGY AND *DOMINUS IESUS*

1. See Pheme Perkins, "Christianity and World Religions: New Testament Questions," *Interpretation* 40 (1986) 367-378.

2. See the exegesis of Rom 1:18-32 and its subsequent history in patristic interpretation by Kathy L. Gaca ("Paul's Uncommon Declaration in Romans 1:18-32 and Its Problematic Legacy for Pagan and Christian Relations," *Harvard Theological Review* 92 [1999] 165-198).

3. *Dominus Iesus* speaks with the voice of a church that can apologize without admitting that it has done real evil to God's people over the centuries in its persecution of Jews. See James Carroll, *Constantine's Sword: The Church and the Jews. A History* (Boston: Houghton Mifflin, 2001).

4. William L. Lane, *Hebrews 9–13* (Word Biblical Commentary; Dallas: Word, 1991) 235-252; Harold Attridge, *Hebrews* (Philadelphia: Fortress, 1989) 244-252.

5. Attridge, *Hebrews,* 246.

6. David Lyon, *Jesus in Disneyland: Religion in Postmodern Times* (New York: Polity Press, 2000) 43.

7. Joseph A. Fitzmyer, *The Gospel According to Luke (I–IX)* (Anchor Bible 28; New York: Doubleday, 1981) 359-361. Fitzmyer detects possible allusions to Job 12:19 (also 1 Sam 2:7) and 5:11 in this verse (368). That allusion would confirm our general point that the language of triumphant exaltation is appropriate only from the mouth of the lowly.

8. Lyon, *Jesus in Disneyland,* 145.

9. Among the seminal works in this area of research, see Jonathan L. Reed: "This picture of Galilee fits the world portrayed in the sayings tradition, where concern for sustenance, poverty, and landlessness are dominant. Though the cities are not in any systematic way targeted for criticism, the wealthy are deemed arrogant or idolatrous, and wealth in general scorned as transitory and ephemeral" (*Archaeology and the Galilean*

Jesus: A Re-examination of the Evidence [Harrisburg: Trinity Press International, 2000] 219); also Richard A. Horsley, *Galilee: History, Politics, People* (Harrisburg: Trinity Press International, 1995); Gerd Theissen, *The Gospels in Context: Social and Political History in the Synoptic Tradition* (Minneapolis: Fortress, 1991) and *Social Reality and the Early Christians: Theology, Ethics and the World of the New Testament* (Minneapolis: Fortress, 1992); Wayne A. Meeks, *The First Urban Christians: The Social World of the Apostle Paul* (New Haven: Yale, 1983).

10. See Pheme Perkins, "The Gospel of Mark," in *The New Interpreter's Bible. Volume VIII. General Articles on the New Testament; Matthew; Mark,* ed. Lee Keck (Nashville: Abingdon, 1995) 694.

11. RM 9; *Catechism of the Catholic Church,* 846-847.

12. See Pheme Perkins, *Peter: Apostle for the Whole Church* (Columbia: University of South Carolina, 1994) 177-178.

13. For a discussion of the debate over whether Paul means that at the end-time God will complete the covenant with his people in its original terms or will bring them together with Christians in Christ see Joseph A. Fitzmyer, *Romans* (Anchor Bible 33; New York: Doubleday, 1993) 618-635. We concur with Fitzmyer's view (620) that Paul has some form of salvation "in Christ" in view. Contrary to the doctrinal position taken in *Dominus Iesus,* Paul's example raises the issue of extending this conclusion to other religious traditions. One may continue dialogue, even opening the possibility of conversion to individuals and groups in other religions, without anticipating that prior to the end-time large numbers will be converted to Christ. Fitzmyer's sketch (622-624) of the traditional interpretations of 11:26, "so all Israel shall be saved," highlights the difficulty of appealing to tradition as the norm for exegesis. Patristic exegetes tend to favor reading "Israel" in a spiritual sense, which, as Fitzmyer remarks, "is scarcely correct; it goes against the meaning of *Israel* in the rest of Romans" (624).

14. This question remains debated. For a discussion of the issues which finally decides that Israel remains included see W. D. Davies and Dale Allison, *The Gospel According to Saint Matthew. Volume III. Commentary on Matthew XIX–XXVIII* (International Critical Commentary; Edinburgh: T. & T. Clark, 1997) 682-684.

15. Again, a strong witness against the repeated assertions in *Dominus Iesus* that "obedience of faith" which implies explicit cognitive acceptance of dogmatic propositions about God and faith are what the New Testament authors understand as required for salvation. Of course, Matthew considers belief in Jesus to be God's intended way of salvation. But speaking from the margins to a world which God may bring to an end at any time makes the existence of such "righteous non-believers" a basic fact in every Christian's experience.

16. Which, given the parallel saying in Luke 10:16, was probably the conclusion of the missionary discourse in Q; see Davies and Allison, *The Gospel According to Saint Matthew. Volume II. Commentary on Matthew VIII–XVIII* (International Critical Commentary; Edinburgh: T. & T. Clark, 1991) 225.

17. Davies and Allison avoid concluding that Matthew has adopted this saying from Mark 9:41 as a promise to sympathetic outsiders (a relationship with the "other" which was certainly familiar to first-century diaspora Jews at least). They advance a convoluted argument for the conclusion that those offering aid are Christians who were not called to engage in the mission (*Matthew VIII–XVIII,* 229-230).

18. See Arland J. Hultgren, *The Parables of Jesus: A Commentary* (Grand Rapids: Eerdmans, 2000) 314-316. Hultgren draws the conclusion from this parable in a way that strikes at the heart of Christian claims to monopolize salvation: "Gone is the view here that the only way one can serve Christ (or God) is a prior commitment to him

...The down-to-earth service of the person in need—without any sense of religious obligation or motivation—*that* is service to Christ! Christ's true servants, then, know nothing about him but only seek to serve the neighbor" (326-327).

19. See the discussion of the phrase and its use in tandem with an anathema dividing those who do not love the Lord from those who do in Anthony C. Thiselton, *The First Epistle to the Corinthians* (New International Greek Testament Commentary; Grand Rapids: Eerdmans, 2000) 1347-1352.

20. Also 1 Corinthians 11:23. When Paul does not have such a tradition or saying from the Lord, he is willing to make a determination but suggests a difference in its authority (1 Cor 7:6, 11 and 25 as opposed to the saying of the Lord in v. 10, for example). On the whole question of how Paul uses various authorities in formulating his argument see A. Eriksson, *Traditions as Rhetorical Proof: Pauline Argumentation in 1 Corinthians* (Stockholm: Almqvist & Wiksell, 1998).

21. For instructive suggestions from an exegete on how Paul deals with conscience in this section of 1 Corinthians see Jerome Murphy-O'Connor, "Freedom or the Ghetto (1 Cor VIII:1-13, X:23–XI:1)," *Revue biblique* 85 (1978) 541-574.

22. On the relationship between Paul's labor and his apostolic mission, see Ronald Hock, *The Social Context of Paul's Ministry: Tentmaking and Apostleship* (Philadelphia: Fortress, 1980) 50-68; on the issues of patronage see J. K. Chow, *Patronage and Power* (JSNTSS 75; Sheffield: Sheffield Academic Press, 1992) 106-107.

23. The "woe to me, if I don't preach" refers to a divine requirement which cannot be evaded without danger of divine retribution (Thiselton, *First Corinthians,* 695-696).

24. Thiselton, *First Corinthians,* 697-698.

25. See James D. G. Dunn, *The Epistle to the Colossians and to Philemon* (New International Greek Testament Commentary; Grand Rapids: Eerdmans, 1996) 114-115.

26. A point that Paul presses against the over-realized eschatology in Corinth that denied resurrection of the body in 1 Corinthians 15:27-28, a text which *Dominus Iesus* reads quite against the apostle's meaning as though it demonstrated the truth of the proposition that the "kingdom" is not to be sharply distinguished from the church (§18).

27. Dunn, *Colossians* 116. For first-century examples of the concept that a sum of sufferings is somehow required to "trigger" the end-time, see Revelation 6:9-11; *4 Ezra* 4:33-43.

28. For a discussion of this aspect of Pauline eschatology see James D. G. Dunn, *The Theology of Paul, the Apostle* (Grand Rapids: Eerdmans, 1998) 317-333.

29. See Margaret Thrall, *The Second Epistle to the Corinthians. Volume II: II Corinthians VIII–XIII* (International Critical Commentary; Edinburgh: T. & T. Clark, 2000) 657-666.

30. Thrall provides a concise description of the rhetorical use of *pathos* in this section of the epistle (*2 Corinthians,* 698-699). She points out that the anger which Paul directs at the opposing missionaries is tempered by the apostle's love for the Corinthians themselves. Paul can make that emotional connection with his audience credible by recalling the sufferings he endured as an apostle (2 Cor 11:16-33).

31. For a more detailed discussion of this passage see Pheme Perkins, "Ephesians," in *The New Interpreter's Bible, Volume XI,* ed. Lee Keck (Nashville: Abingdon, 2000) 450-452.

32. David E. Aune, *Revelation 17–22* (Word Biblical Commentary 52C; Nashville: Thomas Nelson, 1998) 1120-1122.

33. Aune, *Revelation 17–22,* 1144-1146.

34. Aune, *Revelation 17–22,* 1146.

35. Aune, *Revelation 17–22,* 1186.

36. Aune, *Revelation 1–5* (WBC 52A; Dallas: Word, 1997) lxiii-lxiv, lxxxvii-lxxxviii, 162-164. False prophets also figure in condemnation of abuses in the churches of Asia Minor as in the attack on a prominent woman teacher and her followers at Thyatira (Rev 2:18-29; Aune, *Revelation 1–5,* 203-206, 214).

37. A conviction that includes demonizing of the Jewish population of cities where tensions existed between Christians and Jews. Only the church can lay claim to be "Israel," God's elect. Such phrases as "synagogue of Satan" and "those who say they are Jews but are not" (Rev 2:9; 3:9) will make a nasty contribution to the history of Christian anti-semitism. When combined with the crusades and millennial expectations in the Middle Ages, this heritage becomes "deadly." Carroll (*Sword,* 255-256) ties this millennialism to Hitler.

5. "THERE'S A WIDENESS IN GOD'S MERCY"

1. *Enchiridion Symbolorum Definitionum de Rebus Fidei et Morum,* ed. Henricus Denzinger, rev. Adolfus Schönmetzer, 32nd ed. (Barcelona, Freiburg, Rome, New York: Herder, 1963) #150, p. 66 (Greek), p. 67 (Latin).

2. Bernard Lonergan, "Christology Today: Methodological Reflections," *A Third Collection: Papers by Bernard Lonergan, S.J.,* ed. Frederick E. Crowe (New York/Mahwah: Paulist Press, 1985) 93.

3. Ben F. Meyer, *The Church in Three Tenses* (Garden City, N.Y.: Doubleday, 1971) 80.

4. See, for example: Ben F. Meyer, *The Church in Three Tenses; Christus Faber: The Master-Builder and the House of God* (Allison Park, Pa.: Pickwick Publications, 1992); E. P. Sanders, *Jesus and Judaism* (Philadelphia: Fortress, 1985); *The Historical Figure of Jesus* (London: Penguin, 1993); N. T. Wright, *Christian Origins of the Question of God,* vol. 1: *The New Testament and the People of God* (London: SPCK, 1992), vol. 2: *Jesus and the Victory of God* (Minneapolis: Fortress, 1996); Francesco Rossi de Gasperis, *Comminciando da Gerosalemme* (Lc 24, 47): *La sorgente della fede e dell'esistenza cristiana* (Edizione Piemme, 1997), together with innumerable pastorally oriented biblical meditations by Carlo Maria Cardinal Martini.

5. Hans Urs von Balthasar, *Razing the Bastions: On the Church in This Age,* trans. Brian McNeil of *Schleifung der Bastionen: Von der Kirche in Dieser Zeit* (1952), with a foreword by Christoph Schönborn, O.P. (San Francisco: Communio Books/Ignatius Books, 1993) 93-94.

6. See Ben F. Meyer, *The Early Christians: Their Mission and Self-Discovery* (Wilmington, Del.: Michael Glazier, 1986); James T. Burtchaell, *From Synagogue to Church: Public Services and Offices in the Earliest Christian Communities* (Cambridge: Cambridge University Press, 1992).

7. LG 17. English translation from *The Documents of Vatican II,* ed. Walter Abbott, S.J. (New York: Guild Press, America Press, Association Press, 1966) 37.

8. See Christopher Dawson, *The Formation of Christendom* (New York: Sheed & Ward, 1967); Hans von Campenhausen, *Ecclesiastical Authority and Spiritual Power in the Church of the First Three Centuries* (London: Black, 1969); Henry Chadwick, *Early Christianity* (Harmondsworth: Penguin, 1993); Peter Brown, *The Rise of Western Christendom: Triumph and Diversity AD 200–1000* (Oxford and New York: Blackwell Publishers, 1997).

9. See Robert Markus, *From Augustine to Gregory the Great* (London: Ashgate Publishing Co., 1983), *The End of Ancient Christianity* (Cambridge: Cambridge Uni-

versity Press, 1990), *Gregory the Great and His World* (Cambridge: Cambridge University Press, 1997); Karl Frederick Morrison, *The Two Kingdoms: Ecclesiology in Carolingian Political Thought* (Princeton, N.J.: Princeton University, 1964).

10. Joseph A. Komonchak, "History and Social Theory in Ecclesiology," in *Foundations in Ecclesiology,* Lonergan Workshop monographs series (Chestnut Hill, Mass.: Lonergan Institute of Boston College, 1995) 9-10.

11. See Yves Congar, *A History of Theology,* trans. H. Guthrie (New York: Doubleday, 1968), *Église de Saint Augustin à l'époque moderne* (Paris: Cerf, 1970); Jean Delumeau, *Catholicism between Luther and Voltaire* (Philadelphia: Westminster Press, 1977); Klaus Schatz, *Papal Primacy from Its Origins to the Present* (Collegeville, Minn.: Liturgical Press, 1996).

12. Hermann J. Pottmeyer, *Towards a Papacy in Communion: Perspectives from Vatican I and Vatican II, Ut Unum Sint: Studies on Papal Primacy* (New York: The Crossroad Publishing Co., 1998).

13. Translated from the German of J. Neuner and H. Roos, *Der Glaube der Kirche in der Urkunden der Lehrverkündigung* (Regensburg, 1965), 225-226: "Die Kirche besitzt alle Eigenschaften einer wahren Gesellschaft... Die Kirche ist nicht Glied oder Teil irgend einer anderen Gesellschaft, mitkeiner anderen irgendwie vermengt. In sich selbst ist sie so vollkommen, daß sie sich von allen menschlichen Gemeinschaften abhebt und weit über sie hinausragt Die Kirche ist in ihrer Verfassung so völlig abgegrenzt und bestimmt, daß keine Gesellschaft, die von der Einheit des Glaubens oder von der Gemeishcaft dieses Leibes getrennt ist, irgenwie Teil oder Glied der Kirche genannt werden könnte. Die Kirche ist auch nicht durch die verschiedenen Gesellschaften, die sich christlich nennen, zerstreut und geteilt; sie ist ganz in sich gesammelt und zur Einheit geschlossen."

14. Bernard Lonergan, *Method in Theology* (New York: Herder & Herder, 1972) 359.

15. Komonchak, "History and Social Theory," 9-10.

16. Franz-Xaver Kaufmann, *Zukunftsfähigkeit: Suchbewegungen im Christentum,* authored with Johann Baptist Metz (Freiburg: Herder, 1987) 34.

17. The comments in Avery Dulles's introduction to the American publication of *Lumen gentium* are to the point here: "Among all the documents of Vatican II, probably none underwent more drastic revision between the first schema and the finally approved text. The successive drafts of the Constitution, compared with one another, strikingly reveal the tremendous development of the Church's self-understanding which resulted from the dialogue within the Council. The original schema, prepared by the Theological Commission before the first session in 1962, resembled the standard treatise on the Church as found, for example, in most of the theological manuals published between the two world wars. Influenced by centuries of anti-Protestant polemics, the writers of this period placed heavy emphasis on the hierarchical and juridical aspects of the Church, including the supremacy of the Pope.

"When the Council Fathers came together, they immediately saw the need of setting forth a radically different vision of the Church, more biblical, more historical, more vital and dynamic."

18. The issue raised here is underscored in the contribution of Francis A. Sullivan to the present collection. Note especially his reference to the contrasting view of John Paul II in *Ut unum sint.*

19. Lonergan, "Aquinas Today: Tradition and Innovation," *A Third Collection* 35-54 at 53.

20. Bernard Lonergan, "The Response of the Jesuit as Priest and Apostle in the Modern World," *A Second Collection,* ed. W. Ryan and B. Tyrrell (Philadelphia: Westminster Press, 1974) 163-187 at 174. The full citation reads: "I am inclined to interpret

the religions of mankind, in their positive moment, as the fruit of the gift of the Spirit, though diversified by the many degrees of social and cultural development, and distorted by man's infidelity to the self-transcendence which is given." See Frederick E. Crowe, "Son and Spirit: Tension in the Divine Missions?" and "Son of God, Holy Spirit, and World Religions" in his *Appropriating the Lonergan Idea,* ed. Michael Vertin (Washington, D.C.: Catholic University of America Press, 1989) 297-314, 324-343.

21. Crowe, "Son and Spirit," 308.

22. The internal quotation is from Lonergan, "Response of the Jesuit," 174, cited by Crowe, "Son and Spirit," 307.

23. Crowe, "Son of God, Holy Spirit, and World Religions," 335.

24. Crowe, "Son and Spirit," 308.

25. Lonergan, "Mission and the Spirit," *A Third Collection* 23-34 at 32.

26. *Summa theologiae* III, q. 3, art. 8.

27. Lonergan, "Response of the Jesuit," 175.

28. Cited by Carlo Maria Martini, *Communicating Christ to the World,* trans. Thomas M. Lucas (Kansas City: Sheed & Ward, 1994) 58.

6. THE REAFFIRMATION OF THE CHRISTIC CENTER

1. Paul Wilkes, "Only Catholics Need Apply," *The Boston Globe,* Focus Section, September 10, 2000. Francis A. Sullivan, S.J., of Boston College, wrote an effective rejoinder to Wilkes's irresponsible charges. It was printed in the "Letters to the Editor" section of *The Boston Globe,* September 12, 2000. But incalculable harm had already been done.

2. The phrase is from a review by Joseph A. Komonchak of a recent book about Cardinal Joseph Ratzinger: *Commonweal* 117, no. 19 (November 3, 2000) 32.

3. Kilian McDonnell, O.S.B., "Imperial Claims?" *The Christian Century,* October 18, 2000, p. 1041.

4. Richard John Neuhaus, "To Say Jesus Is Lord," *First Things* 107 (November 2000) 69.

5. John Paul II, "Angelus Address," October 1, 2000. See p. 34 of this volume.

6. A point rightly insisted upon by Eugene Fisher, associate director for the American Bishops' Secretariat of Ecumenical and Interreligious Affairs in his exchange with the Jewish ecumenist, Edward Kessler. See "A dialogue of head and heart," *The Tablet,* 18 November, 2000, pp. 1556-1559. S. Mark Heim's essay in this volume clearly perceives the intended audience and purpose of the declaration.

7. For a rich discussion of the relation between normative doctrine and theology and the crucial role of doctrine in articulating the church's public identity, see Reinhard Hutter, *Suffering Divine Things: Theology as Church Practice* (Grand Rapids: Eerdmans, 2000).

8. In his critical treatment of *Dominus Iesus* in *Commonweal* (October 20, 2000, p. 15), Philip Kennedy, O.P., states that the declaration "perpexingly [*sic*] overlooks" article 16 of *Lumen gentium*—a charge reiterated by Frederick Lawrence in this volume. In point of fact, *Dominus Iesus* prominently refers to article 16 of *Lumen gentium* in footnote 23. Moreover, it is important to note that LG 16, for all its positive assessment of the religions, concludes with the risen Lord's injunction: "Preach the gospel to every creature" (Mk 16:16); and the following section then begins with the imperative: "Go, therefore, and make disciples of all nations, baptizing them…" (Mt 28:19).

9. RM 18.

10. Luke Timothy Johnson, *Living Jesus: Learning the Heart of the Gospel* (San Francisco: Harper, 1999) 34.

11. Luke Timothy Johnson, *The Real Jesus* (San Francisco: Harper, 1996) 168-169.

12. Frans Jozef van Beeck, *Catholic Identity After Vatican II* (Chicago: Loyola University Press, 1985) 56-57; italics in the original.

13. See Rahner's essay, "Christian Living Formerly and Today," *Theological Investigations,* vol. VII, translated by David Bourke (New York: Herder and Herder, 1971) 15.

14. I find confirmation of this view in Harvey Egan's fine exposition, in the present volume, of Rahner's strikingly Christocentric theology. Egan writes: "Only Jesus of Nazareth is that than which nothing greater can be thought because God himself can do nothing greater."

15. See Lonergan's essay, "Theology in Its New Context," *A Second Collection* (Philadelphia: Westminster Press, 1974) 67.

16. Irenaeus of Lyon, *Against Heresies,* V, 6, 1; V, 28, 4.

17. Yves Congar, *The Word and the Spirit* (San Francisco: Harper, 1986) xi.

18. Congar, *The Word and the Spirit,* 71.

19. John Zizioulas, "Christ, the Spirit and the Church," in *Being as Communion* (Crestwood, N.Y.: St. Vladimir's Seminary Press, 1985) 139, 129.

20. I have serious misgivings with the view proposed by John Pawlikowski in the article cited in Philip Cunningham's contribution to this volume. Pawlikowski contends that implicit in Vatican II's *Nostra aetate* is the position that "Jews can attain salvation apart from the Christ event" (*The Ecumenist* 37, no. 1, p. 5). This sentence of Pawlikowski (not directly quoted by Cunningham) seems to exemplify the sort of stance that *Dominus Iesus* (and *Redemptoris missio*) seeks to correct. The consistent teaching of the church's magisterium is that all grace is Christic.

21. I have developed this perspective at greater length in "New Adam and Life-Giving Spirit: The Paschal Pattern of Spirit Christology," *Communio* 25, no. 2 (Summer 1998).

22. A recent study that illuminates this "paschal depth grammar" of salvation in Christ is Thomas G. Weinandy, O.F.M. Cap., *Does God Suffer?* (Notre Dame: University of Notre Dame Press, 2000), especially chapters 9, "The Redemptive Suffering of Christ," and 10, "Suffering in the Light of Christ."

7. METHOD AND MEANING IN *DOMINUS IESUS*

1. I want at the outset to register my thanks to Margaret O'Gara and Michael Vertin of St. Michael's College, University of Toronto, for their generosity in helping me understand what I had and had not understood in an earlier version of this essay.

2. "Statement by the Archbishop of Canterbury concerning the Roman Catholic Document 'Dominus Iesus.'" See p. 27 of this volume.

3. John Paul II, "Angelus Address," October 1, 2000. See p. 34 of this volume.

4. One notable exception is the verb *believe,* as I shall discuss in a moment.

5. More exactly, the notion of assent to (propositional) truths belongs to the declaration's conception of Christian faith, which is what I am discussing here. Rather confusingly, as Francis Clooney points out, "belief" is also used in a rather deprecating way when *Dominus Iesus* treats non-Christian religions; but the present point is not affected.

6. Francis Sullivan discusses this question in his essay.

7. See Frederick Shriver, "Councils, Conferences and Synods," in *The Study of Anglicanism,* ed. S. Sykes and J. Booty (London: SPCK and Philadelphia: Fortress Press, 1988) 188-199, esp. 189-191; Henry Chadwick, "The Status of Ecumenical Councils in

Anglican Thought," in *The Heritage of the Early Church*, ed. D. Nieman and M. Schatkin (Rome: Orientalia Christiana Analecta 195, 1973) 393-408.

8. More exactly, Chalcedon quotes both the creed of the council of Nicaea and the somewhat expanded creed promulgated some fifty years later at the first council of Constantinople. It is the latter which is commonly called the "Nicene" Creed, and is said or sung in eucharistic worship today. The text of the creed quoted in *Dominus Iesus* matches Chalcedon's by omitting, deliberately and perhaps significantly, the phrase "and the Son." See Francis Sullivan's essay.

9. It may be significant that among the dogmatic *topoi* that are touched on, justification, atonement, and grace do not appear. Something more will be said on this score in my final section.

10. For the interpretation of Chalcedon's decree as a rule of speech—more exactly, a second-order proposition—see Bernard Lonergan, "The Origins of Christian Realism," in his *A Second Collection*, ed. W. F. J. Ryan and B. J. Tyrrell (Philadelphia: The Westminster Press, 1974) 239-261, esp. 252-253; and "The Dehellenization of Dogma," ibid. 11-32 at 26. The point is that the meaning of the decree does not depend on any particular metaphysical philosophy; it depends on the meaning of the Nicene Creed—as the decree itself says it does.

11. Bernard Lonergan, *Method in Theology*, 2nd ed. (New York: Herder and Herder, 1972) xi. See also 124, 300-302, 326, 363. For a brief overview of Lonergan's views on cultural shifts in relation to theology, see "The Transition from a Classicist World-view to Historical-mindedness," in his *A Second Collection*, 1-9. Most of the other essays in this volume also deal with related topics.

12. The theological principle here is *gratia perficit naturam non tollit*, methodological criteria being regarded as belonging to *natura*. To claim that only a Roman Catholic can truly assess a Vatican teaching with regard to its method—and, to that extent, with regard to its convincingness—is to claim that grace replaces intelligence and that the Roman Catholic Church has a monopoly on grace. To the best of my knowledge, that church itself is not committed to either claim, though each has been made by some of its theologians.

13. On the New Testament as evidence, and the implications for a doctrine of inspiration, see Lonergan, "Christology Today: Methodological Reflections" in his *A Third Collection*, ed. F. E. Crowe (New York/Mahwah: Paulist Press, 1985) 74-99, esp. 80-82, 86.

14. See Margaret O'Gara, *The Ecumenical Gift Exchange* (Collegeville, Minn.: Liturgical Press, 1998) 117-119.

15. Lonergan, *Method in Theology*, 270.

16. Lonergan, "Theology in Its New Context," in *A Second Collection*, 55-67 at 63.

17. Bernard Lonergan, "Dimensions of Meaning," in *Collection*, 2nd ed., Collected Works of Bernard Lonergan, vol. 4 (Toronto: University of Toronto Press, 1988) 232-245 at 244.

18. David Kelsey, *The Uses of Scripture in Recent Theology* (Philadelphia: Fortress Press, 1975) 193, 215; esp. 163: "At the root of every theological position there is an imaginative act in which a theologian tries to catch up in a single metaphorical judgment the full complexity of God's presence in, through, and over-against the activities comprising the church's common life and which, in turn, both provides the *discrimen* against which the theology criticizes the church's current forms of speech and life, and determines the peculiar 'shape' of the 'position.'"

19. The bull of Boniface VIII, significantly entitled *Unam sanctam*, is cited in article 16, note 51 of *Dominus Iesus*. The original text reads: "Porro subesse Romano Pon-

tifici omne humanae creaturae declaramus, dicimus, diffinimus omnino esse de necessitate salutis." DS 872.

20. William J. Abraham, *Canon and Criterion in Christian Theology* (Oxford: Clarendon Press, 1998) 115-116.

21. Ibid., 115.

8. A JEWISH RESPONSE

1. As quoted by Y. A. Korff, "Jewish-Catholic Relations: Dangerous or Wasted Effort?", *The Jewish Advocate* 190:37 (September 15-21, 2000) 1; and by Eric J. Greenberg, "Sainthood Moves Could Harm Catholic-Jewish Ties," *The Jewish Week*, September 8, 2000.

2. Pope Pius IX entertained such measures and even ordered the razing of the ghetto gates and the cessation of forced attendance at conversionary sermons before the 1848 uprisings and temporary overthrow of the Roman Republic. This made the Jewish reception of his enforcement of these same measures after his return to power all the harder. See David I. Kertzer, *The Kidnapping of Edgardo Mortara* (New York: Alfred A. Knopf, 1997) 49, 81-82, 89. Kertzer suggests (*Kidnapping* 138) that the church came to identify Jewish rights as part of the liberalism that it was combating in the latter half of the nineteenth century.

3. For a detailed analysis of this case, see Kertzer, *Kidnapping.*

4. For the situation in Italy, see Kertzer, *Kidnapping,* 48-49, 61-62.

5. For a description of one such case within my own extended family, see Rachel Sarna Araten, *Michalina: Daughter of Israel* (Jerusalem: Am Yisrael Chai Press, 1986).

6. Eric J. Greenberg, "Sainthood Moves Could Harm Catholic-Jewish Ties," *The Jewish Week,* September 8, 2000.

7. I refer here particularly to the issues around Holocaust-era figures, most famously Edith Stein and Pope Pius XII. In general, the Jewish world understands neither the function of saints in the Catholic Church nor the processes of their identification.

8. See the sidebar in *Origins* 30/17 (October 5, 2000) 263-264, quoting Roman rabbi Abramo Piatelli, a spokesman for the union of Italian Jewish Communities, and Tullia Zevi, director of inter-religious relations for the European Jewish Congress, pointing to the combined impact of this declaration and the beatification of Pope Pius IX.

9. Ed. Tikva Frymer-Kensky, David Novak, Peter Ochs, David Fox Sandmel, and Michael A. Signer (Boulder and Oxford: Westview Press, 2000). The document itself may also be found in *Origins* 30/15 (September 21, 2000) 225, 227-228, and at www.icjs.org, there with its list of signatories.

10. See, for instance, Eric J. Greenberg, "One Step Forward, Two Steps Back," *The Jewish Week,* September 15, 2000.

11. Greenberg, "One Step," A22.

12. "The Future of Catholic-Jewish Relations," *The Jewish Advocate,* September 29, 2000. Signed by Robert Leikind, Diane Kolb, and Carl Axelrod of the New England Region of the Anti-Defamation League, Nancy Kaufman of the Jewish Community Relations Council, Sheila Decter of the American Jewish Congress, Lawrence Lowenthal of the American Jewish Committee, Rabbi Samuel Chiel, and myself. Note also that the paper never printed an op-ed submitted by the Archdiocese of Boston that attempted to clarify the intent of the document. However, as the author of that piece and I discussed privately, this is likely because Jewish papers are justifiably hesitant to print discussions of Christian theology.

13. "Dialogues Will Continue," *Origins* 30/15 (September 21, 2000) 228-229. His remarks apply to the church's dialogue with others in general, among whom he does specify Jews. Compare also Archbishop Rembert Weakland of Milwaukee, "On the Document's Ecumenical Impact," *Origins* 30/17 (October 5, 2000) 266-267, reprinted from the Milwaukee *Catholic Herald* (September 14, 2000), who also regrets that the declaration makes no reference to post-conciliar ecumenical dialogues. Archbishop Weakland's article can be found on p. 32 of this volume.

14. Emphasis mine, reflecting an earlier statement: "In [announcing to the world the good news of Jesus] we encounter our brothers and sisters of other religions. Our dialogue with them is sincere and based on a constant search to understand better God's design for all human beings." "Statement on the Document of the Congregation of the Doctrine of the Faith: *Dominus Iesus*," *Pilot*, September 5, 2000. Also published as "What 'Dominus Iesus' Reaffirms," *Origins* 30/15 (September 21, 2000) 229-231.

15. In a letter read for him by Cardinal Edward Idris Cassidy at the closing ceremony of the Thirteenth International Meeting of Representatives of the Christian Churches and Communities and of the Great World Religions in Lisbon on September 26. I have seen two translations, one copied from the Sant'Egidio web site (the conference's sponsors), and another attributed to Walter Harrelson of Dallas. My text here mostly follows the former, although I have inserted phrases from the latter where they seemed clearer. To my knowledge, the Vatican itself has not issued an official English text.

16. See also: the September 17 statement of Bishop Robert Lynch of St. Petersburg ("Text's Impact on Ecumenical and Inter-religious Dialogue," *Origins* 30/17 [October 5, 2000] 263-265), who pledges to continue ecumenical and inter-religious dialogue "with the deepest respect and affection for their religious beliefs"; and the article written by Bishop Anthony Pilla of Cleveland for his archdiocesan newspaper, the *Catholic Universe Bulletin* (reprinted in *Origins* 30/17 [October 5, 2000] 267-268), voicing his absolute commitment to continued dialogue, citing the instruction "Dialogue and Proclamation" (Pontifical Council for Inter-Religious Dialogue and the Congregation for the Evangelization of Peoples, 1991), and commenting that "the Catholic Church does not expect participants in dialogue to abandon the convictions of their religious beliefs, but to face each other honestly to discuss the beliefs that give meaning to their lives."

17. "Understanding This Document's Context and Intent," *Origins* 30/15 (September 21, 2000) 234.

18. "Understanding This Document's Context and Intent," *Origins* 30/15 (September 21, 2000) 234.

19. NA 4. All citations of the documents of the Second Vatican Council are from *Vatican Council II: The Conciliar and Post Conciliar Documents*, ed. Austin Flannery, O.P. (Northport, N.Y.: Costello Publishing Company, revised edition, 1992).

20. "Text's Impact on Ecumenical and Interreligious Dialogue," *Origins* 30/17 (October 5, 2000) 264.

21. "On File," *Origins* 30/14 (September 14, 2000) 210.

22. "On File," 210. Note that although the Pope's letter does not directly address *Dominus Iesus*, this newly issued declaration with its implications for ecumenical dialogue lay in the forefront of the consciousness of the community the Pope was addressing.

23. NA 2.

24. NA 3.

25. NA 4.

26. *Humanae personae dignitatem*, Introduction, 2.

27. *Humanae personae dignitatem*, §IV.1.g.

28. LG 16.

29. See Eugene J. Fisher, "Pope John Paul II's Pilgrimage of Reconciliation: A Commentary on the Texts," in *Spiritual Pilgrimage: Texts on Jews and Judaism 1979-1995*, ed. Eugene J. Fisher and Leon Klenicki (New York: The Crossroad Publishing Co., 1995) xxxiii and the sources to which he makes reference there.

30. In private correspondence and in "Dialogue of Head and Heart" with Edward Kessler, *The Tablet* (London, November 18, 2000) 1556ff.

31. Cardinal Ratzinger, prefect of the Congregation for the Doctrine of the Faith, has stated recently that "Catholic dialogue with Jews belongs to a unique category because the Jewish faith 'for us is not another religion, but the foundation of our faith.'" John Norton, "Cardinal Ratzinger Links Christian Anti-Judaism to Holocaust," *Catholic News Service* (December 29, 2000), quoting a front page article in the Vatican's newspaper. However, this does not quite answer our question.

32. "Cardinal Tells Jewish Audience Media Distorted Vatican Text," *Catholic News Service*, October 16, 2000.

33. See Philip A. Cunningham's essay in this volume for an articulation of this derived from various church pronouncements.

34. Pontifical Commission for Religious Relations with the Jews, "Guidelines and Suggestions for Implementing the Conciliar Declaration *Nostra Aetate*, No. 4" (1974), III.

35. Pontifical Commission for Religious Relations with the Jews, "Notes on the Correct Way to Present Jews and Judaism in Preaching and Catechesis in the Roman Catholic Church" (1985), VI, 25.

36. See, particularly, Mark Heims's discussion of this point in this volume.

37. See the sixth and eighth paragraphs of *Dabru Emet*.

38. "Cardinal Tells" (note 32 above).

39. See particularly Charles Hefling's discussion of cultural change and communications issues in this volume.

9. IMPLICATIONS FOR CATHOLIC MAGISTERIAL TEACHING ON JEWS AND JUDAISM

1. See *Origins* 30/14 (September 14, 2000) 222-224.

2. John Paul II, *Tertio millennio adveniente*, 53. See *Origins* 24/24 (November 24, 1994) 414.

3. Edward Idris Cardinal Cassidy, "The Future of Jewish-Christian Relations in the Light of the Visit of Pope John Paul II to the Holy Land," address delivered at the Annual General Meeting of the Interreligious Coordinating Council in Israel, Jerusalem, March 13, 2001.

4. Walter Cardinal Kasper, "*Dominus Iesus*," address delivered at the 17th meeting of the International Catholic-Jewish Liaison Committee, New York, May 1, 2001, §2.

5. Joseph Cardinal Ratzinger, "The Heritage of Abraham: The Gift of Christmas," *L'Osservatore Romano*, December 29, 2000. Trans. Murray Watson.

6. Pontifical Commission for Religious Relations with the Jews, "Guidelines and Suggestions for Implementing the Conciliar Declaration *Nostra Aetate*, No. 4," 1. See Eugene J. Fisher and Leon Klenicki, eds., *In Our Time: The Flowering of Jewish-Catholic Dialogue* (New York/Mahwah: Paulist Press, 1990) 29-37.

7. Commission, "Guidelines," 1.

8. Joseph Cardinal Ratzinger, *Many Religions, One Covenant: Israel, the Church and the World* (San Francisco: Ignatius Press, 1999) 109; emphasis added.

9. Ratzinger, *Many Religions,* 111.

10. Pontifical Commission for Religious Relations with the Jews, "Notes on the Correct Way to Present Jews and Judaism in Preaching and Catechesis in the Roman Catholic Church" (1985), 27. See Fisher and Klenicki, *In Our Time* 38-50.

11. David Berger, "*Dominus Iesus* and the Jews," paper delivered at the 17th meeting of the International Catholic-Jewish Liaison Committee, New York, May 1, 2001. See p. 39 of this volume.

12. Berger, "*Dominus Iesus* and the Jews."

13. Berger, "*Dominus Iesus* and the Jews."

14. Walter Cardinal Kasper, "*Dominus Iesus,*" §3.

15. Walter Cardinal Kasper, "*Dominus Iesus,*" §2.

16. Many of these documents, together with numerous statements from other Christian churches, can be found in the Documents Library on the website of the Center for Christian-Jewish Learning at Boston College at www.bc.edu/cjlearning.

17. John Paul II, "Address to the Jewish Community in Mainz, West Germany" (November 17, 1980) in Eugene J. Fisher and Leon Klenicki, eds., *Spiritual Pilgrimage: Pope John Paul II—Texts on Jews and Judaism, 1979–1995* (New York: The Crossroad Publishing Co., 1995) 13-16.

18. Fisher and Klenicki, *Spiritual Pilgrimage,* 13-16.

19. John Paul II, "Address to Jewish Leaders in Miami" (September 11, 1987) in Fisher and Klenicki, *Spiritual Pilgrimage,* 105-109.

20. Commission, "Notes," 10.

21. Commission, "Guidelines," Prologue.

22. Edward Idris Cardinal Cassidy, "Reflections on the Vatican Statement on the *Shoah,*" *Origins* 28/2 (May 28, 1998) 31.

23. "Service Requesting Pardon," *Origins* 29/40 (March 23, 2000) 647.

24. John Paul II, "Mass of Pardon Homily" (March 12, 2000), *Origins* 29/40 (March 23, 2000) 649ff.

25. John Paul II, "Western Wall Prayer" (March 26, 2000), *Origins* 29/42 (April 6, 2000) 679 sidebar.

26. John Paul II, "Address to Delegates to the Meeting of Representatives of Episcopal Conferences and Other Experts in Catholic-Jewish Relations: Commission for Religious Relations with the Jews" (March 6, 1982), in Fisher and Klenicki, *Spiritual Pilgrimage,* 17-20.

27. Commission, "Notes," 25.

28. John Paul II, "Address at the Great Synagogue of Rome" (April 13, 1986), in Fisher and Klenicki, *Spiritual Pilgrimage,* 60-66.

29. Commission, "Notes," 6-7; emphases added.

30. Bishops' Committee on the Liturgy, National Conference of Catholic Bishops, *God's Mercy Endures Forever: Guidelines on the Presentation of Jews and Judaism in Catholic Preaching* (Washington, D.C.: United States Catholic Conference, 1988) 31, b, c, i.

31. John Paul II, "Address to Jewish Leaders in Warsaw" (June 14, 1987) in Fisher and Klenicki, *Spiritual Pilgrimage,* 98-99.

32. Ratzinger, *Many Religions,* 27-28; emphasis added.

33. Ratzinger, *Many Religions,* 104.

34. Commission, "Guidelines," Prologue.

35. Bishops' Committee on Ecumenical and Inter-religious Affairs, National Conference of Catholic Bishops, "Catholic Teaching on the Shoah: Implementing the Holy See's *We Remember*" (Washington, D.C.: United States Catholic Conference, 2001) B, 2.

36. Commission, "Notes," II, 11.

37. Commission, "Notes," 10.

38. Walter Cardinal Kasper, "*Dominus Iesus*," §3.

39. Walter Cardinal Kasper, "*Dominus Iesus*," §3.

40. Michael B. McGarry, "A Question of Motive: A Conversation on Mission and Contemporary Jewish-Christian Relations." Unpublished paper read at the Christian Study Group on Jews and Judaism, November 1989. See also his "Roman Catholic Understandings of Mission" in Martin Cohen and Helga Croner, eds., *Christian Mission-Jewish Mission* (New York/Ramsey: Paulist Press, 1982) 141.

41. Richard Grein, John Cardinal O'Connor, and James Sudbrock, the respective bishops of the Episcopal, Roman Catholic, and Lutheran churches of New York City, issued a public statement on June 25, 1996 committing themselves to dialogue with Jews and warned that "an aggressive direct effort to convert the Jewish people would break the bond of trust built up for over thirty years and recreate enmity with our 'elder brothers and sisters.'" While composed in response to a June 13, 1996 resolution of the Southern Baptist Convention that called for the missionizing of the Jewish people, it did not develop a theological counter argument. Tommaso Federici had devised the beginnings of such a theological exposition against the Christian missionizing of Jews for a 1977 meeting of the International Catholic-Jewish Liaison Committee. However, his working paper has not been utilized in a subsequent Catholic magisterial document. (See Tommaso Federici, "Study Outline on the Mission and Witness of the Church," *SIDIC Review* 11/3 [1978] 25-34.)

42. Walter Cardinal Kasper, "*Dominus Iesus*," §3.

43. See my *A Story of Shalom* (New York/Mahwah: Paulist Press, 2001).

10. CHALLENGES TO MUSLIM-CHRISTIAN RELATIONS

1. For an elaboration on the concept of *tawhîd,* see the *Encyclopaedia of Islâm* or Kevin Reinhart, *Before Revelation: The Boundaries of Moral Thought* (Albany: SUNY Press, 1995); and William Graham, *Beyond the Written Word in Early Islâm: A Reconsideration of the Sources, with Special Reference to the Divine Saying or Hadîth Qudsî* (The Hague and Paris: Mouton, 1977).

2. For recent works on the subject of *jihâd,* see Reuven Firestone, *Jihâd: The Origin of Holy War in Islâm* (London: Oxford University Press, 1999); Harfiya Abdel Haleem, Oliver Ramsbotham, Saba Risaluddin, and Brian Wicker (eds.), *The Crescent and the Cross: Muslim and Christian Approaches to War and Peace* (New York: St. Martin's Press, 1998); Fred Donner, "The Sources of Islamic Conceptions of War," in *Just War and Jihad: Historical and Theoretical Perspectives on War and Peace in Western and Islamic Traditions,* ed. John Kelsay and James Turner Johnson (Newark: Greenwood Press, 1991); and Stephen Humphreys, *Islamic History: A Framework for Inquiry* (Princeton: Princeton University Press, 1991).

3. The Qur'ân uses the word *jihâd* about thirty-five times, with the majority of obvious references to specific historical situations for the first Muslim community members who were under siege by the ruling Quraish tribe and their political allies.

4. DI 1. Also in Mt 28:18-20; Lk 24:46-48; Jn 17:18, 20, 21; Acts 1:8.

5. See Qur'ân 62:6

6. For similar verses see also Qur'ân 2:111-13; 7:169; 3:24; and 4:53-55.

7. Qur'ân 5:19.

8. For more on pluralism and Islam see, Farid Esack, *Qur'ân, Liberation and Pluralism* (Oxford: Oneworld Publications, 1997); Toshihiko Izutsu, *Ethico-Religious Con-*

cepts in the Qur'ân (Montreal: McGill University Press, 1966); Richard Martin, "Understanding the Qur'ân in Text and Context," *History of Religions* 21 (1982) 361-384; and Mahmoud Ayoub, "Islâm Between Tolerance and Acceptance," *Islâm and Christian Relations* 2 (1991) 171-181.

9. See Francis Cardinal Arinze, *The Risks and Rewards of Inter-Religious Dialogue* (Huntington, Indiana: Our Sunday Visitor Publishing, 1997).

10. 'Alî ibn 'Uthmân al-Jullâbî al-Hujwîrî, *Kashf al-Mahjûb,* Ulama Fazal ud-din Gohar, Urdu translation (Lahore: Zia al-Qur'ân Publishers, 1989) 410.

11. IMPLICATIONS FOR THE PRACTICE
OF INTER-RELIGIOUS LEARNING

1. This essay draws on a briefer reflection which appeared in *America* 183, no. 13 (October 28, 2000) 16-18.

2. In the sections to which I limit my consideration, its focus is on other religions; I leave to other contributors to this volume reflection on the ecclesiology and ecumenical implications of the document and its likely reception among Christians.

3. For an expression of my own view of a proper practical Catholic response to religious pluralism, see for instance my essay, "Goddess in the Classroom," *Conversations in Jesuit Higher Education,* October 1999, 29-39. There I argue that we Catholics are better off when we are well informed about the beliefs and practices of other traditions, particularly as these are presented to us by persons of other traditions among whom we live and work. As theories, both relativism and exclusivism lack real grounding and fail to do justice to either our own tradition or the traditions of others. On the tensions inherent in the Catholic view of pluralism, see also my "Openness and Limit in the Catholic Encounter with Other Faith Traditions," in *Examining the Catholic Intellectual Tradition,* ed. Anthony J. Cernera and Oliver Morgan (Fairfield: Sacred Heart University Press, 2000) 103-132.

4. That is, according to the usage of the declaration, which refers without comment to "the sacred writings of other religions" (§8).

5. Throughout this essay I refer to the example of the Hindu tradition which worships Narayana as God, since this is a tradition I have studied in some depth. But the same points regarding specificity can be made with innumerable other examples from other traditions.

6. *New Revised Standard Version* (New York: Oxford University Press, 1991).

7. The declaration footnotes the 1 Corinthians citation by a reference to *Redemptoris missio,* 55, but neither there nor anywhere else in the encyclical does John Paul II cite 1 Corinthians 10.

8. See Francis X. Clooney, *Seeing through Texts: Doing Theology among the Srivaisnavas of South India* (Albany: State University of New York Press, 1996) 239.

9. My translation of verse 68 in the *Nanmukan Tiruvantati* of Tirumalisai Piran. One of Tirumalisai Piran's major goals in the *Nanmukan Tiruvantati* is to reject the idea that Brahma and Shiva are equal to Narayana. Attanjiyar is commenting on Tirumalisai Piran's verse in the course of a longer commentary on verse X.2.1 from the *Tiruvaymoli* of another ninth-century saint, Shatakopan, a verse in which exclusive devotion to the name of God is highly praised.

10. John Paul II, in a speech in Madras, India, February 5, 1986, as reprinted in *Interreligious Dialogue: The Official Teaching of the Catholic Church (1963-1995),* ed. Francesco Gioia (Boston: Pauline Books and Media, 1997) 326.

12. A TIMELY REAFFIRMATION AND CLARIFICATION OF VATICAN II

1. This essay is a modified version of a public lecture given at the Seminary of Saints Peter and Paul, Bodija-Ibadan, Oyo State, Nigeria, on November 30, 2000. My profound appreciation goes to members of the audience whose questions and comments challenged me to clarify my position.

2. Cf. DI 5; DV 2.

3. DV 4, quoted in DI 5.

4. Cf. DV 4; DI 6, with citations of Council of Chalcedon, *Symbolum Chalcedonense* (DS 301); Athanasius, *De Incarnatione* 54.3.

5. DI 7.

6. FR 13.

7. DI 8. The previous magisterial documents that back up this doctrinal stance are listed. See Council of Trent, *Decretum de libris sacris et de traditionibus recipiendis* (DS 1501); Vatican I, Dogmatic Constitution *Dei Filius*, ch. 2 (DS 3006); DV 11. The point must not be overlooked here that there is no denying the fact that the sacred books of the Jewish religion are canonical. Their canonicity is implied in the affirmation of the canonicity of the books of the Old Testament.

8. See RM 55 and 56; and EN 53.

9. RM 6, quoted in DI 10.

10. Cyprian of Carthage, Letter 63, 13.1-3 in *The Letters of St. Cyprian of Carthage,* translated and annotated by G. W. Clarke, vol. 3 (Ancient Christian Writers, vol. 46; New York/Mahwah: Paulist Press, 1986).

11. See the beautiful study of J.-M.-R. Tillard, *Chair de l'Église, chair du Christ. Aux sources de l'ecclésiologie de communion* (Paris: Cerf, 1992) ch. 2: "Tous saisis en un seul Corps, corps eucharistique, corps ecclésial."

12. See LG 8.

13. DI 16. For further indications of reaffirmation of Vatican II see LG 15: "these Christians are indeed in some real way joined to us in the Holy Spirit for, by his gifts and graces, his sanctifying power is also active in them and he has strengthened some of them even to the shedding of their blood"; UR 3: "some, even very many, of the most significant elements and endowments which together go to build up and give life to the Church itself, can exist outside the visible boundaries of the Catholic Church: the written Word of God; the life of grace; faith, hope and charity, with the other interior gifts of the Holy Spirit, as well as visible elements. All of these, which come from Christ and lead back to him, belong by right to the one Church of Christ." The importance of these texts for ecumenism is underlined by John Paul II in his encyclical letter *Ut unum sint* 13.

14. DI 17. For attestation of Vatican II inspiration, see UR 3 and 22. *Dominus Iesus* repeats Vatican II when it speaks of the defects of these communities: "Therefore, these separated Churches and communities as such, though we believe they suffer from defects, have by no means been deprived of significance and importance in the mystery of salvation. For the spirit of Christ has not refrained from using them as means of salvation which derive their efficacy from the very fullness of grace and truth entrusted to the Catholic Church" (UR 3).

15. LG 14, quoted in DI 20. The following are teachings of the Second Vatican Council which reiterate this view: AG 7: "The reason for missionary activity lies in the will of God, 'who wishes all men to be saved and to come to the knowledge of the truth. For there is one God and one Mediator between God and men, himself a man, Jesus

Christ, who gave himself as a ransom for all' (1 Tim 2:4-5), 'neither is there salvation in any other' (Acts 4:12)."

UR 3 asserts that "it is through Christ's Catholic Church alone, which is the universal help towards salvation, that the fullness of the means of salvation can be obtained. It was to the apostolic college alone, of which Peter is the head, that we believe that our Lord entrusted all the blessings of the New Covenant, in order to establish on earth the one Body of Christ into which all those should be fully incorporated who belong in any way to the people of God."

16. This position finds support in two Church fathers: Cyprian, *De catholicae ecclesiae unitate* 6; Irenaeus, *Adversus haeresus* III, 24.1.

17. See RM 10; AG 7.

CONTRIBUTORS

ANTHONY AKINWALE, O.P., a priest of the Dominican Province of Nigeria, obtained his Ph.D. from Boston College and teaches systematic theology at the Dominican Institute, Ibadan, Nigeria. Apart from being a consultant to the Symposium of Episcopal Conferences of Africa and Madagascar (SECAM), he is also a consultant on ecumenism to the Nigerian Conference of Catholic Bishops, and current president of the Catholic Theological Association of Nigeria (CATHAN). His research interests include theological methodology, Christology, and ecclesiology.

FRANCIS X. CLOONEY, S.J., is a professor of comparative theology at Boston College and coordinator for inter-religious dialogue for the Jesuits of the United States. His most recent books are *Hindu Wisdom for All God's Children* and *Preaching Wisdom to the Wise: Three Treatises by Roberto de Nobili, S.J., Missionary and Scholar in 17th Century India* (co-authored with Anand Amaladass, S.J.). Oxford University Press will shortly publish his *Hindu God, Christian God: How Reason Crosses the Boundaries among Religions*. He is currently researching the earliest Jesuit encounters with people of other religions and beginning a book on the theology of goddesses in traditional Hinduism.

PHILIP A. CUNNINGHAM is executive director of the Center for Christian-Jewish Learning and an adjunct professor of theology at Boston College. Interested in the intersections of biblical studies, religious education, and Jewish-Christian relations, he is the author of several articles and two forthcoming books from Paulist Press: *The Hebrew Scriptures in the Lectionary: Interpreting the "Old Testament" as a "Shared Testament"* and *A Story of Shalom: The Calling of Christians and Jews by a Covenanting God*. He is a member of the advisory committee on Catholic-Jewish relations for the National Conference of Catholic Bishops and of the Catholic Biblical Association of America.

HARVEY D. EGAN, S.J., received his doctorate under the direction of Karl Rahner from Westfälische Wilhelms-Universität and is currently a professor of systematic and mystical theology at Boston College. His books include *Christian Mysticism: The Future of a Tradition, An Anthology of Christian Mysticism, Ignatius Loyola the Mystic,* and *Karl Rahner: Mystic of Everyday Life.* He is widely known for his studies on Christian mysticism and on the thought of Karl Rahner.

S. MARK HEIM is the Samuel Abbot Professor of Christian Theology at Andover Newton Theological School. He has been deeply involved in issues of religious pluralism and Christian ecumenism. He is the author of *Salvations: Truth and Difference in Religion* and *The Depth of the Riches: A Trinitarian Theology of Religious Ends*. An ordained minister in the American Baptist Churches, he represents that denomination on the Faith and Order Commissions of the World Council of Churches and the National Council of Churches of Christ. His research interests include science and theology, Baptist history, and global Christianity, and he is currently working on a study of the atonement.

CHARLES HEFLING is an associate professor of systematic theology at Boston College and an editor of *Method: Journal of Lonergan Studies*. He received doctorates from Harvard University and from the Joint Doctoral Program of Boston College and Andover Newton Theological School. He is an extra-parochial priest of the Episcopal diocese of Massachusetts, and teaches in its program for the vocational diaconate. The author of books on Austin Farrer and the nature of Christian doctrine, he is currently at work on *The Meaning of God Incarnate: Christology for the Time Being*.

QAMAR-UL HUDA is an assistant professor of Islamic studies and comparative theology at Boston College and writes about medieval Islamic texts and mystical sûfî treatises. He received his doctorate from UCLA, Department of History, in the history of Islamic religious thought and Middle Eastern history. His book *Striving for Death: Spiritual Exercises for the Suhrawardî Sûfîs* will be published in 2002. He is currently working on sûfî commentaries of the Qur'ân and translating a number of sûfî treatises dealing with the Suhrawardî inner path.

ROBERT IMBELLI is a priest of the Catholic archdiocese of New York and an associate professor of systematic theology at Boston College, where he directed the Institute of Religious Education and Pastoral Ministry for six years. His areas of particular concern are Christology and trinitarian theology. He has published articles on the Holy Spirit and the Incarnation, and is a member of the United States Anglican-Roman Catholic Dialogue and has served on the board of the Catholic Theological Society of America.

RUTH LANGER is an associate professor of Jewish Studies at Boston College. She received her Ph.D. in Jewish liturgy in 1994 and her rabbinic ordination in 1986 from Hebrew Union College–Jewish Institute of Religion in Cincinnati. She is the author of *To Worship God Properly: Tensions between Liturgical Custom and Halakhah in Judaism* and her current research focuses on the development and interpretation of the liturgies surrounding the reading of the Torah. At Boston College, she is involved in the development of the Center for Christian-Jewish Learning dedicated to promoting learning about and research on issues of Jewish-Christian relations.

FREDERICK LAWRENCE is an associate professor of systematic theology at Boston College, where he also directs the annual Lonergan Workshop. He studied with Karl Barth, Hans-Georg Gadamer, and Heinrich Ott as well as with Bernard Lonergan, and received his doctorate at the University of Basel. He has been involved in judicial education and the development of undergraduate core education, and his research interests include postmodernism, hermeneutics, theology as political, and the Triune God.

PHEME PERKINS is a professor of New Testament at Boston College. She has served as president of the Catholic Biblical Association of America and is an associate editor of the New Oxford Annotated Bible. She holds a Ph.D. from Harvard University and is the author of over twenty books on the New Testament and early Christianity including the commentaries on John and the Johannine epistles in the *New Jerome Biblical Commentary; Peter, Apostle for the Whole Church; Jesus as Teacher;* and *Reading the New Testament.*

STEPHEN J. POPE is an associate professor of theological ethics and chairs the theology department at Boston College. He received his doctorate at the University of Chicago. He is the author of *The Evolution of Altruism and the Ordering of Love* and edited *The Ethics of Aquinas.* Currently he is working on a book entitled *Human Evolution and Christian Ethics.*

FRANCIS A. SULLIVAN, S.J., studied at Boston College, Fordham University, and the Gregorian University in Rome, where, after obtaining the STD in 1956, he taught ecclesiology for thirty-six years, serving also as dean of the faculty of theology from 1964 to 1970. After being declared emeritus of that faculty in 1992, he returned to Boston College as an adjunct professor of theology. He is the author of *Creative Fidelity: Weighing and Interpreting Documents of the Magisterium; Magisterium: Teaching Authority in the Catholic Church;* and *Salvation Outside the Church?*

INDEX

Abraham, William, 121
Abrahamic faith, 40, 89-93, 142-43
Alliance of Reformed Churches, viii
Anglicans: orders of, 53-56; responses of, x, 27, 107-23
anti-semitism, 43, 89-90, 124-26, 139, 142, 184n. 37
apostolic succession, 36-38, 53, 85, 120-23, 131
Aquinas, Thomas, 49
Arians, the, 58, 173
Athenagoras, Ecumenical Patriarch, 37

Balasuriya, Tissa, ix
baptism, 17, 33, 36, 49, 70-71, 119-20, 125-26
Baptism, Eucharist and Ministry, 70-71, 181n. 3
Barth, Karl, 103
Berger, David, 139-40
Boff, Leonardo, 52, 179n. 1
Boston College, 57, 66
Boston *Jewish Advocate*, 126-27, 189n. 12
Brunett, Alexander J., 128-29
Buddhism, 32, 64, 74-77, 162-63

Cassidy, Edward Idris, viii, 136
Catechism of the Catholic Church, 83
Catholic Church: central to salvation, viii-ix, 5, 12, 17-18, 20-22, 32-33, 35-38, 49-53, 82, 86-88, 118-23, 174-78, 179n. 1; doctrinal authority in, 47-48, 110-11; historical continuity of, 71; and the Jews, 124-49; and kingdoms of God and Christ, 5, 18-20, 48-49, 51, 83, 86-88, 119, 157; and other religions, 20-22, 32-33, 124-33, 155-56; sinfulness of, 93; unicity of, 15-18, 120-23; universal mission of, 3-4, 22-23, 68, 80-88, 97-99

"Catholic Teaching on the Shoah" (U.S. Bishops' Committee on Ecumenical and Inter-Religious Affairs), 146
Chalcedon, Council of, 10, 102, 111-14, 119, 121, 123, 171, 172-76, 188nn. 8, 10
Christianity in Jewish Terms, 126
Christological doctrine, x, 61-63, 96-106, 108-109, 171-74
"Christological drift," 108, 111-13
"Christomonism," 103
Church, Charism and Power (Boff), 52
"churches," other than Catholic, vii-viii, 17-18, 30-31, 33, 53-56, 92-93, 152, 174-78
classicist foundations of DI, 115-16
Congar, Yves, 104
Congregation for the Doctrine of the Faith (CDF), vii, 30-31, 35-36, 47-49, 51-56, 79, 111, 166-67
Constantinople, Council of, 98, 102, 171
conversion, necessity of, 156
Crowe, Frederick, 94
Cyprian of Carthage, 174-76

Dabru Emet advertisement, 126
Dalai Lama, the, 74-77
Day of Prayer, Assisi 1986, viii, 28
D'Costa, Gavin, 74-77
"Definition of Faith" of Chalcedon, 111-14, 121, 123
Dei Verbum, 97-98, 105, 171
dGe lugs tradition of Tibetan Buddhism, 75-77
Dignitatis humanae, 99
discrimen of DI, 118-23
doctrinal authority, 47-48
Dupuis, Jaques, ix, 179n. 8

"ecclesial communities," 30, 34, 53-56, 92-93, 176-77

Piran, Tirumalisai, 164-65, 194n. 9
Pius IX, 38, 125-26, 134-35, 189nn. 2,
    8
Pius XII, 49, 52, 91
pluralism, ix-x, 9, 48-49, 62, 66-67, 74-
    77, 117-18, 153-56, 163-64, 194n. 3
Pontifical Council for Promoting Chris-
    tian Unity, viii
Protestant: communions, viii, 36-37,
    53-56, 71-72, 152; evangelicals, 43,
    148; responses, x, 68-79

Qur'an, the, 151-56, 193n. 3

Rahner, Karl, x, 58-67, 102, 180nn. 5,
    7, 187n. 14
Ramanuja (theologian), 160, 163-67
Ratzinger, Joseph, vii-viii, 40-43, 48,
    53-54, 89, 135, 137-40, 145-46,
    191n. 31
Redemptoris missio, 6-7, 51, 57, 105,
    132 , 173
Reformation, the, 30-31, 33
relativism, 6-7, 21-22, 51, 78-79, 82,
    161-62
revelation, 6-9, 60-61, 171-73
Roos, H., 91-92

salvation: and the Church, 49-51, 120-
    23, 174-78; means of, 77-78, 117;
    and other religions, 20-22, 74-77,
    117-18, 150-56; paschal pattern of,
    105-106; Rahner on, 58-67; unicity
    of, 11-15; universality of, 14, 48-49,
    73-74, 77-79, 17
scripture, interpretation of, x, 5-6, 80-
    88
Second Vatican Council, 4-6, 8-10, 12,
    14-17, 21, 32-33, 35-37, 48-57, 69,
    90, 92-93, 96-106, 150, 169-78,
    195-96nn. 13-15
Shoah, the, 43, 90, 145-46
Society of Jesus, 58
Soloveitchik, Joseph B., 41, 43

Southern Baptist Convention, 148,
    193n. 41
style of writing in DI, 134-35
"*subsistit in*" expression, 52-53, 175-76
Sullivan, Francis, 71
supersessionism, 41, 139-40
systematics, 109-11, 115, 116, 122, 170

tawhîd concept, 151
theological reasons for controversy, ix-x
tiqqun 'olam, 124, 132
tone of DI, 96-97, 107
Torah, 41, 90, 132
"Toronto Statement" (World Council of
    Churches), 70-71
Toward a Theology of Pluralism
    (Dupuis), ix
Transfiguration, the, 104-106
Tridentine Reform, 91, 97
Trinitarian theology, x, 89-93

unicity, 5, 11, 13-18, 37-38, 118-23,
    172
"unitarianism of the Spirit," 99-100
Unitatis redintegratio, viii
*Unity of the Churches: A Real Possibil-
    ity* (Rahner), 59
universality: of the Church, 5, 49-51; of
    mystery of Christ, 13-15, 73-74, 77-
    79, 96-106, 118-23, 172-74; and the
    Word, 9-13
U.S. Bishops' Committee on Ecumeni-
    cal and Inter-Religious Affairs, 146
Ut unum sint, ix, 34, 47, 55-56, 72

Vaishnavas, the, 160, 163-65
Vatican I, 37-38
Vatican II, *See*, Second Vatican Council
Vedartha Samgraha, 160

World Council of Churches, viii, 70-71

Yom Kippur, 81